617 -495-1155

Gils-

→

D0931238

- when is the last day.
- how should I inform you.

→ David
→ 6 May   end of June.
          May 31st
call Jason Smith
[617-496-6542]

Discourses HM281, J2

Paris J25538. P2

Chapra J26374. P7

Maintaining Order, Making Peace

Also by Oliver P. Richmond

MEDIATING IN CYPRUS

THE UN AND HUMAN SECURITY (*edited with Edward Newman*)

THE WORK OF THE UN IN CYPRUS (*edited with James Ker-Lindsay*)

Maintaining Order, Making Peace

Oliver P. Richmond
Department of International Relations
University of St Andrews

First published 2002 by
PALGRAVE
Houndmills, Basingstoke, Hampshire RG21 6XS and
175 Fifth Avenue, New York, N. Y. 10010
Companies and representatives throughout the world

PALGRAVE is the new global academic imprint of
St. Martin's Press LLC Scholarly and Reference Division and
Palgrave Publishers Ltd (formerly Macmillan Press Ltd).

ISBN 0–333–80049–4

This book is printed on paper suitable for recycling and made from fully managed and sustained forest sources.

A catalogue record for this book is available from the British Library.

Library of Congress Cataloging-in-Publication Data
Richmond, Oliver P.
   Maintaining Order, making peace / by Oliver P. Richmond.
      p. cm. — (Global issues)
   Includes bibliographical references and index.
   ISBN 0–333–80049–4
      1. Pacific settlement of international disputes. 2. Peace.
   3. Conflict management. 4. Security, International. I. Title.
   II. Series

JZ6010 .R53 2001
327.1′72—dc21
                                                                        2001032126

10   9   8   7   6   5   4   3   2   1
11   10   09   08   07   06   05   04   03   02

Printed and bound in Great Britain by
Antony Rowe Ltd, Chippenham, Wiltshire

Contents

Preface

This study outlines and explores three generations of approaches to ending conflict culminating in the broadening concepts of, and approaches to, peace and human security in the post-cold war era. It aims to develop a useful typology for analysis, as well as detailing and critiquing an emerging approach to ending so-called 'intractable' conflict, which in the post-cold war environment is dominated by questions of legitimacy related to identity, representation, powersharing, and claims to sovereignty. This development has occurred within the static framework of territorialism and state-centricity as the basic foundation for the attempted organization of political community. Classic forms of peacekeeping, international mediation/negotiation, and conflict resolution approaches constitute the first two generations of activity, and are essentially mono-dimensional activities. In the contemporary environment in which local, regional, and global actors and the norms pertaining to human security and human needs have accrued enhanced legitimacy through a growing consensus at most levels of political interaction, space and access has been created for the utilization of more sophisticated tools. This was implicit in the emergence of a third generation of multidimensional and multilevel approaches to ending conflict, exemplified by the UN peace operations of the 1990s. These multidimensional approaches to ending conflict may seem to have a clearer potential to unravel 'intractable' conflicts when compared to mono-dimensional approaches, though they also lead to some serious dilemmas for international society, particularly as approaches to ending conflict have become more interventionary in nature, especially in the context of humanitarian operations. The three generations outlined here indicate the progression of peace strategies into more diverse multidimensional approaches in a global environment in which a wider recognition of human needs has led to a conceptual shift towards forms of human security rather than state security. This, however, raises the suspicion that the creation of peace is a totalizing practice based on universal claims that are difficult to substantiate or justify (though there seems to be little alternative). Finally, some conditions are proposed for a fourth generation approach that may emerge from this debate.

Acknowledgements

This book was prompted by a long-standing interest in various 'protracted' and 'intractable' conflicts that have been a significant part of the daily diet of news in Western media for many years. These conflicts have seemed indicative of the fact that there are zones of conflict that are perceived to be all but hopeless because they are afflicted by issues which are almost impossible to resolve or even manage within the conventional framework of the Westphalian international system. My thinking about these issues has benefited from a wide range of inputs, from friends, colleagues, and many other writers, most of whom are named in the bibliography. I would like to thank my colleagues at the University of St Andrews, and in Cyprus. I would particularly like to thank Costas Constantinou whose hospitality and conversation in the foothills of Troodos was particularly helpful. I would also like to thank Roland Bleiker, Dan Jones, and Tarja Vayrynen, for their helpful comments on several chapters at various stages of their development. Finally, I would like to thank Myria for her invaluable contribution, support and vivacity. Of course, all errors are my own responsibility.

Abbreviations

ASEAN	Association of South East Asian Nations
CIS	Commonwealth of Independent States
ECOMOG	Economic Community Cease-fire Monitoring Group
ECOWAS	Economic Community of West African States
EU	European Union
HCNM	High Commissioner on National Minorities
HRFOR	UN Human Rights Field Operation (Rwanda)
ICRC	International Committee of the Red Cross
IFOR	International Force
IGOs	Inter-Governmental Organizations
INGOs	International Non-Governmental Organizations
IOs	International Organizations
IR	International Relations
KLA	Kosovo Liberation Army
LAS	League of Arab States
MCPMR	Mechanism for Conflict Prevention, Management and Resolution
MICIVIH	UN–OAS International Civilian Mission
MSF	Médecins Sans Frontières
NATO	North Atlantic Treaty Organization
NGOs	Non-Governmental Organizations
OAS	Organization of American States
OAU	Organization of African Unity
OIC	Islamic Conference
ONUC	Operation des Nations Unies au Congo
ONUSAL	UN Observer Mission in El Salvador
OSCE	Organization for Security and Cooperation in Europe
PLO	Palestinian Liberation Organization
RENAMO	Resistência Nacional Moçambicano
ROs	Regional Organizations
SAARC	South Asian Association for Regional Cooperation
SADC	South African Development Community

SFOR	Stabilization Force
UK	United Kingdom
UN	United Nations
UNAMIR	UN Assistance Mission in Rwanda
UNAVEM I, II and III	UN Angola Verification Missions
UNDOF	UN Disengagement Observer Force
UNEF	UN Emergency Force
UNFICYP	UN Force in Cyprus
UNHCR	UN High Commission for Refugees
UNIFIL	UN Interim Force in Lebanon
UNITAF	Unified Task Force
UNMIK	UN Interim Administration Mission in Kosovo
UNOGIL	UN Observer Group in Lebanon
UNOMIL	UN Observer Mission in Liberia
UNOSOM I/II	UN Operation in Somalia
UNPREDEP	UN Preventative Deployment Force (Former Yugoslav Republic of Macedonia)
UNPROFOR	United Nations Protection Force
UNTAC	UN Transitional Authority in Cambodia
UNTAG	UN Transition Assistance Group in Namibia
UNTSO	UN Truce Supervision Organization
US	United States

Introduction

Peace, conflict, war and order have always been contested concepts, carrying diverse and politicized connotations often derived from a need for the stability of political structures, clearly endorsed legitimacy and justice, and acceptable to the dominant actors in the international system. Making peace in 'intractable' conflict has perhaps emerged as one of the fundamental challenges to the restructuring of the Westphalian international system, improving upon an inflexible concept of territorial sovereignty which promotes competition and conflict over both territory and sovereignty. In response, this may see a shift towards a post-Westphalian international society[1] in which a diversity of actors interact in a just and legitimate system of global interdependence, and diverse political communities coexist while also preserving their distinctiveness. The application of approaches to ending conflict creates and recreates a particular international order. Thus it is ever more apparent that how we think about 'peace', 'conflict', 'war' and 'order' and how they are created or sustained is a crucial global issue.[2] In this context approaches to conflict need to be able to address conflict over identity, representation and status, political, economic and social resources, and the environment in the context of the contemporary blurring of the distinctions between war, conflict, crime, and violations of human rights.[3] Yet many of the issues that are being grappled with (or are being studiously ignored), treated with ambiguity and so forth, which constitute the reform of the post-cold war, late-Westphalian environment are encompassed by the intractable conflicts that mark many regions of the world. According to mainstream IR theory such issues can be located in 'zones of conflict' as opposed to western, liberal democratic zones. Yet they exist and are replicated partly because of the failure of the international system as it developed during the cold war,

1

and because of problems arising from the exploitation of the Westphalian system during the process of decolonization.

The mainstream literature on ending conflict has responded to its own identification of forms of intractable conflict in a number of ways. Firstly, the strand derived from the Realist tradition has seen intractable conflicts over identity and representation as somewhat beyond the pale (of the Westphalian system) and argued that solutions should be found in the reconstitution of existing states through neutral or coercive diplomatic or military methods leading to a negotiation of territorial and constitutional arrangements – sometimes by creating new states. The liberal, neo-liberal, and functionalist school indicate that the roles of intergovernmental organizations may facilitate this process within an implicitly universal normative system and there was a general concurrence that the ending of conflict could be aided by conditions of a hurting stalemate – which could even be externally induced. The pluralist world society/human needs school argues that such state-centric approaches only replicate the very issues at the roots of the conflict and point to the need to include citizens in peace processes, while structuralists and peace researchers concentrate on the violence produced by economic systems and political structures and on issues of justice derived therein.

Some of the assumptions made, and the challenges raised, by such analyses illustrate how the international system itself may have framed, created and replicated conflicts, and attempts to resolve them. More critical approaches to ending conflict locate its practice in a language infused by power in the defence of an international order constructed through exclusionary discourses; from a critical perspective peacekeeping, peacemaking and peacebuilding should contest such tendencies because resolving conflict requires normative and emancipatory projects to overcome the binaries that power discourses produce. From a postmodern perspective even this may be suspect, as all approaches to ending conflict may imply a problematic imposition.

Making peace, the international system, and intractable conflict

The concept of protracted social conflict describes intractable, seemingly irresolvable conflicts, which involve sporadic outbreaks of violence resulting from communal and ethnic cleavages. According to Azar such cleavages are derived from the denial of fundamental human needs.[4] Kriesberg has argued that intractable conflicts involve a clash of group identities and can be characterized as multiple, simultaneous conflicts.[5] These definitions, while clearly underlining the roots of such conflicts, have tended to denote the fact that 'special' measures are required to deal with them because they fall outside the remit of 'normal' conflicts in the Westphalian international system. Burton developed the concept of 'deep-rooted conflict' to refer to conflicts based on uncompromisable human needs (which are paradoxically, not in short supply). According to Burton, such conflicts tend to occur where social inequality exists and where needs for identity and participation are blocked. This may result in communities resorting to violence to preserve their culture and values.[6]

This is an important starting point for a critique of 'intractability' within the framework of the Westphalian system, which leads to the toleration of levels of injustice and insecurity in order to manage conflicts that its frameworks could not resolve (and so are defined as intractable). Consequently, many conflicts drift somewhere between the realms of open violence and uncomfortable (or relatively comfortable) status quos, contributing to a general 'balance of power' which lacks in legitimacy and justice. The concept of intractability has come to be a euphemism for the perpetuation of injustices, often with the subtle acquiescence of global and regional powers that may have or had substantial interests in not upsetting a regional and global ideological and military balance. Thus, 'intractability' as a concept refers to the possibility,

(i) that no states in the international system have the resources or the will to resolve a conflict;

(ii) that the disputants themselves differ fundamentally on core issues of status (state or non-state) and the distribution of legal, political, social, and material resources;

(iii) that statist third parties have conducted protracted efforts to manage or resolve the conflict and consistently failed;

(iv) and most significantly that the mechanisms and frameworks of international law, politics, and the norms of the international system cannot offer a clear way out of conflicts based on subjective issues like identity, ethnicity, and subsequent claims for representation. Clashes between interests and notions of justice are characteristic of intractable conflict, this in itself being related to fact that Westphalian perspectives of justice lead to organization along the lines of territorial forms of sovereignty.

Intractability is a reflexive term that mirrors the psychosis of the Westphalian imaginary and its inability to understand or address issues outside of rigid statecentric organization. It is often a pejorative label applied to conflicts which its mechanisms fail to manage, involving issues beyond the pale of the international system. The normative implications of this appear to cancel out any obligation to intervene on the basis of responsibility to fellow human beings beyond sovereign borders, except in exceptional circumstances dictated by national interest. The term is therefore a label of frustration, convenience, and/or hopelessness, and has often been used to refer to the many civil conflicts over powersharing, territory, reform and ideology which exist, as well as historical enmities between identity groups, and the conflicts caused by the perceived balance of power between the West and the Warsaw Pact countries. Since the end of the cold war, many such tensions have become more obvious – though it would be dangerous to ignore the historical and ideological tensions which still exist, as well as tensions caused by armaments, differing rates of economic, social and political development between north and south, and the distribution of resources. It is also apparent that some interstate conflicts continue to exist, such as that between India and Pakistan (which went nuclear in 1998–9),[7] between Greece and Turkey, in the Balkans, difficulties about the status of Taiwan with China, regional interstate tensions in the Middle East, and in Africa. However, many contemporary conflicts revolve around territorial constructions of community, identity and human security and it is in ethnic and secessionist conflicts that the normative dimensions of conflict have received emphasis since the end of the cold war. Likewise, it is these tensions which threatened the stability of an increasingly obsolescent international system, moulded during an era of interstate threat. It has become pertinent, though not less problematic, to talk of a global civil society or a post-Westphalian international society in which the normative dimensions of human security have begun to gain heightened levels of legitimacy in the eyes of some states, intergovernmental organizations, NGOs, social groups and movements, and individuals. A crucial factor which separates Westphalian from late-Westphalian perspectives has been the broadening of security debates from state security, delegated from citizen to state, to a more normative version of human security which includes human rights, economic development, freedom from identity and representational constraints in the context of a globalizing and fragmenting environment.

Clearly, the term intractable has been used as a convenient label for many different types of conflict, operating on different levels, impinging on ethical and legal norms and structures, and the nature of political, economic, social and resource-based interests, and in particular on political arrangements (and their ambiguity) for the distribution of political representation, legitimacy, legality and territory. The reasons why such conflicts have defied a Westphalian framework of understanding and management can be blamed on a diverse range of reasons, including;

(i)   the failure of constitutional arrangements within a state because of a lack of flexibility vis-à-vis identity and representation and territory on the part of the disputants, and the lack of a negotiating culture;

(ii) the existence of a coercive and oppressive majority regime predicated on the nation-state's 'unity' as a medium for coherence, stability and survival;

(iii) the desire for impermeable borders based on the notion of the Westphalian imaginary, incorporating both the norms of non-intervention, territorial sovereignty and integrity and self-determination;[8]

(iv) the regional geopolitical environment, and the existence of transborder identity forces, particularly in unstable regions characterized by nationalism and underdevelopment;

(v)   the promotion of secessionist forces by either internal entrepreneurs or external actors which harbour irredentist sentiments;

(vi) the difficulties in applying the framework of international law and the norms of the international system in order to arrive at an unambiguous set of guidelines for resolution and/or management;

(vii) the lack of will (with respect to dominant actors) and resources (with respect to regional and international organizations);

(viii) the application of monodimensional[9] frameworks for the management and resolution of multidimensional conflicts.

Both security and conflict when viewed through the Westphalian prism are seen as essentially monodimensional. Yet, it is patently obvious that conflicts are multidimensional and impinge upon many different aspects of interaction or levels of analysis as well as subjective issue areas. The impulse to reduce the organization of societies to power/law frameworks has therefore become somewhat restrictive of the development of approaches to ending conflict.[10]

The Westphalian international system has been characterized by state-centric notions of sovereignty and self-interest via a communitarian world view. Inflexible versions of sovereignty blocked responsibility for humanitarian issues, and focused on state interests in a narrow sense, providing little space in which actors, official or private, could address the roots of conflict. Indeed, this system often replicated conflicts over identity and representation by focusing on state rather than human security. Pluralist approaches introduced the concepts of human needs as constituting navigation points for policy; functionalism and regime theory introduced a neo-liberal conception of an order in which institutions could play a role in setting the limits of acceptable international behaviour and development; and with the end of the cold war there has been an increasingly critical and normative reaction to the international system, relating to the wider existence of political communities, a development of international society and a global civil society that hinges on a wider recognition of human needs and thus, human security. Because identity, representation and human security issues are becoming priorities (even if only for reactionary reasons), a complete rethink of our understanding of peace and order and the way they are sustained are required.

The critique of approaches to ending conflict in this study begins with an examination of the literature on peacekeeping, international mediation and negotiation within the mainstream of IR approaches, drawing upon the subsequent critique of this 'paradigm' from the perspective of disputants.[11] Third party intervention could be used as an avenue for the facilitation of the disputants' original objectives, hence drawing the third party into the issues of the dispute. Consequently, the subsequent failures of such approaches may be attributable to the inflexibility of both parties to the conflict and their devious objectives which might pervert the rather simplistic assumption that disputants value such processes because of their objective of attaining a compromise, as the literature would have it. The irony of this insight is clear, especially when placed into the context of the view that the disputants tend to create of their negotiating positions vis-à-vis their perceptions of the international system. This indicates that it is also necessary to examine the cultural contexts in which both third parties and disputants operate, and furthermore that the basis for the projection of peace and order which occurs through forms of intervention needs to be re-evaluated.

The emergence of relatively low-level conflict, often about identity, and complex emergencies, has spurred new developments for ending conflict, once normally confined to high-level diplomatic efforts, peace-keeping, or citizen-based projects. Increasingly such activities are becoming more coordinated and widespread, and occurring in the context of other projects, such as peacekeeping, economic development and democratization, and through IOs/ ROs/ NGOs, as well as involving the burgeoning of social movements. These activities are emerging in the context of human rather that state security, within the context of a late-Westphalian framework in which sovereignty is increasingly loosing its primacy, and while they are embryonic it is important that they are theorized, developed and critiqued, at least in a preliminary manner. One of the main characteristics of the literature, which runs in parallel with the general tendency not to question the dominance of various forms of political realism (or neo-liberalism) is the reliance on state-centricity, with respect to roles played by intergovernmental organizations and also with non-state actors. Conflict resolution approaches, for example, ultimately seem to aim at contributing to state-centric efforts towards management even though they may appear to conceptually contradict state-centricity. At the very least this scope needs to be broadened: state support, creation and recreation as solutions to conflict ignore the role of the state in replicating the binaries which often create or reinforce conflict in the first place.

In the contemporary environment the notion of intractable conflict has become almost synonymous with ethnic conflict. Efforts to create constitutional settlements based upon a reappraisal of identity groupings tend to assume that identity is immutable; yet it is being constantly recreated in the late-Westphalian environment by individuals, political, social, economic, and geographic influences, and also the ubiquitous forces of globalization, fragmentation, development, democratization and integration, within the context of a growing 'ideological' human security discourse. A lengthy period of trying to avoid including the individual and the normative as factors, agents or structures in resolving conflict seem now to be giving way, and there has arisen an increasing acceptance of the fact that radical change and strategies are required to meet the challenge of identity at its most basic level.

The challenges of making peace arise not just from the deep-rooted nature of conflict, and the difficult issues that have been involved over many generations, but also from the general failure of the Westphalian international system itself. Indeed it might be said that there has been a systemic blindness in the face of the modalities of identity politics, ethnic groups and their needs, and the blindness of state and sovereignty in one important respect mirrors the structurally inherent imbalance pertaining to domestic individual and group inequalities, which have marked the international system from the perspective of both dominant and repressed actors since the emergence of the first feudal societies, empires, democracies, dictatorships and totalitarian governments. Barriers to diversity of identity have been structurally built into the Westphalian version of the international system in the way that elitism or sexism have been in socio-political and economic systems. They have been related to the basic requirement for security; hence the securitization of actors, identities, roles, territory and resources.[12]

Since the end of the cold war, the challenges posed by conflict-torn societies are generally perceived as being vast, although this must of course be ascribed to a level of relativity vis-à-vis the challenge that maintaining the cold war balance presented. In the context of the previous era (of comforting symmetry, as Waltz argued[13]), it is fairly clear that the traditional diplomatic approach of *Realpolitik* allowed a maximum practical objective of stability, not justice, and a normative order was constructed on the basis of the value of the status quo. However, given the reduction in the priority of maintaining a balance of power, there has been much more pressure to try to evolve strategies to deal with conflict for which formerly a status quo without justice would have been acceptable. So far the record has been poor, though it is possible to see in which direction practices for the ending of conflict have been moving: the UN's retreat from Angola, and its uncertain achievements in Cambodia, Somalia, Bosnia, Rwanda, Haiti and elsewhere, serve to underscore this.

The long-awaited reform of the UN system mirrors a much-needed rethink of both the practice and the theory of ending conflict in the context of the systems in which is it applied, particularly regarding the role of the state, the nature of political community (particularly the balance between 'cosmopolitan' and 'communitarian' forces for peace), responsibility beyond borders, and the role of supranational institutions and organizations. This requires the examination of possible alternative approaches – described here as third generation approaches – to which a growing literature is dedicated, revolving around the development of preventive regimes, peace-maintenance and peace-building, as strategies for ending conflict in a new, normalized environment. Such developments are not without their own contradictions. Do third-generation approaches depend upon a coherent, universal, blueprint, perhaps developed under the auspices of the UN, to be applied in every case? Will such activities, derived from neo-liberal and neo-institutionalist concepts of post-cold war order, totalize? Will they lead to forms of global governance? How far can the tensions between the local and the global be resolved in the context of such operations? Finally, can claims for identity, representation, and human security be resolved by reconstituting Westphalian states in conflict environments?

Developing approaches

Thus far, two generations of monodimensional activities have emerged, while a third generation of multidimensional activity has developed in response to the perceived inefficiency of earlier approaches, in particular since the end of the cold war. It is acknowledged here that the term 'generation' provides only a loose typology. It is used to reflect both a general historical progression, but more definitely, a categorization of approaches to ending conflict and their responses to their own inadequacies.

Traditional peacemaking and peacekeeping is described in the typology put forward here as 'first generation' (which includes and is derived from standard diplomatic practice, defined by the norms of state interaction and international law). According to *Realpolitik* approaches, conflict is ameliorated at the state level by negotiation and tactical bargaining or coercive third-party intervention, and is therefore dependent on the state-centric framework of international relations which is subject to a security dilemma, managed through the balance-of-power mechanism, or in its neo-liberal form, pacified by the spread of capitalist democracy and the intervention of international institutions. Thus, the individual, subnational, or substate group has little input into such processes, except through the democratic process, if it exists. Conflict resolution approaches based on a human needs/world society framework and drawing on the insights provided by peace researchers, which here are described as 'second generation', developed out of a need to find a process which could facilitate the 'resolution', rather than the management, of intractable conflicts – often ethnic conflict – and was derived from a grassroots movement that decries the state-centric and power-political leanings of high politics as described by dominant theories of the international system and *Realpolitik* approaches to conflict. Conflict resolution approaches attempted to bring the individual back into the realm of conflict management and made the case that conflict can be resolved at the diplomatic level only with the consent of the individual citizen.[14] Consequently, it has been argued that conflict resolution approaches may actually help facilitate diplomatic comprom- ises and, more significantly, provide a critique of traditional conflict management approaches. It is well known that traditional diplomacy and conflict resolution approaches have differing views of what is de- noted by the word 'peace', diplomacy assuming no more than status- quo management, while conflict resolution, more optimistically, sees a natural harmony of interests being plausible. Peace research approaches confirm this division, seeing the roots of conflict in the structural defi- ciencies of the international system, examining the tension of structures and individual needs and desires.

One of the most obvious problems with standard debates on conflict management and resolution,[15] apart from reliance on coercion, ripe moments or hurting statemates, and the application of vast external resources (as at Camp David and Dayton), is the lack of complementar- ity between classical peacekeeping and forms of peacemaking,[16] and between what is often described as Track I and Track II diplomacy (and their derivatives). One long-standing objective has been to reduce the conceptual and practical blockages in third party peacemaking at official and unofficial levels. Furthermore, because of the existing literature's general failure to examine the views, objectives and strategies of direct and indirect disputants with respect to third parties or the local, regional and international environment, this undermines work that has been carried out on the post-conflict search for a solution and the variants that such a solution could take,[17] because both the process of ending conflict, and the envisaged solution, tend to reflect the structures of the Westphalian international system and its dominant actors, rather than the disputants themselves, their perceptions of the conflict and of that system. Consequently, there is a need to examine the direct and indirect impact of the structure of the system, which illustrates the general failure of state-based theories and methods of conflict management, resolution and settlement, in dealing with conflict through the prism of territory, sovereignty, and legitimacy – this being the legacy of Westphalia and *Realpolitik* in its hard and soft vari- ants.[18]

The implications contained here are that there are several distinct levels in world politics, including that of the state and that of the individual, and one cannot operate in harmony without the other. In the post-cold war world, however, this description is somewhat limited, and what parts of the following discussion is predicated upon is the view that there are developing – however fragile – ethical regimes[19] and norms of democratic civil society, at the citizen level, at the global level,[20] within the international system, and to a certain extent at the level of international society.[21] The contemporary (Western-centric) belief in the benefits of democratization, together with an elevated concern about human rights and human rights-based-intervention illustrate these twin developments, which run parallel with each other. Somewhere in between is located the traditional international system in which power politics conditions diplomatic discourse about international and substate intractable conflict.[22] This system is sandwiched between emerging democratic societies split by intractable, civil or ethnic conflict and a developing international society,[23] both of which have much in common. Also emerging and complicating this picture is a growing but contested global civil society. All of this may lead to a development of an international society in which actors at all levels find a normative basis for their interaction, in the context of a late, and emerging, post-Westphalian system. This indicates that it is more practical to view the role of the spectrum of conflict resolution and management activities as one of mediation between global and local civil societies, and the still predominant international state system (through which many official actors still view conflict).

A third generation

Third generation activity has been characterized by its complex and multilevel, multidimensional nature, and has occurred in the context of a post-cold war shift in the international system. This has influenced UN peacekeeping with the shift from the traditional interpositionary peacekeeping system (in parallel with high-level mediation and negotiation) to the integrated and multidimensional operations which have marked the post-cold war era (including the aberration of the paradoxical 'peace-enforcement' missions). In many cases, it has been multidimensional UN peacekeeping forces which have provided the foundations for a plethora of humanitarian, preventive, and peacebuilding activities, and it has been through the UN framework that it has become possible to regard peace operations as achieving more than strategic settlements, but as part of the social fabric of former conflict environments. In this, the UN has become by far the most significant actor (also obviously flawed) in the post-cold war era, partly because of its recognition of the multiple political, social, economic and humanitarian dynamics of 'peace' via the concept of human security. Thus, third generation approaches to peace, though problematic because of their totalizing potential, signify the attempt to create an operational, normative, just, democratic fabric of mediation in and between civil societies.

However, such coordinated activity and intervention implies that there is a common, perhaps even universal, basis for such action agreed by the vast majority of the world's actors, states, organizations, governments, administrations and communities. This revives the problematic debate of the universal versus the particularist normative basis for such action and the possibility that such mechanisms would be viewed as neo-colonial.[24] However, the multidimensional framework highlights the direction in which peace operations have moved since the end of the cold war, with the experience of UN missions in Namibia, Cambodia, Mozambique, Somalia, the former Yugoslavia, Western Sahara and El Salvador. UN peacekeeping, peacemaking and peacebuilding operations have shown an accelerated response to change since the end of the cold war, and multidimensional operations concentrating on humanitarian and normative issues – at the deep roots of conflict – have begun to emerge in parallel with the standard status-quo operations of the previous era. A multiplicity of actors, interests and issues areas are now frequently involved in UN operations, from within and without conflict environments and at diverse levels of global interaction. These approaches are highly problematic, however, and hint at clear normative limitations which may again reproduce the conditions they have set out to resolve. In the late-Westphalian environment, a discussion of humanitarian intervention has been a logical outcome of the gradual broadening of peace operations, meaning that approaches to ending conflict are now less consensual and more interventionary in their nature. It is argued in this study that for approaches to ending conflict to retrieve themselves from such pitfalls they must incorporate inter-subjective perspectives of sovereignty, territory, law and order, justice and histories, and aim at promoting a democratic discourse based on a post-conventional morality in the context of interdependent political communities. This may form the basis for the emergence of a fourth generation approach.

Defining the book

This study attempts to unravel the complexities of making peace in 'intractable' conflict by viewing it from a late/post-Westphalian perspective of human security, international and global civil society. Much of what follows is predicated on the view that many 'intractable' conflicts become so because the disputants locate their negotiating positions and

neo-colonial

objectives in their perceptions of what the Westphalian international system, its norms and political and legal structures offers them.[25] This means that identity, be it nation, national, communal or ethnic, finds much of its meaning, and therefore dynamism and legitimacy (and abrasiveness) in this construction, in particular in the tension between sovereignty, human rights, territory, identity and self-determination, and security. Thus, a meaningful evaluation of disputants' positions, which can contribute to effective approaches, must occur through an examination of their views of their role, status, positions and leverage in international society, and through what they believe to be their rights vis-à-vis the contemporary system as it stands.

As a result, this book addresses a gap in the evolving field of conflict theory. It aims to chart and critique the development of the field in the context of shifting global norms, and examine the consequences and implications of new types of peace activities that are emerging in response to the shifting nature of the 'international system' and the changes brought about by the end of the cold war, including the highly significant elevation of normative concerns and rhetoric. This elevation, much like the similar trend that was apparent at the end of the First World War, appears to be backed by the military might of the West, as the NATO action over Kosovo in mid-1999 indicated (although the events in East Timor and Chechnya in the same year seem to qualify this proposition somewhat). This is actually in contrast to the post-First World War situation in that force was not used to back up the emergent idealism/neoliberalism of some of the dominant world powers, which feared long-term engagement. (There may be a heavy price to pay for the elevation of normative concerns, however, in the same way that the ideological struggle of the cold war led the US into the quagmire of Vietnam in the 1960s.)

Implicitly, this study examines the question of the relationship between theory and practice in the field, something which has tended to be ignored in the mainstream literature at least.[26] Has the predominance of a state-centric, first generation methodology exacerbated the very problems that such approaches attempt to solve? In other words, does theory influence, create or recreate the practices of ending conflict? This indicates that it is pertinent to examine the development of the debates surrounding making peace in the context of epistemological and methodological debates relating to positivist and non-positivist approaches to IR. It has become a point of contention over the value of each approach, with non-positivist standpoints seemingly indicating that positivism in IR leads to the emergence of security dilemmas, status quo oriented policies and forms of diplomacy, which are unable to provide justice in international society. Such positions point to the fact that this perhaps leads to self-fulfilling zero-sum prophecies. Proponents of such approaches argue that managing conflict is the best that can be achieved, given the nature of states and the international system. Opponents argue that non-positivist approaches pertaining to identity, justice and normative issues may promote a better understanding of conflict and how it should be resolved. This feeds into the debates around ending conflict, in that peacekeeping, international mediation and conflict resolution approaches are essentially positivist, though the latter has begun to straddle the subjective and normative divide by focusing on individuals as actors. I argue here that the emergence of a third generation approach is occurring partly because of the elevation of intersubjective approaches, relating to identity, justice, and normative issues. This has led to a re-emphasis of issues pertaining to *human* security. Thus, third generation approaches claim to incorporate both positivist and intersubjective perspectives, though not uncontroversially. Yet it may well be that the emergence of third generation approaches represents the expansion of positivist approaches, thus continuing to replicate conflict.

This study therefore concentrates on a series of questions:

(i)   How far has the development of peace approaches from first through to third generation approaches enabled a response to the full scale of problems which intractable forms of conflict raise?

(ii) What sort of international order is envisaged by such approaches, and what sort of order is actually achieved?

(iii) What issues in particular need to be addressed if peace processes are to result in sustainable outcomes?

(iv) How far has the evolution of UN approaches to making peace enabled it to address the issues referred to in (iii) and what kind of order results from UN intervention?

(v)   What are the prospects for international society, and how may approaches to ending conflict continue to develop?

Chapter 1 outlines the practical, normative, ethical and other shifts in the global environment that have prompted this study, and which can be traced in the development of world politics in two main phases. These two phases, those of the Westphalian/cold war and late/post-Westphalian/post-cold war environment have witnessed significant shifts in both the theory and the practice of ending conflict. The main changes which are important in this context relate to: the development of states; the metamorphosis of the concept of sovereignty; the emergence of the forces of fragmentation, regionalization and globalization; the developing cosmopolitan role of IOs, ROs and NGOs; the shift towards human security; humanitarian intervention and the elevation of normative perspectives in the analysis of global politics on the part of dominant actors (including states, international and regional organizations which project different permutations of legitimacy, legality, and military and economic power).

Chapter 2 analyses the debates about, and critiques of, the theory and practice of traditional forms of peacekeeping and international mediation. It examines in particular the theoretical debates surrounding classical peacekeeping, state-backed mediation and the role of the UN Secretary-General and his Special Representatives. It argues that such activities can be described as 'first generation' forms of making peace of a monodimensional nature.

Chapter 3 examines the theory and practice of conflict resolution, both as a response to the shortcomings of tradition diplomacy, and as an independent approach to 'intractable' conflict. It draws upon instances of private attempts at conflict resolution, as well as those that are backed by international organizations and NGOs, and indirectly by states, and concentrates mainly on the conceptual and practical obstacles to this type of activity. Second generation conflict resolution approaches take a radically different view of conflict when compared to first generation approaches; the assumption is made that conflicts can be (and ought to be) solved rather than merely managed. Conflict resolution approaches see difficulties in the way first generation approaches attempt to deal with conflict and therefore propose to address the civil level of conflict in the context of compromise, reconciliation, and deconstruction of stereotypes, rather than in the context of rearranging limited resources between self-interested and competing actors. Conflict at this level, it is argued, can be viewed in a win-win perspective. Despite this, second generation activities are also monodimensional.

Chapter 4 examines the weaknesses of the first two generations of activity as outlined in the previous chapters, in order to develop a clear critique of what I have defined as monodimensional attempts to deal with multidimensional conflicts. It is argued that traditional peacekeeping, mediation and negotiation, which are derived from traditional state-centric diplomacy and conflict resolution provide only narrow frameworks only capable of addressing a single dimension of conflicts which in their very nature are multidimensional. This is partly as a consequence of the emphasis of both approaches on rationalizing conflict with 'manageable' frameworks so that they can be reduced to their dominant dynamics. However, in doing so, both first and second generation approaches become victims of reductionism and consequently undervalue significant aspects of conflict, and ignore the possibilities for addressing these aspects. First and second generation approaches operate by prioritizing the issues that need to be addressed; this leads their essentially monodimensional nature, and their subsequent theoretical inflexibility. This in turn has led to these approaches tending to reproduce 'intractable' conflicts, partly because of their inability to recontextualize themselves in a shifting global, regional and local environment.

Chapter 5 examines the development of, and significant problems with, emerging multidimensional peace operations, addressing local, regional and global issues which impinge upon conflict in an interdependent world in which normative frameworks, though contested, are clarifying.

Finally, Chapter 6 discusses the sensitizing of approaches to making peace to the many problems faced by the concept of multidimensional peace operations, and discusses the problems uncovered in the way we think about making peace and creating and recreating order in the international system. Some thoughts are offered about the possible qualities of a fourth generation approach that might resolve some of the problems inherent in approaches to ending conflict.

This study concludes that traditional forms of diplomacy were established with an eye to the Realist nature of the international system from the Treaty of Westphalia until the end of the cold war and the creation of an order of 'fact'. From a liberal perspective a normative value was added to this order. Because the post-cold war order is fundamentally different from that of the previous era by virtue of the re-emergence of humanitarian and normative issues, approaches to ending conflict in theory and practice need to be re-examined and reformulated. The opportunity to critically readdress long-standing debates in this field represents an important challenge. While making peace may well be seen as an attempt to impose a universal sovereign discourse in conflict environments, there is the opportunity to view peace processes not as an overlay to be placed in conflict environments, but as a long-term sustainable discourse about a local, regional and global fabric of mediation to resolve human security issues and prevent the creation and recreation of conflictual binaries. The link between making peace and order depends upon the nature of the envisaged order and the nature of 'peace' and 'conflict' need to be problematized.

1
Order, Security and Conflict in a Changing Global Environment

Introduction

Making peace in the international system has traditionally been dependent upon the nature of diplomacy and the selective use of direct or indirect coercion, in turn defined by the framework of international politics created by the interactions of the states, in particular, great powers and regional hegemons. Thus, recent shifts in the international system have had important implications for the utilization of, and the methods of ending conflict. Increasing diverse private and official actors and organizations have been called on to respond to the inadequacies of the states-system vis-à-vis certain forms of conflict, no longer easily distinguishable by the traditional concepts of war, insurgency, belligerency, secessionism, irredentism, revolt, and other concepts related to political violence. This chapter aims to draw out the main characteristics of the Westphalian/Cold War and late-Westphalian/ post-Cold War environment[1] with respect to the implications held for the theory and practice of making peace. It must be noted however, that long debate about the 'international system', 'international society', 'world society' or 'global society' indicates that the task of describing the changing global environment in the light of conflicts which tend to emerge, and its effects on conflict practice and theory, are contestable and tenuous right from the start. However, it is my contention here that certain significant changes can be teased out to provide a useful basis for the discussion of the evolution of theory and practice of making peace in the chapters that follow.

The end of the Cold War was greeted with triumphalism in the West, despite the fact that there was an almost complete lack of recognition of the subsequent need for rethink of what might follow. The collapse of the Soviet Union took analysts by surprise, and it may well be that the emergence of a 'new world order' will do the same.[2] Changing approaches to conflict have perhaps been most pronounced in the conceptual shift from state security to human security in the rhetoric of many of the actors in the system, led partly by the UN-inspired discourse of the early 1990s about human rights and sustainable development aspired to by many states after the removal of the crushing imperatives provided by global conflict and a Soviet threat (misperceived or not).[3] This has stimulated the broadening of security concerns away from purely state-centric interests with important implications for any discussion of conflict and making peace. This may have been interpreted in international society as providing an opportunity to create a 'modern cosmopolis', as Danilo Zolo has argued, in which 'peace and stability are to be guaranteed by a legitimized power hierarchy'.[4] This has been a possible scenario ever since 1815 and the Congress of Vienna, was taken up by the League and later the UN, and implicit within this tendency is the creation of a 'universal order'. This, Zolo argues, has been mistakenly based on the 'domestic analogy' and defies the deep roots of conflict, raising the question of whether 'any cosmopolitan project [such as the Congress of Vienna, the League of Nations, and the UN] can ever be anything other than an inherently hegemonic and violent undertaking?'[5] This problem is a vital component of any attempt to understand or create peace.

The apparent strengthening of the international system provided by the UN has been something of an illusion, although the potential of cooperation between intergovernmental organizations and NGOs seems to present increased possibilities. The changing discourses about sovereignty, identity and security also appear to be increasingly significant, as evidenced by the progress seen in Northern Ireland, Spain, and the Middle East after the end of war, though this may be discounted somewhat by the outbreaks of conflict in Algeria, East Timor, Yugoslavia, Kosovo, and Sierra Leone. The instability in the Eastern Mediterranean, Greco-Turkish relations, and the potential for backsliding both in Northern Ireland and the Middle East peace process are also implicit in this changing dialogue. Will humanitarianism and shared norms overtake crude nationalism and ethno-nationalism and their association with inflexible concepts of sovereignty, which tend to be entwined in so-called zones of intractable conflict?[6] What does the shift in the definition of security since the end of the Cold War imply for areas that traditionally have been viewed from western perspectives as zones of intractable conflict, underdeveloped, historically violent, and filled with seemingly insurmountable religious and identity conflict? Over the centuries and as a result of the emergence of nationalism,[7] the shifting of boundaries and conquest (often as a reaction to perceived insecurity), the demographic characteristics of these political units and areas have often moved from multiethnic and cosmopolitan to mono-ethnic. The current trend of fragmentation may continue, as is evidenced by the events over Kosovo, itself long a flashpoint, and in East Timor in 1999. This chapter develops this discussion in the dual context of the changing nature of security issues in the light of contemporary critical debates related to states, claims to sovereignty, identity, security, justice and responsibility. It charts the shift from a discourse about the 'international system' to a late-Westphalian discourse about an 'international society' in order to provide a basis for the analysis in the rest of this study.

The Westphalian system and order

States have been constructed in part to exercise and monopolize organized violence. The fact that every major systemic war (in the traditional sense of the term) has ended with a peace treaty, an attempt to create a regional or global balance of power, and a conflict management system, is indicative of the significance of tools for ending conflict throughout the history of international politics for the creation and recreation of a version of order prominent in the minds of third parties (and disputants who have consented to the process). Traditional tools of conflict management associated with state-centric diplomacy revolve around peace-keeping, mediation and negotiation frameworks, and incorporate actors defined in terms either of states or of insurgents.[8] They are products of the practice of *Realpolitik*, and of the balance of power system. These traditional tools of conflict management were always suspect (one only has to examine the application of peacekeeping and mediation by the UN throughout the cold war to see this), partly because they were confined by the parochial imperatives of a state-centric and conservative order.

The Treaty of Westphalia offered the notion that statehood was sacrosanct, and that this was guaranteed through a system of reciprocal sovereignty, conducted by political leaders rather than religious leaders. Conflicting claims and desires for global and regional domination led to the need for the recognition of certain levels of interdependence in the international system if the status quo was to be preserved and managed through the Concert system instigated by the victors of the Napoleonic Wars at the Congress of Vienna at 1815. Thus, the principles of diplomacy

dictated that state interests were paramount and that diplomatic relations and communication could be conducted to prevent conflicts from
escalating, in the context of an international system in which the rights
of states were well defined (although the rights of individuals were to be
defined only by the government apparatus of the states that they in-
habited). This system broke down catastrophically in 1914; the outcome
of the First World War allowed the victors (and principally the US) to
redefine a new version of order and a new system of conflict management, elucidated in two main parts including the <u>territorial reforms</u> that
were instigated at Versailles[9] and the <u>normative elements that were</u>
added to legal and diplomatic practice by aspects of the League of
Nations.[10] These reforms were to be endorsed by a new international
institution that was the culmination of several centuries of diplomatic
dialogue to prevent conflict from threatening the status quo, and about
the debate between interests and morality in the international system.
Yet the response at Versailles was revolutionary because of the sheer
scale of the First World War. It also clearly represented state-centric
practices, although cracks in the state apparatus had begun to appear,
only to be rapidly covered over. Conflict between states was a planned-
for and manageable part of the international environment, but conflict
within states or challenging statehood and sovereignty was something
beyond the pale and far more subversive. The establishment of the
League and later the UN was indicative of the failure of states to manage
conflict through previously more informal balance of power mechanisms. The legacy of the Congress of Vienna in 1815 provided the concept
of diplomatic consultation in a zero-sum environment moderated by
the balance of power, while the Versailles settlement in 1919 added
normative notions (and tensions) related to democratization, self-
determination, and minority rights – but in a framework within which
the victors squabbled over territory and future influence.[11]

The first half of the twentieth century also saw the development of
alternative ideologies and views. Notably liberal, social, peace and disarmament movements, and internationalism with its associations with
humanitarianism, socialism, feminism and so on, contributed important opposing discourses to mainstream and top-down diplomatic and
international practices. However, many of these alternative debates,
seen as based on 'unworkable ethics' were contained, defined and constrained by the legal, national and liberal order which the League
created.[12]

The failure of the League,[13] and the establishment of the UN indicated
that preventing conflict between states was perceived as a worthy cause

to follow, while conflict which was perpetrated by non-state actors was undesirable; one of the UN's main tasks was to help create *new* states in the process of decolonization – in other words to release the pressure on the state-centric international system from non-state actors by providing them with notional sovereignty (and therefore equality and legitimacy), even if it was only 'quasi-sovereignty'[14] and therefore only a legal fiction. The UN became a vehicle through which 'quasi' and other, 'negative', forms of sovereignty, moderated by international treaties of guarantee, emerged and through which third states (or alliances) were given authority over supposedly new 'sovereign' actors. The UN soon became a vehicle for the mediation of sovereignty at a political, normative and legal level, through the General Assembly declarations, in particular relating to human rights and self-determination.[15] The nature of diplomacy was changing, and required a radical rethink of the nature of conflict management. The UN Charter limited self-determination to former colonies,[16] and endorsed the principle's linkage with the legitimacy of sovereignty, statehood and the principle of non-intervention, in a world in which security was to be guaranteed by a council of its most powerful members. All of these somewhat contradictory principles made the practice of making peace fraught with practical, legal and normative pitfalls.

During the cold war states used political ideology and military force to manipulate the rule of international law and to uphold a system that often ignored the use of force (against other states as well as against their own populations) in an attempt to maintain the status quo.[17] Democracy was viewed by western states as the only way of regulating states' internal behaviour (unless there was 'no alternative'). In the post-cold war world, what impact have the emerging norms of human rights had on the traditional view of sovereignty, and therefore on the realist vision of the international system and security? Article 2(7) of the UN Charter codified the norms of sovereignty and non-intervention that had emerged from Westphalia, offering a legal model based on the sovereign equality of states. However, the UN system began to alter Westphalia: international law is no longer applicable only to relations between states but to individuals too, as several war-crimes tribunals have demonstrated. The UN system is also concerned with orchestrating economic, social and environmental matters, as the UN Economic and Social Council, the World Bank, the International Monetary Fund, the International Whaling Commission, the Food and Agriculture Organization, the World Health Organization and a battery of human rights conventions have illustrated. On the other hand, the UN Charter, in many respects, has just extended the Westphalian interstate system, by serving to legitimate the interests of Security Council members,[18] as illustrated in particular by the difficulties seen in the process of UN reform and the expansion of the Security Council since the end of the cold war.

It is not surprising that the international system has, since the end of the cold war, been increasingly viewed as flawed, because it only recognizes states and implies that states are equal and autonomous.[19] There is also a conflict between the principle of self-determination in Article 1 (2) of the UN Charter and the preservation of a state's domestic jurisdiction as outlined in Article 2(7). Clearly differing rates of development, armaments, access to resources, and of course interdependence and fragmentation, makes the equality of states somewhat of a fallacy. Furthermore, the existence of substate interest groups threatens the preservation of the domestic jurisdiction of states.[20] The question then becomes, how can political, social and economic development and interdependence lead to security, defined as being situated in the realms of physical security for states, groups and individuals, and cultural, religious, economic and social security – in other words, human security? The most recent answer to this question, as proposed by the UN Secretary-General and the US President in 1999 at the General Assembly, has been a re-endorsement of the principle of collective security based on universal norms.[21]

Theorizing order and security in a Westphalian environment

During the cold war, classical security debates of a strategic nature remained at the heart of traditional International Relations (IR) theory. IR theory has seen the development of a number of frameworks through which the issue of order and security could be viewed, and which carried significant implications for the practice and development of approaches to ending conflict.[22] The starting point for this analysis is to make clear that, despite the simple definitions of order and security that stemmed from strategic and military debates, security as a concept has always been confused – almost essentially contested.[23] In a classic article, Wolfers, however, defined it as the absence of threat to acquired values.[24] This implies the 'acquired values' will of course be those of dominant actors, both within states and within the states-system.

The primary traditional framework draws on the works of the Realist school including the later variants of structural and neo-realism. This school attempts to view security and order through a narrow positivist theoretical framework, which attempts to reduce the behaviour of the main actors in the international system – the state, and its associated economy – to models in which behaviour can be simply analysed and predicted. In this debate, international politics revolves around the states-system, the state being the highest unit of analysis, and its behaviour only modified to a greater or lesser extent by the existence of other actors in the international system. The nature of individual states revolves around the notion of the pursuit of the national interest; thus states are self-interested, self-serving, and exist in an international environment of Hobbesian anarchy. As Waltz argued, in anarchy security is the highest end and it is only if survival is ensured that states can seek other goals such as tranquillity, profit, and power in a self-help system.[25] Thus, states pursue power and prestige in order to guarantee their security from the unwanted attentions of other states, which are also engaged in a race for power and prestige. From this is derived the hierarchical nature of the international system, and also its shape and stability. However, from this is also derived the security dilemma in which one state's achievements in its chase for power and prestige presents other states with an imperative for relative success, in the face of the threats from other, more powerful states. Neo-realists argue that security is achieved through being the most powerful actor; states compete for security in a self-help system, this being their most important goal.[26] Such frameworks tend to be reductionist in that many actors and variables are ignored in the face of the overwhelming control of the state; furthermore, internal issues, relating to the legitimacy of a state's regime, and the viability of its economy are ignored insofar as such elements do not impinge on the state's quest for prestige, power and influence at the international level. Waltz argued that the Cold War bipolarity, which seemed to be modelled by derivatives of realist thought, had 'stark simplicities and comforting symmetry'[27] and that 'peace' prevailed at the centre of the international system. In his view the cold war bipolar system had demonstrated its structural durability through its ability to survive major wars.[28] His characterization of the post-cold war system as being bipolarity in an altered state[29] placed the emphasis on technological and economic competition. Realists would argue that this is the best that can be achieved, while liberalist opponents would argue that this is the reason why so little is achieved. Security, therefore, was defined by the realist school as pertaining to the relations between states, and was to be guaranteed by global and regional balances of terror (power), which were to be managed, rather than eradicated. Realists and liberal analysts met with agreement upon the role of international organizations in setting guidelines for state behaviour, via a western view of the post-Second World War inter--

national system. Thus, approaches to ending conflict were derived from within this framework.

Traditional security debates, and those debates surrounding the stabilization of local, regional and global systems through the incremental adjustments offered by first generation approaches worked predominantly at the state level, though other levels were addressed in a secondary manner on occasion. Figure 1.1 illustrates the tools available within the Westphalian context:

GLOBE–Addressed through international conferences, congresses, organizations, peace talks between great powers, arms reduction talks.

REGION–Addressed through international and regional conferences, organisations, congresses, peacekeeping, peace talks between great powers/regional powers and mediation.

STATE–Addressed through international and regional conferences, congresses, peace talks between great powers, bilateral and multilateral talks. Occasionally by peacekeeping and mediation.

GROUP–Addressed through substate negotiations, democratization, minority rights provisions, etc. Sometimes by peacekeeping and/or mediation.

INDIVIDUAL–Addressed through substate negotiations, democratization, Minority rights provisions and human rights norms and law.

Figure 1.1   Levels of analysis and traditional forms of making peace

The state theoretically provides the fulcrum on which the entire substate and international political system rests, and from which authority, power, legitimacy, decision-making and implementation stems; normative, psychological, environmental and identity-based levels of analysis are all addressed through this mechanism.

The modern history of the international system has been one of an increasing awareness of the fact that the 'national interest' cannot be sustained independently. The First World War indicated that war was to be avoided wherever possible and the League of Nations was established in order to facilitate conflict management and settlement. The response to the Second World War was to strengthen the role of international organizations in order to police world politics and try to guarantee peace and security. During the cold war UN peacekeeping filled the gap that was created by the lack of consensus in the Security Council in order to prevent small-scale conflicts from upsetting the status quo. It has been argued that states have progressively adjusted their policies on security affairs, based on perceptions of interests, in ways that increased the importance of international organizations. The process was not a zero-sum game in which the state lost and the United Nations won. Rather, states won in the sense of greater barriers against armed attacks on them, and the UN won in the sense of being given more authority and tasks than the League of Nations once had.[30]

States came for the most part to hold in common an interest in maintaining a status quo in which they were the predominant actors; this was achieved through a balance between independence in many aspects of political decision-making and interdependence in economic matters. Consequently, power, authority and legitimacy was deemed to emanate from states, though decisions and decision-making processes were deemed to be more legitimate if groups of states concurred, often through supranational forums and particularly when intervention was under discussion. What this meant was that order was to be defined as state-centric, and as a hierarchical modification of anarchy dependent upon the interests of powerful states, which had a duty to impose their own version of order to protect themselves and their allies.

Thus, the cold war was characterized by state-centric conflicts, such as in the Middle East, Latin America, Africa, and in Asia, that revolved around the interests of existing states. It was characterized by the repression of non-state groups or territories which were claimed by states, such as in south-eastern Turkey, Northern Ireland, or Kashmir and Tibet, while proxy wars, such as in Vietnam, provided a forum for ideological conflicts between East and West.

Alternative discourses within the Westphalian framework

While Realist approaches have formed the core of international relations debates since the Second World War, particularly in US circles (this being of significance in itself), such frameworks have been challenged from several angles.[31] David Mitrany placed the emphasis on the promotion of values and habits of cooperation by functional institutions,[32] and Karl Deutsch argued that a North Atlantic–European 'security community' could be created to transcend traditional security dilemmas in the region, through the integration of communities, the logic of community and peaceful dispute settlement, rather than the logic of anarchy.[33] Structural approaches argued that security is merely the product of the grand forces that autonomously define the shape of the international economy and the rise and fall of hegemonic powers. Functionalists, liberalists and pluralists also challenged the view that a mechanism of self-help in the international system, and an anarchy controlled by the great powers is a viable, scientific and just formula for stability. Instead, they focused on the economic, social, political, structural, and other inequalities that lead to conflict, not necessarily between states, but also at a substate or trans-state level.

Some analysts emphasized the value of functional institutions that were viewed as able to relieve the pressures which individuals, states, and other actors found themselves caught up in.[34] This seemed to be born out in these circumstances by the contribution the UN was able to make. In Egypt, after the Suez war, the UN Secretary-General played an important face-saving role for Britain and France. The UN played a controversial role in the Congo; the Secretary-General played a face-saving role in the Cuban Missile crisis; he mediated an end to the conflict between Iran and Iraq; and many flashpoints such as in Cyprus, were dampened by UN peacekeeping forces or observer missions, such as in Kashmir and on the Golan Heights.

The role of supranational institutions in facilitating regional integration has also been indicative of the changing nature of the international system, in stable regions at least. Some proponents saw the development of an interdependent world society or cosmopolitan international system which would eventually negate the emphasis on power-politics between states, replacing it with an emphasis on individuals, economic cooperation, and functional regional and global institutions to facilitate the transactional relationship which would form a new international system. The 'English School' of IR argued that despite the anarchy of the international system, common norms did exist and were generally adhered to, thus indicating the existence of an international society, despite the prevalence of strategic interests.[35] Liberalist and pluralist approaches redefined security in a much broader sense (though still bowing to the hegemonic discourse of Westphalia), positing that it was dependent not only on the actions of states towards one another, but on the satisfaction of the basic needs of individuals. This contributed to the recent discussions related to the development of international regimes, ethics and norms, and also the debates about the qualities of an international cosmopolitan society, global democracy and justice. The recent debates on globalization, ethics, ethical regimes and international norms[36] all point to an understanding of order in world politics as being constituted by a wider variety of issues, forces and actors. It is clearly apparent that the dominant issues of IR transcend the mere security needs of states, that structural forces related to the international economy and globalization are at play, that the voices of individuals and identity or interest groups cannot be overlooked, and that states and the supranational institutions and organizations that they belong to have levels of practical and normative responsibilities to each other, and to future generations that cannot sensibly be overlooked in the manner that state-centric security debates allow.[37] 'Order' is therefore being redefined by necessity.

Rosenau depicted the shift from cold war to the post-cold war era as a 'bifurcation of world politics' between a *sovereignty bound* world to a *sovereignty free* world.[38] The questioning of the rhetoric of sovereignty, as well as demands for subnational reorganization and the elevation of humanitarianism has been crucial, particularly in the context of the paradoxical phenomena of globalization and fragmentation. It is not only the order of Yalta (bipolarity and the cold war) and the Order of Versailles (the borders and states that emerged from the collapse of the Ottoman and Austro-Hungarian Empires, plus the principle of national self-determination) that have been challenged:

> A new pattern of conflicts is prevailing in the post-Cold War period, which is evoking a fresh pattern of responses. The main focus used on international wars; now it is on internal conflicts. Much of the theory of conflict resolution developed in response to symmetric conflicts: now asymmetric conflicts are dominant. International wars have typically been Clausewitzean affairs, fought out by power centres which use organized force directed against enemy forces in order to break the opponent's will to continue. But many post-Cold War conflicts are post-Clausewitzean, involving fragmented decision-making and disorganized forces directed against civilian populations.[39]

As Kaldor has pointed out, these are 'new wars' which entail multiple forms of violence, not necessarily controlled by state actors, in the context of the integration and fragmentation brought about by the nature of globalization.[40]

In the contemporary environment, and as reflected in the utterances of governments,[41] social movements and NGOs, normative issues have raised their heads: discussions about justice and humanitarianism are beginning to contribute to policy-making; and the notion of 'ethical regimes',[42] 'good international citizenship' and ethical dimensions to foreign policy[43] have buttressed (and exploited) the case for the development of a just international society, most notably proposed via cosmopolitanism. Such developments, however incremental, underline the weaknesses of a framework based on the sanctity of sovereignty and statehood (and therefore nationalism), in an environment where identity issues, humanitarianism, regionalization and globalization are altering patterns of transactions. International organizations and NGOs are becoming highly specialized, and questions of justice and humanitarianism permeate the distribution of social, political, and practical resources in an interdependent environment.

Indications of these changes emerged as far back as the conferences on disarmament at The Hague at the end of the last century. Such specialized conferences were indicative of the need for states to observe a set of mutual rules in international society in order to manage their relationships and avoid conflict, as were the meetings that brought about the systems elucidated by the Treaty of Westphalia and the Congress of Vienna, the League of Nations, and later the UN, which has attempted to moderate the results of the 'eighty years crisis'.[44] The development of a new international constitutional structure of permanent and universal conferences of states was vital in subsequently shaping modern international society,[45] as it was also important that the states were coherent units (though this was achieved through the exploitation of nationalism to a certain extent). Such permanent multilateral conferences were indicative of the need for a basis from which all states can approach a range of security issues in order to promote a mutual order.

The 'internationalist' debate is important here. Lynch has argued that it continues to exist with four main strands: the democratic peace, led by the US and the UN; humanitarian interventionists in the UN and NGO communities; neo-liberalism and the anti-globalization debate.[46] The post-cold war UN, it has been argued, could become a blueprint for a new international framework to oversee the activities, externally and internally, of states, and those of other, non-state actors as part of a development of a cosmopolitan, global democracy, and of humanitarianism.[47] The EU has also shifted the level of analysis in Europe towards a regional, supranational institution, while the Organization for Security and Co-operation in Europe suggests a broadening of the sphere of interests of multilateral actors, and the emergence of a framework that incorporates the state, but also transcends individual states' interests with a view to the promotion of human security, which requires action to prevent and remove structural and direct forms of violence. However, strategic debates continue to dominate behaviour in uncertain regions. At least at the level of rhetoric, human security competes with state security in the constitution of order. Yet this has underlined the vast difficulties of constructing an order, via forms of intervention and tools for ending conflict, which reflect local, regional and global sensitivities.

The subsequent critique of statecentricity, and the rise of transnational actors, has been an important part of this development. Generally speaking, however, this discourse has been a neo-liberal discourse in which 'should' statements were made about conflict, but according to predominantly western 'universal' norms by powerful actors and their coalitions.

Beyond the Westphalian discourse?

Since the end of the cold war, there seems to have been a reduction of the ability of states to monopolize violence by its 'privatization' from beneath.[48] In this context, violence is often motivated by identity issues, which require a rethinking of traditional approaches to the international system and conflict therein. Thus, recent approaches have challenged traditional formulations of order and security on the basis of identification of a broader range of serious and pressing issues related to the triad of socio-political, military and economic competition, ignored by realist formulations. These include identity, justice, humanitarianism, the environment, and development of a sustainable nature. Globalization and fragmentation, interdependence and normative issues have become a significant part of such debates despite the fact that most states still focus primarily on national interests. Yet power-politics may lead to a self-fulfilling prophecy of international *dis*order lurking within the superficial order of the system. This normative undercurrent is indicative of a point of view in which some actions, circumstances and policies may be viewed as 'just' or 'unjust', but with varying emphasis on the responsibility of actors for the levels of justice of which they may be victims or recipients. A primary question at this level becomes, 'whose formulation of justice will dominate?' the mainstream approach is often opposed as being western-centric, status quo oriented, and thus consolidating global inequalities in its favour. This leads into criticisms that challenge existing frameworks on methodological and epistemological grounds as they are seen to be based on a Western rationale derived from a positivist approach to knowledge. Thus the concept of 'might is right' is at once a theoretical framework with certain explanatory and predictive power and a prescription for policy-making in an uncertain world. As Buzan has argued, intersubjective considerations in security discourses, such as perceived threats against values and norms leads to the securitization of issues at the heart of conflict.[49] This means that socio-cultural issues are increasingly becoming re-securitized, producing dynamics in the international system that do not respond to traditional approaches to ending conflict.

In the human security discourse, 'order' should be derived from the voices of all actors in international society rather than merely from those that dominate in various ways. This means that security has been reconceptualized at multidimensional levels other than the state.[50] So far this has led to multidimensional forms of activity that implicitly create order in the image of the Westphalian system. This human security framework pertaining to states, non-state and individual actors, is based on interdependence within a regional and global economic, social and political framework, and utilizes liberal and functional institutions to coordinate transactions which take place at such levels. However, in the case of Cyprus, Israel and the Palestinians, the Kurds in Turkey, Kosovo and various movements in the Near East, Egypt, Indonesia and East Timor, India, Pakistan and Kashmir, and Algeria, it can be seen that if the integrity of the state is threatened, then insecurity is perceived and strategic considerations at the state level immediately are brought to the forefront of the threatened state's priorities. It must be noted that in all of the examples cited above, not one of the state actors has succeeded in completely quelling its difficulties at a substate level. It is therefore in the interest of regional and global security and order that the 'international system' comes to represent the interests of all such groups on a mutually acceptable basis. As Linklater has pointed out, the notion of a post-Westphalian international society requires changes in the modern states-system and the concepts of sovereignty, territoriality, citizenship and nationality.[51] To this I would add the practice and theory of making peace as an order producing mechanism, based on the legitimacy of the intersubjective and socially constructed nature of issues that give rise to conflict.

Consequently, if security is defined narrowly as being of a military and strategic nature, it merely revolves around the ability of states to harness their own resources to develop a military–industrial complex, and strategic foreign policies, and replicates the highly problematic Westphalian system. This tends to lead to nationalistic and self-perpetuating, self-fulfilling security dilemmas. If a broad definition of security is adopted, on the other hand, including environmental and resource security, and the security of individuals from oppression and poverty, security in society, language, culture and identity, then normative questions relating to regional and global standards of human rights, economic aid and development, as well as a coherent environmental policy must also be included in policy responses on the part of all states, regional and global actors. From this type of discourse, regional institutions and organizations emerge which effectively dampen the negative impact of strategic security concerns through the development of cooperation, interdependence, trust-building, and the resultant reduction of structural violence. The price of this fundamentally more dynamic definition lies in the reduction of state autonomy and sovereignty, which states will only agree to initially if they are located in a stable and predictable environment. Consequently international law also becomes conceptually suspect and at odds with socio-political objectives of a humanitarian nature. It is at this point in the debate that the inscrutable logic of *Realpolitik* usually comes to the fore; yet if one looks at the peace process in Northern Ireland, this cycle can be reversed if the broader context (in this case within the European region) itself is secure and predictable, and alternative versions of sovereignty are recognized.

Conflict, order, and peace in a changing environment

As Linklater has argued, a post-Westphalian environment is not constituted by forces that steer actors towards ethical governance or universalism, but does indicate that totalizing projects, fragmentation and globalization have detached sovereignty from many of its 'sub-issues' such as identity and culture. Linklater argues that this is allowing new combinations of universality and difference to arise, leading to forms of political community.[52]

In the current environment, defined as a late-Westphalian framework, 'order' has been subjected to a critical discourse aimed at uncovering how it has been imposed through a universalizing view of the international system, and often through peacekeeping/peacemaking processes. Thus, conflict has often stemmed from the way that order has marginalized groups and communities through the hegemonic discourse of the state. The issues that give rise to conflict are now less likely to be ignored by a state-centric discourse of diplomacy that imposes a non-reflective order. For example, it has become obvious that many ethnic and identity conflicts, taking place in failing, often underdeveloped regions, involve disputes over autonomy and sovereignty,[53] which lead to traditional state-centric security dilemmas for states that aspire to majority rule and policies of assimilation. So called 'ethnic-security dilemmas' also exist for identity groups that respond to their marginalization by seeking to marginalize other groups or by aiming at independence. Often minority groups have claimed, or at least can claim, certain rights which may well conflict with those of states (multilateral conferences have since the League of Nations' Minority Treaties observed that the principle of self-determination jeopardizes the sanctity of the sovereign state, and have thus tended to deal with non-state actors through the framework of states). Hassner has argued that the post-cold war order is itself jeopardized by this dichotomy.[54] The fact that the modern state itself may be responsible for such problems has increasingly become an important focus in the late-Westphalian environment.

In the light of this identification of the contemporary environment as being marked by practical and theoretical flux, it has been tempting for the neo-realist and neo-liberal schools of thought to see regional and global organizations as a panacea for the ills of the 'international system' and as providing an 'agenda for peace'. This might be constituted by agreement by states on normative standards at the international level. This is exactly what filtered through to the UN at the end of the cold war, when it was empowered by its most powerful members to act in the construction of a 'new world order' – against Iraq, and in Somalia. Such activities were actually little more than a protection of the old world order in that sovereignty was re-endorsed and states were (re)built. The failure of such activities, as evidenced in Somalia and Bosnia, illustrated the need for more creative thinking. Some argued that this was firmly dependent on the development of a more flexible state system, which would allow the transfer of some sovereign authority to functional institutions and regional organizations. In particular, it is tempting to view intergovernmental organizations as motivated by a post-national, post-*nationalist* logic of peaceful integration, economic interdependence and social integration. Yet, because of the failure of the UN in the creation of a 'new world order' after the end of the cold war, it is questionable whether the traditional state is compatible with international organizations or institutions which require a shift in the traditional norms of sovereignty.[55] Periods of transition tend to increase the perception of security risks, and states have learned that they cannot afford to take risks in an uncertain world. This means that the state-centric framework remains, but as attention turns to new definitions of security the traditional framework must shift, in order to respond to the new priorities that are emerging.[56]

The UN does play a significant role, however, as a mechanism for global politics and its (somewhat contested) mediation of international values do permeate the system, though its development was effectively blocked for forty years because of the traditional state-centric security concerns of the cold war period. Nevertheless, most accept that increasingly the role of the collectivity of states is based on consensus of values,[57] at least among the most powerful and wealthy states in the international system. However, this has the effect of reinforcing the state in favour of the state-centric and by implication, western, status quo – a status quo which many non-Western states dispute on social, cultural, political, and economic grounds.

The post cold war shift towards regionalization and the supposed revitalization of the UN was to be indicative of the new sovereignty-free order. Yet, as the UN suddenly became more significant in attending to and reformulating old sources of insecurity as a consequence of the burgeoning of old rivalries and conflicts which the cold war had kept refrigerated, the UN's effectiveness did not mirror that optimism. After the relative success of Namibia and Cambodia, the cases of Somalia, Bosnia and Rwanda reduced its credibility. The war in the Gulf also served to provoke accusations that the UN was western and status-quo oriented. The UN has, at the inter- and intra-state level, increasing been regarded as impotent. UN efforts in former Yugoslavia, and in Cyprus, illustrate exactly this, being indicative of the continuing prevalence of traditional security debates, which exist side by side with the new issues that have emerged. The authority of the UN and the EU in the ex-Yugoslav conflict, for example, was paralysed early on in the conflict by the inherent contradiction between the right of national self-determination claimed by ethnic minorities and national groups to legitimate their statehood, and the principle of territorial integrity.[58]

It is notable that the UN Security Council decided that human rights repression in Iraq threatened international peace and security, that the failed state of Somalia should be subject to UN intervention and enforcement, and that humanitarian assistance should be provided in Bosnia. These operations, along with efforts addressing the situations in Rwanda and Haiti occurred on a growing fault-line between conceptions of state sovereignty and the growing pressure for legitimate forms of intervention to be applied.[59] This pressure seemed to be developing into a series of new norms in world politics, related to different (and often previously ignored) levels including civil society, and local and regional political structures, and in response to the needs of many different actors and the diverse security related issues that affect them. Increasingly, authority and legitimacy in international society can be ascribed to the networks that connect such actors, many of which converge upon the UN. Yet there are also occasions when the legitimacy of UN authority is circumscribed on the grounds of humanitarianism, as NATO action over Kosovo in 1999 seemed to show.

The OSCE is an important example of the growing concurrence between institutional approaches to making peace and broader forms of security. As Adler has noted, it fulfils several community-building functions that contribute to security by implicitly accepting and acting upon a broad definition of security.[60] These include the promotion of political consultation and bilateral and multilateral agreements among its members; the establishment of liberal standards – applicable both within each state and throughout the community – that are used to judge democratic and human rights performance, and monitors compliance with them; conflict prevention; developing the practices of peaceful settlement of disputes within the region; building mutual trust by promoting military transparency and cooperation; supporting the building of democratic institutions and the transformation to market-based economies; and assisting in re-establishing state institutions and the rule of law after conflicts.[61] Consequently this aids in the development of transnational identities based on mutual and liberal values, and on the normative structure embodied in OSCE documents, the 1975 Helsinki Final Act, the 1990 Copenhagen Declaration, and the 1990 Charter of Paris. Through its 'demilitarized' security concept, the OSCE has elevated the status of human security based on confidence and cooperation, peaceful means of dispute settlement between states, justice and democracy in civil society, the advancement of human freedom and rights.[62]

The developing cooperation between the UN and such regional organizations, Boutros Boutros-Ghali argued, is crucial for new approaches to making peace. Since the end of the cold war, the then CSCE was able to begin a process of reform, becoming involved in making peace in the Nagorno-Karabakh dispute, and establishing a High Commissioner on National Minorities (HCNM). It was also declared that the CSCE was a regional arrangement under Chapter VIII of the UN Charter, as well as instigating a new link to NATO to which NATO responded in mid-1992, at a foreign ministers conference in Oslo, by pledging to try to support OSCE peacekeeping efforts. The OSCE security regime that emerged after the end of the cold war addressed less overt types of security issues, reflecting growing concern about ethnic conflicts, economic dislocation, and environmental issues.[63] The OSCE also became involved in activities normally associated with NGOs. Its diverse security activities are a consequence of the Helsinki norms on democracy, basic rights, and the rule of law, and low-key preventive diplomacy. Consequently, of particular interest to the OSCE are those NGOs specializing in conflict prevention and management, mediation and confidence-building,[64] which enables it to operate at a grassroots level, as well as at a diplomatic level, through both formal and informal coordination networks.[65]

The debates over globalization and fragmentation are also significant here. A common theme relates to gradual undermining of the Westphalian state. David Armstrong has argued that this is an over-simplification, as there are two main forces at work: globalization and interstate interaction.[66] Globalization tends to 'break down territorial boundaries and replace them with new, uniform configurations of power, money and culture, while the interactions of states reconfirms territorial boundaries and the structures and processes contained by them'.[67] Related to these developments is another level of change relating to culture. Westphalian states have traditionally been seen as frameworks and guardians for distinct national cultures, and it was through this general assumption that much of the state's internal and external legitimacy and coherence arose. Modernity, capitalism or westernization seem to promote global assimilation while also prompting local cultural fragmentation. Post-cold war conflict, as Kaldor argues, are 'wars between exclusivism and cosmopolitanism'.[68]

Human security in the contemporary environment

Human security in the contemporary environment seems to have been constructed with reference to human needs in an international society in which states are increasingly subject to normative expectations of citizens and non-citizens. At the same time, there has also been an emergence of a global civil society constituted by non-state actors and international or local NGOs whose objectives are shaped by a human needs framework. Their work has revolved around humanitarian issues, justice and human security, and their amelioration and monitoring of conflict. The community of NGOs has been brought together in a global civil society framework in the context of the UN General Assembly. This development has become most notable in the context of conflict management mechanisms for IOs and ROs, the reform of UN peacekeeping operations and the UN's attempts to play a greater role in preventive diplomacy and peacebuilding, and of course, in the work of many NGOs in complex crises and conflicts.[69] This seems to have crucial implications for the reconceptualization of security and order in the contemporary environment away from the artificial frameworks that states provide and towards the issues which confront individuals, and to which approaches to ending conflict must become sensitized.

Security, therefore, must be defined in the broadest of manners, covering strategic, social, economic, cultural and environmental issues, pertaining both to international and regional organizations, states, groups, and individuals, protecting their diverse values from marginalization at a mutually acceptable level. Actions aimed at increasing security need to be constructed in the light of an overall system which is mutually inclusive – potentially cosmopolitan. Of course this can only be attained with the application of viable resources and states, and organizations may be reluctant to undermine their own foundations as the cost of attaining a broader practical approach to diverse security issues. The UN Security Council itself has increasingly broadened its interpretation to incorporate the security issues that arise from human rights, economic and ecological problems, and it is possible, though still controversial, to argue in the contemporary environment that humanitarian abuses within a state constitute a threat to international peace and security within the UN framework.[70] This has important implications for the 'order' aspired to by approaches to ending conflict.

The result has been that selected conflicts across the world have been addressed in a more comprehensive manner than ever before, as illustrated by independence for Namibia, in the significant steps toward regional peace and reconciliation in El Salvador and Nicaragua, and the role of the UN in Cambodia. However, the fatally flawed attempts to ameliorate disorder in Somalia in 1992–3 and as Yugoslavia broke up, and the efforts of the UN in Rwanda and Haiti, illustrate that such comprehensive efforts were often unrealistic or inherently problematic, as was the bypassing of the Security Council before NATO intervention in Kosovo. The changing international environment has raised new problems for the creation of an order based on a human security framework. This can be seen in Figure 1.2.

While cold war authority structures were derived from the state with respect to a narrow definition of security, post-cold war structures see the state as unable to exert the same authority as before and tend to assume an increasing harmonization between global and local actors, norms and objectives. This is occurring in response to the elevation of new types of security concerns, brought on mainly by the reduction of traditional interstate conflict and a concurrent increase in the political legitimacy of actors and groups which elucidate interests derived mainly from normative issues, pertaining to human security. A critical perspective would tend to concur here, but it must be noted that there is a

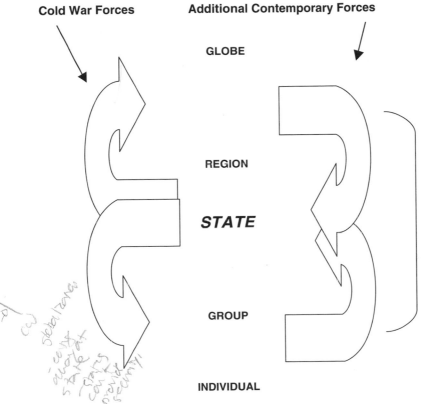

Figure 1.2 Contemporary forces in the global system of politics

critique beyond even this position. This would tend to argue that the international system (and its international texts) has propagated the sovereign, western, rational voices of states, and their version of order, at the expense of other voices and issues, and that any attempt at making peace must therefore open up questions about what peace is, who defines it, and who implements it, in the context of what interests, at what level, through what methodology and in what epistemological context. This would seem to leave an intellectual analysis of ending conflict as a project that must inevitably bow to the interests of those who presume to be making peace, with obvious implications in the post-cold war world.

Conclusion

In the contemporary environment there is an awareness of the potential dangers of a clear elucidation of a new order such as occurred at Versailles in 1919, or in San Francisco in 1945. Yet it is clear that the international system is shifting, as is the nature of diplomacy and the nature of states; other actors are gaining legitimacy, to the displeasure of some states that are still locked in cold war-style security dilemmas and are fearful of internal discordance. The shifting global environment now allows for the expression of substate concerns and states are finding it increasingly difficult to prioritize against them on the grounds that pressing policy-problems take priority. The modifications of the international system towards an international society which have been taking place with respect to security, order, diplomacy and making peace are merely part of a long chain of events reaching back to Westphalia and beyond. The construction of an international system has been motivated by a desire for order and security (even if it is the order of the victors and based on self-interest). The shifts that have occurred can be summarized as follows:

1. Sovereignty and territorialism versus humanitarianism and humanitarian intervention;
2. Human rights versus political interests;
3. International society versus strategic interest;
4. The balance between state sovereignty, individual identity and personal sovereignty;
5. The role of IOs/ ROs and NGOs;
6. A shift of focus towards civil societies and their perceptions;
7. The gradual emergence of what has been described as a global civil society constituted non-state actors working on a range of human security issues;
8. The re-emergence of normative issues as global and regional concerns of states and individuals;
9. The attempted redefinition of the norms of intervention in the post-cold war world;
10. The re-emergence of identity conflicts, spurred often by past injustices and a tendency towards marginalization committed in the name of statehood in the past;
11. The possibility of increasing coordination between traditional levels of diplomacy, and emerging roles played by private actors, international and regional institutions and NGOs in the context of a debate about the emergence of universal norms;

12. The problem of globalization versus fragmentation, of the local versus the global, the universal versus the particular.
13. The use of approaches to ending conflict, to restore 'order', democracy, rebuild states, etc.
14. The use of peace-enforcement to project these norms and values where disputants do not provide their consent.

In the Westphalian international system conflict took on the identity of intractability when the parties to the conflict were able to impede the machinery of the international system in finding a solution through peacekeeping, mediation and negotiation. Intractability was also evident when the disputants were able to make reasonably credible appeals to conflicting principles in the international system and when they were able to exploit the grey areas of the international system and of international law, thus preventing peacekeeping and mediation processes from adopting clear positions. Intractability does not therefore just imply that a conflict cannot be solved because of the inflexibility of the disputants; there are several levels behind this. The basic levels must be related to core issues of individual, group and state rights, primarily relating to status, legitimacy, strategic and economic security for identity groups. Because, as has been shown above, the international system in its various states throughout recent history has claimed to form the basis for all human interaction, it is here that one must look for the roots of intractability. This means that territorial, ethnic, resource and cultural conflicts (defined as being the most intractable by classical realist, liberal and pluralist models) are problems because of the way they are conceptualized through actors perceptions of the international system. It is this discord between the local and the global which traditional diplomacy produces that is a key problem in the search for a stable and normatively acceptable order, and in understanding the notion of intractability in conflict. Levels of intractability are heavily dependent upon the disputant's understanding of their rights vis-à-vis the international system. Thus, the notion of intractability in conflict tends to be applied to conflicts which cannot easily be resolved by the application of the principles of the Westphalian international system. This means that any stand taken by direct or indirect actors, be they states or international institutions or organizations, becomes heavily politicized and ambiguous.

The end of the cold war has allowed multilevel activities to emerge, though not necessarily coordinated, but which have a far greater chance of reducing the knots that emerged under cold war regimes because it has become possible, both practically and theoretically, to address the demands and needs of actors without necessarily concentrating on the level of states (and therefore on traditional diplomatic levels). This means that such activities can now be legitimately directed by private citizens and organizations at private levels, as well as by governmental organizations at a regional and global level, dealing not only with traditional state concerns, but also with private concerns of a social, political, security or economic nature, as well as at a regional and global level. Human security therefore has become the focus of many peace processes, with state-centric strategic concerns losing legitimacy within international society. Making peace in this environment has tended to occur through traditional diplomacy, peacekeeping, problem-solving approaches, and regional strategies for development and reconciliation via NGOs and international organizations and institutions. While such activities seems to be a welcome development they are not without their own problems, as later chapters will outline. The forces of globalization and fragmentation, plus environmental and human security issues, denote the need for new approaches to ending conflict to produce a more sustainable 'order' – but there needs to be general agreement on that order first.

2
First Generation: Conflict Management Approaches

Si vis pacem para bellum[1]

Introduction

The theory and practice of first generation approaches to making peace can be located in an artificial and limited state-centric discourse in which activity in the international system is framed by power politics. This narrow focus excludes other actors and non-statecentric issues in a quest for the establishment and protection of order and security and approaches to ending conflict are constituted by the strategic management and reinforcement of states and their interests. As it evolved during the cold war, UN peacekeeping was supposed to provide the conditions of stability in which mediation and negotiation can occur. Such approaches often led to controversial status quos or solutions based on state-security rather than justice and human security. First generation approaches revolve around the protection of the Westphalian international system, and address the shortcomings of that system through Westphalian tools, potentially replicating that system and the conflicts that it tends to provoke.

First generation approaches are based upon the traditions, norms and culture of western diplomacy as it has evolved since Westphalia, in particular on stylized and formal communication between sovereign representatives and the military and diplomatic tools they control to maintain order. The development of functional institutions added legitimacy. First generation approaches assume that *conflict management* is the best that can be achieved given the existence of competing national interests in an anarchical international system, even where some levels of social development may be observed (though it is essentially viewed

41

as communitarian).[2] They assume that diplomacy, peacekeeping, international mediation, and negotiation are unable to *resolve* differences that potentially may threaten a regional or global status quo, which has been so painstakingly engineered by centuries of diplomatic practice, but are able to manage them. Because this practice has moderated the interplay between national interests and the ability (or inability) of states to attain them, conflict management approaches attempt only to settle conflicts into a status quo.

Clearly the dominant forces of the cold war world stemmed from the bipolar balance, and the need for cohesion and unity in each camp. This was achieved through the mediating function of sovereignty and diplomacy, through the norm of non-intervention, and also through assimilative state frameworks aimed at producing internal cohesion and therefore contributing to the essential balance that managed conflict in the cold war environment (even during periods of détente). Thus, the roles of diplomacy, peacekeeping, mediation, negotiation, and adjudication – the main forms of conflict management practical in this environment – were applied to fine-tune the balance of power and on occasion used for crisis management (for example, during the Cuban Missile Crisis in 1962); more often they were used as a form of 'status quo diplomacy' in that the mediation/peacekeeping framework made the continuation or outbreak of open conflict less likely (as in Cyprus from 1964 until today).[3] On the occasions when mediation succeeded, as with President Carter at Camp David, it was through the application of significant reward or threat structures to one or other parties.[4] Similarly, the negotiations at Dayton over the future of Bosnia in 1995 saw the application of threats against the Serbs and rewards to the Croatians, as well as clear bias on the part of the US and its mediator, Richard Holbrooke, against the Serbs because of their policy of ethnic cleansing.[5]

This approach to making peace has proved to be far from a panacea. As the state-system allocates territory and rights on the basis of national groups which are self-supporting economically, territorially and militarily,[6] conflicts which tend to fall outside of these frameworks (constituting the vast majority) or are even caused by the inadequacies of the system, tend to be labelled intractable. In such cases, conflicts have raged unattended for many years (as in Afghanistan and Sudan) and have been cordoned off from world politics by the sovereign state system (which can be used to justify non-intervention even if humanitarian abuses are taking place in a given state), have been subject to methods of management (status quo diplomacy[7] and peacekeeping forces) or have been quelled by the use of force while the rest of the international community looked in the other direction. However, the objective was to preserve the status quo in the international system by preserving the integrity of states. Thus, first generation approaches' primary aims are normally either to prevent open conflicts, find new constitutional arrangements in torn states, find solutions between war- ring states, or far less often to establish a new regional state system consisting of fragments of one or more failed states. All of this assumes that the attainment of a semblance of peace will contribute to a self-sustaining international order. This chapter examines the development and viability of these debates.

First generation approaches: the role of UN peacekeeping

> The UN is an international body with a contradiction at its core. It is an association of sovereign states brought into existence by those states in order to curb the shortcomings of the state...the UN is a global essay in moderating the interplay between independence and interdependence in a world where interdependence is inescapable but often unpalatable.[8]

The development of international organization in the guise of both the League of Nations and the UN was founded upon the desire for diplomacy to become more effective in halting the escalation of disputes between states into war. The vision of conflict management presented in both the Covenant and the Charter was one bounded by the framework of international law in which war was a last resort in disputes between states where one or other had committed an act of aggression. Civil conflict and political violence were to be resolved by local, democratic and constitutional processes which were assigned as the responsibility of the state and were not subject to international supervision. This meant that peaceful methods of dispute settlement were required in order to solve disputes between states, and according to the structure and framework provided by the international system. An important part of the basic peace and security framework of the UN refers to peaceful methods of dispute settlement, which authorizes the UN to function in a dynamic or procedural mediatory capacity to manage international disputes.[9] The UN has no authority to intervene in such cases, unless under circumstances covered in Chapter VII of the Chapter. Nor has a state any obligation to submit to UN involvement. Internal conflicts that are likely to endanger international peace and security can be the subject of UN involvement, however, if they appear to be in danger of threatening international peace and security, and this loophole has been given an increasingly broad interpretation. UN peacekeeping emerged as a compromise between the UN's diplomatic function as outlined in Chapter VI, and enforcement, as outlined in Chapter VII.

It is important to note that during the cold war, peacekeeping, based upon the principles developed by the UN Secretary-General for the UN Emergency Force from 1956 to 1967, often provided the basis for mediation and negotiation, and was generally applied to placate and refrigerate the conflict environment to allow formal negotiations to take place.[10] Diehl has argued that there are two basic criteria for evaluating traditional peacekeeping operations pertaining to whether an operation deterred or prevented violent conflict and whether it helped resolve the underlying elements of the conflict.[11] The Security Council and the Secretary-General played crucial roles in the development of UN peacekeeping as a creative way of honouring at least part of the UN's foundational commitment to preserving the post-Second World War order. The use of military personnel in peacekeeping, observation, policing and humanitarian roles developed in the context of a compromise between the needs of the era and the superpower balance, and an equally difficult balance between a clear UN role in interstate and intrastate conflicts. On occasions, as with UNEF (UN Emergency Force), the General Assembly took the lead when the Security Council was deadlocked though the use of the veto.[12] Generally, however, the Security Council was responsible for such roles which were divided between operations depending upon the consent of the disputants under Chapter VI of the UN Charter, and those which came under Chapter VII.

Most cold war peacekeeping operations were protracted and contributed little to a settlement: the observer missions in Kashmir and the Middle East have been in place since 1948, and the mission in Cyprus since 1964, the mission on the Golan Heights since 1974, and in southern Lebanon since 1978. UNTSO (UN Truce Supervision Organization), the UN Force in Cyprus (UNFICYP), and the UN Force on the Golan Heights achieved little more than stasis. In 1956 UNEF 1 was established in the Sinai Peninsula, separating Egyptian and Israeli forces.[13] This was the first major peacekeeping force to be set up, and depended upon consent to oversee a ceasefire, yet the Secretary General withdrew UNEF in 1967 upon the request of the Egyptian government despite the fact that many believed that a war between Egypt and Israel would follow. With the problems associated with the decolonization process for the Congo, ONUC (Operation des Nations Unies au Congo) was formed in 1960 after a plea to the Security Council from its government for help. Its role was initially to monitor the withdrawal of Belgium's forces and to restore law and order; its conduct was to provide a hint of the difficulties caused by the location of the UN's role in the preservation of peace and security between consent by, and intervention in, sovereign states. As the situation deteriorated, partly because of cold war rivalry, in 1961 the Security Council controversially authorized the use of force and the UN force became involved in preventing the secession of the communist-led region of Katanga. After a disastrous mission (though attaining the objectives of its mandate) ONUC withdrew in 1964 and the permanent members of the Security Council attempted to rein-in the development of peacekeeping and to make sure that any such forces would be solely controlled by the Security Council.

With the costs of peacekeeping escalating, and controversy over its objectives, there was a hiatus in its development and initiation. After the withdrawal of UNEF I, UNEF II was set up after the October War in 1973 to supervise the ceasefire, and the UN Disengagement Observer Force (UNDOF) was established in 1974 to keep the peace on the Golan Heights. UNEF II was wound up after Camp David led to a rare mediated agreement by 1979. The main UN Interim Force in Lebanon (UNIFIL) was established to restore government authority after the Israeli invasion in 1978 and continued despite the second Israeli invasion in 1982 but again was unable to fulfil its mandate. In the late 1980s, however (after the Soviet Union had finally agreed to pay its contributions towards UNIFIL), a new phase of peacekeeping began. As the cold war came to an end, new missions were deployed in Africa, Asia and South America, to cope with power vacuums left by the collapse of old alliances or the uncovering of identity conflicts which had been dormant during the cold war period.

During this period, however, the use of monodimensional peacekeeping forces hardly provided much impetus for peacemaking, particularly in its traditional, consent-based format, in which peacekeeping was supposed to provide a stable environment for high-level diplomacy to occur in. In the context of these early peace operations, order was clearly defined as retaining a strategic regional and local status quo, rather than human security at the civil level. After the cold war ended this led to a shift from classic approaches to peacekeeping, such as UNDOF or UNEF, to multidimensional operations such as the UN Transition Assistance Group (UNTAG) in Namibia, the UN observer Mission in El Salvador (ONUSAL), and the UN Transitional Authority in Cambodia (UNTAC), which entailed the implementation – again with the consent of the parties – of complex peace agreements.[14] These more complex approaches allowed deployment as part of negotiated political solutions, and broadened the responsibilities of peacekeepers to include tasks such as disarmament, demobilization, resettlement of refugees, police training and supervision, and election monitoring.[15] This led to the linkage of peacekeeping with peacebuilding and towards a multidimensional approach for UN peace operations in general, viewed by some as the fulfillment of the UN's original purpose. However, it should be noted that even during the early phase of peacekeeping, forces were often involved in low-key humanitarian work, as in the cases of ONUC, UNFICYP and UNIFIL.[16]

First generation approaches: the role of UN peacemaking

An important element of the UN's conflict management structure was its call for peaceful dispute settlement before war was resorted to, and its provision of mechanisms through which international peacemaking could take place under the auspices of the UN. The UN Charter states that: 'All Members shall settle their international disputes by peaceful means in such a manner that international peace and security, and justice, are not endangered.'[17] It clarifies exactly how this is to take place: 'The parties to any dispute, the continuance of which is likely to endanger the maintenance of international peace and security, shall, first of all, seek a solution by negotiation, enquiry, mediation, conciliation, arbitration, judicial settlement, resort to regional agencies or arrangements, or other peaceful means of their own choice.' Finally, the Security Council is empowered to call upon the parties to settle disputes by peaceful means.[18] In the light of the experience of the League of Nations, part of the UN's goal was to give such methods credibility though what tended to happen was that 'peaceful' methods of conflict management were resorted to after war had failed to achieve its participants' objectives.

The primary consequence of a disputant's recourse to the UN has tended to be the internationalization of the dispute, aimed at legitimizing a particular claim or position. The even-handed attitude of the UN has tended to ignore the distinction between aggressor and victim,[19] limiting its effectiveness, even if there was a clear mandate and political will for a solution. The typical peacemaking role of the UN during the cold war was often in the unobtrusive context of good offices, mainly on a procedural level, negotiating and providing a place for meetings, providing a chairman, or conveying messages, and involving informal contacts and suggestions on the part of the Secretary-General and his representatives. Occasionally, Secretaries-General acted as direct mediators and presented their own ideas for a solution, and in the regular report of the Secretary-General to the Security Council and General Assembly they usually offered low-key assessments of progress or the lack of it. They occasionally made recommendations to the Security Council for items to be included on its agenda; this was often deemed to be significant by disputants as it often led to Security Council resolutions. Such resolutions (as well as those derived from the General Assembly) tended to be based on a certain amount of horse-trading, in complex behind-the-scenes negotiations, which often resulted in weak resolutions aimed at preserving the status quo. This has been the pattern during the Cyprus problem, for example, and because of the desire of the Turkish Cypriots for the Secretary-General not to become directly involved in the issues of the dispute (UN positions being believed to favour the Greek Cypriots) good offices and mediation appear to have become almost indistinguishable. This has been indicative of an attempt by the Secretary-General to remain directly involved in the settlement process, to the displeasure of the Turkish Cypriot side and the pleasure of the Greek Cypriot side (which believes that the UN reinforces the sovereignty of the Republic of Cyprus which it controls). Because it is generally accepted that a UN peacemaking operation should be derived from the purposes and principles of the organization, the Secretary-General's role as a mediator has depended upon perceptions of his impartiality, skill and tact, and a certain amount of political expediency, recognizing crude power over normative principles.

A good example of the scale of the difficulties facing UN mediation can be found in its attempt to mediate between the Palestinians and the Zionists in 1948. Despite the fact that the UN had clearly proposed partition in 1947, this process led to series of armistices to be supervised by UNTSO. The fact that an African, Soviet and Non-Aligned axis supported the Arabs in the UN was partly responsible for the 1975 General Assembly resolution which equated Zionism with racism[20] and crippled the ability of the UN to act as honest broker between the two parties. Despite the fact that at the end of the cold war the anti-Zionism bloc collapsed and this resolution was rescinded, Israel has continued to distrust the UN – as its rejection of a UN observer role in late 2000 after violence broke out once again between the two communities seemed to show.

UN peacemaking does have certain advantages, however, as the Charter does not allow it to hold any vested interests other than the maintenance of peace and security, and it is a useful face-saving device.[21] Of course, the UN's expression of interests often reflects the interests of its dominant states. States may want to escape a conflict, as with Britain and France in the case of the Suez Canal in 1956. Face-saving provides inexpensive cover when states do not want to engage, as in Cyprus, Palestine, Lebanon.

A further problem has been related to a clash, not of objectives, but of outcomes in conflicts where traditional interpositionary peacekeeping forces were in place to support a peacemaking operation. As has occurred in the case of Cyprus, the United Nations' peacekeeping force provide a status quo more acceptable to one or both sides than any proposed compromise, meaning that the UN becomes entrapped into a long-term peacekeeping and peacemaking commitment. If the UN has been involved in bringing about a ceasefire it is likely that its peacemaking operation will take the ceasefire positions of the parties as its starting point for the establishment of common ground.[22] Thus, if a UN force has frozen the conflict the bargaining dynamics are based on an artificial status quo. A further complication lies in the relationship between the objectives of the disputants, and the different UN bodies – as Boutros-Ghali pointed out, it is necessary that there is a modicum of unity between these actors for peacemaking to be effective (although the Secretary-General's role of good offices has often been most effective when independent of the deliberative bodies).[23]

During the cold war and beyond, it has often been argued that without an enforcement capacity, the ability of the UN to bring about solutions was severely curtailed, and in response after the end of the cold war, the UN turned to coercive techniques (as in Somalia) which have, however, tended to compromise the traditional quiet diplomacy of the Secretary-General. However, most actors still view the UN as an important agent of legitimation, despite the obvious interposition of member states interests into the realms of the UN Charter, often undermining the perceived legitimacy of UN peacemaking efforts.[24] Similarly, the Secretary-General's role as honest broker often suffers because of the interplay of forces between states that have generally refused to countenance the claims of non-state types of actors.[25] However, the UN's main leverage lies in persuasion and partnership with disputants for agreements based on consensus. This means that UN peacemaking has often fallen at the passive end of the spectrum of third party activity, depending mainly on the weight of international consensus behind it, on the trust of the disputants, negotiating symmetry, on its own proficiency in providing a forum for debate, and on its communicational skills.

The effectiveness of this was curtailed during the cold war by super-powers interests,[26] though there were some notable successes, namely in the 1962 Cuban missile crisis during which Secretary-General U Thant called for the suspension of American quarantine around Cuba and Russian arms shipments. This was a face-saving measure for both sides, though each had previously presented uncompromising draft resolutions to the Security Council. The United States convened the Council and introduced a draft resolution, which reasserted its demand for an immediate withdrawal of the Russian missiles from Cuba under Article 40 to be given binding force under Article 25. The Soviet draft called for the immediate revocation of the US decision to inspect the ships of other states around Cuba. However, as the draft resolutions both called for bilateral negotiations between the United States and the Soviet Union to remove the threat to the peace, U Thant was able to call for the voluntary suspension of all arms shipments and the voluntary suspension of the quarantine.[27]

The good offices function of the Secretary-General has been an important contribution because it has tended towards the procedural dimension of peacemaking, has been able to avoid becoming highly politicized and has remained within the sphere of quiet diplomacy. For example, in 1975, after the General Assembly had passed a resolution reaffirming the right of self-determination of the people of the former Spanish Western Sahara,[28] the Assembly requested the Secretary-General to become involved in making the necessary agreements (though the Secretary-General was unable to carry out this task). The case of Sudan illustrates how the UN has been unable to intervene in an ethnic conflict when one of its dominant members has insufficient interests at stake. In contrast, however, in the case of South Africa the UN was able to isolate and delegitimate its racist regime, in particular by its persuasion of member states to adopt diplomatic and economic sanctions, and through Security Council and General Assembly resolutions which served to internationalize the issue. In El Salvador the Secretary-General played an increasingly active role mediation leading to an agreed solution to the civil war. In the Iran–Iraq war patient Secretary-General mediation culminated in a ceasefire in 1989. In his involvement in the conflicts in Afghanistan, Cambodia, the Falkland Islands and Namibia, the Secretary-General played an important role with respect to the strengthening of his role as a credible intermediary, even if this did involve the acceptance of the role of mediator of the last resort and status quo management. However, in the Westphalian order '... [s]tasis, even UN-facilitated stasis, may be preferable to some alternatives...'[29]

though this may have the benefit of keeping the item on the UN's agenda. As with East Timor before independence lip-service, at least, was paid to a principled stand, which certainly had a bearing on events during and after independence.

The UN is part of the traditional win/lose bargaining process[30] in which it has often been viewed as an instrument of national policy within the framework of the international system. It is comprised of actors and constituencies with varying objectives and levels of influence, operating with different cultural and value systems. During the cold war, recourse to the UN tended to lessen the level of conflict though UN peacemaking was generally seen as ineffective.[31] Despite this, the personal skills of the Secretary-General, the moral status derived from the UN Charter and the degree of agreement and will of the permanent members of the Security Council were seen as its most significant assets. However, the UN has tended to be a mediator of the last resort and because of this and its lack of physical resources to guarantee a settlement it is dependent upon the moral consensus it represents, the forum it provides, the diplomatic skills of the Secretary-General and his representatives, and often on the supporting role of peacekeeping forces.

Because of the nature of the Westphalian international system the UN has generally been excluded from involvement in ethnic conflicts because of the interests of its member states, as with Tibet because of the Chinese veto and Corsica because of the French veto. The UN has never become involved in an ethnic conflict because of its ethnic dimension, but always because of a perceived threat to peace and security,[32] as can be observed in the Middle East, Cambodia, Central America, Afghanistan, and the Persian Gulf. As a result of the Congo debacle (in which after three years of continuing conflict, the mysterious death of Secretary-General and the near-bankruptcy of UN, it pulled out), the UN was disinclined to encourage or support intervention in ethnic conflicts. In the Congo a hate campaign was waged against ONUC by the Katanganese, particularly as the UN force became more assertive and recognition was not forthcoming.[33] In the 1970s, the UN was the target of Kurdish lobbying for the revision of the UN Charter in order to allow petitions to the UN from minorities in the 1970s.[34] Lebanon, however, did see UN involvement. In 1958, Chamoun's government complained to the Security Council that the United Arab Republic was interfering in its affairs. This resulted in the Security Council sending in UNOGIL which observed substantial Lebanese military movements in Lebanon. The Secretary-General said there was no evidence for the claim of

Chamoun, who then became disenchanted with the UN.[35] Later, when UNIFIL was installed it was not accepted by several of the players, most notably the PLO and Israel. The Security Council gave UNIFIL an implausible mandate of 'assisting the government of Lebanon in ensuring the return of its effective authority into the area' and did not establish a peacemaking mission at all. Later, as Yugoslavia collapsed, the UN was responsible for peacekeeping and creating the conditions for peacemaking but left the EC with the responsibility of finding a political settlement. This was in part a reflection of the fact that the initiative of the UN was blocked, as Burg has pointed out, by the 'inherent contradiction between the right of national self determination claimed by ethnic minorities and national groups to legitimate their state hood...and...the principle of territorial integrity'.[36]

During the cold war, consent was a key issue, through which disputants met with an implicit assumption that each wanted a strategic settlement in the image of the Westphalian international system in which territorial sovereignty took priority over human rights, development or identity. As in the literature on mediation, this view has dominated UN approaches to peacemaking via a simple formula based on a ceasefire supported by peacekeeping troops, which may then provide the basis for mediation and negotiation. Thus, during the cold war period, United Nation operations usually depended upon the disputants' consent, itself dependent upon maintaining strict impartiality, and on the assumption that the parties intended to make concessions to bring about an agreement.

First generation approaches: negotiation

Viewed from within the framework of the Westphalian international system, the failure of negotiations generally signalled a resort to violence and a hurting stalemate often led to the resumption of negotiation, a process composed of zero-sum forms of bargaining and the rearrangement of interests and resources, which often depends on coercive diplomacy. Because negotiation is so dependent on the factors that can establish a status quo within this framework, there must be an unlikely combination of both common and conflictual interests present,[37] coexisting in an environment of threat. This means that negotiation processes are easily susceptible to deadlock as concessions cannot easily be offered or withdrawn. Consequently, the negotiation process often provided a hiatus for disputants to regroup rather than a clear path towards a peaceful solution to a conflict.

Clearly, state-centric negotiation has little chance of actually resolving conflicts that involve diverse actors and interests. Its aim of reorganizing the balance of power in order to create stability, means that human security issues are often subsumed beneath broader interests in the complex web of forces which constitute world politics. Because of this disputants tend to be motivated by the need to alter the balance of power in their favour.[38] Negotiations only tend to occur, therefore, at moments when the parties have little other choice. All parties are believed to have a preferred set of outcomes based on their understanding of the balance of power, their respective stakes, and the options dictated by these stakes for the discontinuance of negotiations.[39] External systemic influences at local, regional and global levels also impinge upon the process, as well as the demands of the negotiators' various constituencies (though this is heavily dependent on the type of political system which exists within the state or organization/group in question[40]).

Within the first generation framework, negotiated settlements are often built either through a piecemeal method, building agreements through mutual compromise and concessions, or through the establishment of a formula governing the disputed issues and implementation.[41] The most important constraint of negotiation relates, however, to the fact that the negotiator is always faced with a choice between agreeing, refusing agreement, and continuing to talk to improve the terms of agreement.[42] There is little to prevent talks from becoming protracted or one or other party making recourse to open conflict.[43] Whether a piecemeal or a formula approach is used, the literature tends to agree that step-by-step agreements often build more trust than complete agreements, as they allow for withdrawal or reassessment[44] (though the danger is that progress may halt before a total agreement has been reached and parties may be wary of taking a first step for fear of this possibility). As negotiators are vulnerable to dismissal by their constituency through election or a coup, face-saving is vital[45] and its provision is often an important obstacle to progress. However, as negotiation is essentially a symmetrical process in the sense that every tactic is theoretically open to both sides (though their respective status may be far from symmetric) it is very susceptible to deadlock and disillusionment, especially in the context of an international system geared to state-centric forms of conflict, and solutions tend to be founded on mutual fear and threat rather than mutual benefit. The standard solution to these weaknesses is at this point to argue that the addition of a third party mediator to the negotiating process would provide more chances of the disputants attaining a solution. It is to this that the UN framework offered by Article 33 of its Charter, was aimed.

First generation approaches: international mediation

> At a time of international crisis, mediation serves the task of cultural and historical reproduction. It rescues the historical moment from the threat of destruction at the hands of a failing political order. Mediation processes are part of a mature international order.[46]

International mediation is dependent upon the third party's creativity, sensitivities, resources and experience, and is susceptible to the vagaries of the local, regional and global environments, and their linkages with the dispute in question. It has generally been accepted that international mediation is dependent upon successful communication, which itself is dependent upon many factors, including culture, and is often subject to misperception and misunderstanding.[47] It is derived from a tradition of diplomacy from within the state or organization which backs the mediation process, and represents a combination of its strategic interests and understanding of what constitute peace and order. In the context of the Westphalian international system, however, these may be contradictory, particularly as mediation tends to support the most powerful actor.[48] In this sense, a mediator's objective of a compromise contradicts the disputants' objective of winning. This indicates that mediators need leverage and that third party intervention may be a defeat for the objectives of both parties.[49] This is compounded by the problem of the parties' status and of implied recognition, both of which derive from the legalistic framework of the Westphalian international system.[50]

The dominant view of international mediation has been that a mixture of carrot and stick is necessary, and control of the process and procedure is dependent on the mediator's own objectives and resources, the level of skill in controlling the process of interchange, and the flexibility of the disputants. One fact that is inescapable, however, is that mediation occurs in the context of the norms, structures and interests of the dominant actors in the system and the process. From this stems Bercovitch and Langley's argument that what is important is not to categorize the mediator's behaviour, but that mediation can be any process that involves disputing parties, a mediator and a specific conflict management context.[51] Thus, in the Westphalian context, the dominant norms emanate from hegemonic mediation and its ability to create and maintain short-term status quos which are normally extremely fragile and related to external reward structures (e.g. military or financial incentives from a powerful state) or external structures of coercion.[52]

The use of mediation often aims at ending an international conflict in the short or long term, in the context of a conflictual environment normally involving two or more states (although the same techniques were often rather hopefully applied to conflicts between a state and a non-state actor), without the use of physical force. Bercovitch and Houston defined mediation as 'a process of conflict management where disputants seek the assistance of, or accept an offer of help from, an individual, group, state or organisation to settle their conflict or resolve their differences without resorting to physical force or invoking the authority of the law'.[53] This definition reflects the changes which had taken place at the end of the cold war in that it concentrated on the creation of a peaceful solution to a conflict, rather than reflecting the more common cold war reality that the disputants had fought themselves into a stalemate, or that a third party had intervened in order to prevent the conflict from upsetting the cold war status quo. International mediation has been subjected to a tyranny of definitions, however, and most such attempts to provide a succinct definition of a very complex process have underestimated the fact that it is unlikely that the disputants will have identical requirements of a third party, that they may find it difficult to agree on one particular mediator, that mediation is often imposed from the outside, and finally that a third party brings with it additional interests, values and cultural dissonances. It is also important to note that mediators are required, whatever their status, to conform with the prevalent norms of the international system (which themselves are contradictory), not to upset the perceived balance of power, and not to move beyond the interests of their sponsors.

The traditional academic debates surrounding mediation have therefore tended to focus on the skills and personality of the third party, issues related to conflict ripeness, bias and impartiality, the level of the conflict's intensity, the nature of the issues in the conflict,[54] and the resources that can be applied (both coercive and non-coercive) in order to reconfigure the issues in the dispute to the equal and mutual satisfaction and dissatisfaction of all of the parties in the dispute. Though a general consensus exists that the parties to the dispute need to be properly identified for diplomatic reasons, mediation has often ignored key indirect players. More importantly however, the basic assumption underlying all efforts at international mediation has been that that a *compromise* is the objective of all. This is based on the rationale that if parties are engaged in mediation then they must be willing to accept some form of compromise. It is based on the deeper rationale that conflict must be mitigated in some way and that communication (as opposed to fighting) can only take place in an environment of compromise. This, however, means that mediation could be defined as successful if it had merely held off open violence in the short term and had achieved little in dealing with the underlying causes of the conflict, or providing a just settlement; in effect mediation was little other than what has been referred to in another context as a refrigeration operation.[55] How could it achieve more if the foundation for the international system was riddled with an orrery of errors and inconsistencies?

The literature surrounding international mediation provides a variety of standpoints. It is a non-coercive and voluntary form of conflict management[56]: it depends upon the paradox of cooperation in conflict in the light of the threat of escalation[57]; it does not involve force, should be neutral and requires improved forms of communication between the opposing sides[58]; it requires that mediators suggest compromises, negotiate and bargain to induce them[59]; and also that equality should be accepted as the basis for settlement with the mediator acting as a catalyst, providing objective insights into a complex situation.[60] Mediators have to walk a tightrope between a dynamic role based on the carrot and stick, and more of a procedural role based on their contribution to the communication process. Thus, the process is dependent upon the mediator's access to resources, and inevitably leads to zero-sum outcomes.

Because mediation in the Westphalian context is viewed as an extension of the negotiation process where a mediator acceptable (though often grudgingly) to both sides becomes a third party[61] it is important to examine how the mediator influences the positions of the two sides and the negotiating environment. The argument has been made that a neutral third party with no interests other than finding a solution carries an implication of legitimacy based on the mediator or its sponsors, and the disputants' perceptions of the international system itself. This is because it is the Westphalian international system that provides the conceptual, political, legal, and normative framework for managing and solving conflict. However, it is also accepted that if a mediator is not neutral the interests and resources brought into the conflict environment are still defined by the same international system, though a high level of resources may enable mediators to play a far more dynamic role in interpreting (perhaps in favour of itself or its backers) how the international system, the political, legal, and normative structure can be applied in order to find a solution to the problem.

The traditional debates around mediation also concerned themselves with how the third party's interests might affect the bargaining positions of the disputants and factions contained therein. It has also been noted that the third party's constituency plays an important role in influencing decision-making, that his/her role develops as the negotiations continue, and that one alternative method of leverage would be to withdraw (or threaten to withdraw) from the proceedings. In this way, mediation has been regarded as comprising a series of interactions between three parties and their constituencies in which the mediator, the process of mediation and the context of mediation are vital in determining the nature and effectiveness of mediation,[62] within the limitations and constraints imposed by the traditional international system. It has also been argued that mediation could be facilitated if the parties and their constituencies have a stable and cohesive relationship, preferably a democratic one.[63] Therefore, the strategy of the mediator should ultimately be to intervene with the appropriate third party method at the appropriate time in order to de-escalate the conflict.[64] Yet this is unlikely in conflicts which straddle the conceptual weaknesses and irregularities of the international system and diplomatic practice therein. This means that the failure or inefficiency of international mediation has often been misdiagnosed as stemming from the personal and tactical flaws of the third party, or from its lack of coercive resources. This has led to the suggestion that mediators who use coercive tactics are not mediators, but disputants themselves.

Bercovitch and Langley have argued that 'protracted' conflicts need to be approached in a different manner, as the short-term effectiveness of mediation is reduced by the nature of the conflict.[65] It is clear that many conflict management efforts have led only to short-term *status quos*, though mediation has often been labelled a success if it has achieved a reduction of the severity of a confrontation. Such debates are framed by traditional concepts of the international system which themselves define the limits of international mediation as a first generation approach.

Obstacles for international mediation

The Westphalian mediator operates in a complex environment overshadowed by the threat of violence, in which the state system reproduces its own version of order, and imposes its strictures on all those who work within its framework. It is delineated by a complex series of relationships between the parties and their constituencies and internal factions. These relationships are constituted by resource distributions, historical and cultural perceptions and beliefs, and internal and external legality and legitimacy. Mediation conducted in the Westphalian framework tends to focus on the political, legal, military and territorial requirements of disputants, and many factors, such as culture, are undervalued or ignored.

Thus, the mediator's primary goal is limited to an agreement between the conflicting parties within the confines of his/her own objectives and resources, and within the confines delineated by the local, regional or global system. Mediators try to gain a solution at the least cost to themselves, even if they had the ability to apply a high level of resources. They would therefore initially tend towards controlling communication processes and rearranging the disputants' resources by establishing an interaction between the negotiators, to establish and enforce a protocol for their interaction.[66] The literature argues that the initial attempt to establish a mediation process would be perceived by both sides as a sign of weakness. Consequently, a stalemate is required to offset these costs. But as in the case of the negotiations near the end of the Yom Kippur war where the Egyptians were reluctant to enter talks as it would have implied direct recognition of Israel, these costs can be very high. To overcome these initial difficulties the mediator can concentrate on the benefits to both parties of a negotiated solution, using his/her own status and resources. The mediator must find a suitable environment for the talks, establish a protocol that can be followed, and clarify the overall issues in the conflict as a starting point for negotiation. A series of separate meetings between the mediator and the parties to the dispute can be held in which the mediator attempts to clarify his/her understanding of the nature of the dispute, and the negotiating positions of each party. The third party may also explain precedents set by similar situations in the past. The mediator may then concentrate on areas where the two sides are closest to agreement in the hope that if an initial agreement can be reached this may enhance both sides' perceptions of the process and the rewards of further agreements.[67] The mediator may attempt to promote consistency and a spirit of cooperation through the medium of face-to-face meetings or, if these are not likely to be productive (often because one party, usually the state/government, refuses to recognize the legitimacy of the other), proximity talks. All of this, of course, assumes that there is the possibility of a solution in the context of the framework of the Westphalian international system and that the parties themselves actually have accepted the necessity of a compromise.

The mediator must decide how far he/she is to become involved in the issue of the dispute and whether to table his/her own proposals[68] or just to aid in procedural aspects. For example, Carter's coercive mediation at Camp David was based on an American vision of peace in the Middle East; in contrast the Secretary-General's mediation of the Cyprus problem has since 1965 tended towards the procedural, with the exception of Boutros-Ghali's efforts in the early 1990s. Tabling proposals guides the process, allowing the parties to haggle over them, though they may also react to the fear that the mediator is attempting to impose a settlement (although this may be clear if the mediator is also applying his/her own resources). Rejection of such proposals can also lead to a weakening of the mediator's position with one or both sides.

Whatever the nature of the mediation process, the control of information is a vital asset allowing the mediator to be anything from a postman to a decoder, and exert some control over the perceptions of the two sides, keeping them focused on the potential rewards of the process.[69] Secrecy is important. Premature disclosure of the positions of the disputants may lead to domestic pressure on the negotiators who may then find it difficult to retreat from their public positions.[70] In turn this means that the mediator must also expect to play a face-saving role, as with the agreement signed between Egypt and Israel at the military talks at Kilometre Marker-101, which succeeded precisely because it was secret, so enabling Egypt to save face.[71] A shroud of secrecy, though, is difficult to enforce as though it has the advantage of enabling the negotiators to pursue a discourse with the mediator that is relatively free from political rhetoric, often negotiators may feel that political rhetoric protects them somewhat from the attempts of the mediator to make them compromise. It is also clear that Milosevic and his negotiating partners at Dayton were successful in persuading the American mediators that popular rhetoric back home was a powerful constraint (even to the extent that the lives of the negotiating teams might be threatened in the future).[72]

Previous relationships with one or other of the parties to the dispute are also deemed important, though Milosevic's relationship with US diplomatic teams seems to indicate that this can be of uncertain providence in the light of the war over Kosovo in mid-1999. The mediator's history certainly indicates to the parties what type of approach and solution he or she might favour. During and after Holbrooke's involvement in the Balkans he also played a role in mediating in Cyprus; given his approach in the Balkans, the Greek Cypriot side (which favoured the Serbs) was particularly wary about his attitude to 'secession' and Muslim minorities.

In this framework of mediation resources are vital. Bercovitch and Rubin have categorized this in the following way: reward resources are based on the mediator's ability to offer benefits in the event of an agreement, while coercive resources signify the mediator's ability to back threats to withdraw, to make public deficiencies in one side's approach to the negotiations, and to enforce his/her own vision of a solution on the disputants. Legitimacy resources are related to the disputants' perceptions of the mediator's position while informational resources and resources of expertise depend on the mediator's ability to uncover relevant information and bring past mediation experiences into play.[73] Varying levels of access to these resources therefore influences the mediator's choice of strategies. Mediators with basic resources tend to rely on the ability to highlight the common interests. For example, Dag Hammarskjöld's mediation of a dispute between Israel and Jordan in 1957 led to an agreement on the initial problem of transporting petrol and led to a pacification of the whole area.[74] President Carter's offer to build airbases for the Israelis in exchange for their withdrawal from the Sinai was an important prerequisite of peace with Egypt as was Carter's provision of a guarantee for the agreement by the United States. This was the only way that a solution could be found in a situation where both disputants were answerable to constituencies that were hostile to an agreement, as was the case in Israel and most of the Arab world. However it is rare that mediators have access to such high levels of resources, and in situations where a mediator has limited resources he or she can attempt to form a coalition with other interested parties. This can increase the pressure on the disputants to settle but can also further complicate mediation efforts by including a more diverse set of interests.

Drawing on empirical evidence, the factors which influence the effectiveness (defined in the Westphalian sense of reaching a compromise and preventing disorder which threatens to revise the status quo) seem to be diverse, and it is difficult to draw clear lessons. In the case of Angola, with respect to the interstate and intrastate aspects of the conflict, Chester Crocker's ability to mobilize resources had a direct bearing on the third party's ability to exert pressure.[75] In the case of the Afghan conflict, mediators attempted to remove external constraints and then work on the internal conflicts.[76] It was clear that in Northern Ireland and the Israel/Palestine conflict, there was no precise formula for settlement while the disputants and the third party thought in terms of absolute sovereignty (though it is clear that in these two cases the main problem lies in implementation). In the Iran–Iraq war the passage of time seemed to have increased pressure on leaders to compromise, though in some cases, as in Northern Ireland, Palestine,

Lebanon and Cyprus, the disputants have learned to adapt to high levels of physical and structural violence, and many years may pass before a hurting stalemate becomes unbearable.

Debates locating international mediation in the framework of the Westphalian international system have recognized that the nature and number of the issues on the table provide analysts with insights into the propensity for a conflict to be solved: issues involving the national interest, territory or honour have long been identified as being of a particularly problematic nature, along with security, identity and independence, resources and ideology.[77] Because some of these are intangible issues that stem from the disputants' need for identity and representation, it has been argued that as they resist measurement they are therefore inclined to resist bargaining approaches. Because of this, 'intractable' disputes tend to be characterized by a large number of issues of both a tangible and an intangible nature which increase the complexity of the dispute.

It has also been recognized that language used in international mediation, negotiation and subsequent agreements is problematic, being dependent on traditional diplomatic ambiguity to complement the mediator's efforts to rearrange the disputants' resources and apply his/her own.[78] This is linked to a growing recognition of the fact that cultural differences can present difficulties, and this relates to why disputants construct their negotiating positions vis-à-vis other actors in the dispute, how they interpret demands, and the constraints and norms of the framework provided by their interpretation of the international and regional system. For example, at Camp David in 1978 the Egyptians exploited ambiguity to enable them to save face, while in contrast the Israelis wanted the agreement to be clearly defined beforehand. The Arab habit of allowing large bargaining margins also confused the Israeli negotiators who tended to bargain with much smaller margins, which in turn confused the Egyptians, leading to a deadlock that was finally overcome only by the resource-based mediation of President Carter.[79] Thus, the mode of interpretation that the opposing sides use to attempt to understand and explain their dispute may lead to the dispute becoming characterized as 'intractable', because of a reliance and exploitation of unwavering and established beliefs based on historical evidence and past atrocities.

Because mediation has essentially been viewed in the literature as a fragile procedural or dynamic coercive activity, the level of intensity of the conflict in terms of its physical or psychological nature has also been the subject of much debate, particularly related to the success of the process and how the level of intensity shapes the environment in which the mediator operates. This approach held the glimmerings of a recognition of the importance of the local, regional and global environment in the mediation process, though there has not been a clear acknowledgement of this. Rather, the link between 'successful' mediation and the conflict environment has led to an emphasis on the strategies, resources and personal skills and qualities of the mediator. Success was taken to mean incremental and final agreements. One review of the literature on mediation argues that as the level of conflict increases, the likelihood of successful mediation decreases, leading to an increased propensity for the mediator to use coercion.[80] Another position indicates that as it is difficult to measure and therefore categorize the level of intensity,[81] it is impossible to generate anything other than generalities from this perspective. This seems to represent a surrender in the face of trying to define success. However, first generation approaches tend to agree that if power and resource asymmetries exist then there is little chance that the mediator will succeed in terms of producing a solution.[82] Therefore, the definition of success gradually shifted to include 'lesser' forms such as a ceasefire, a break in hostilities, the start of dialogue,[83] or the emergence of a negotiating culture. The success of the mediation process has also been viewed in terms of short and long-term outcomes relating to the goals of the disputants and their initial level of satisfaction towards the solution, and whether the solution is self-sustaining. Bercovitch and Rubin argue that success is a subjective concept as it depends upon the parties' satisfaction with the settlement. They point out that as the aim of mediation is to produce a change in the nature of a dispute and the parties' interactions, examining the consequences of mediation in terms of success or failure is fraught with difficulty in conceptual and methodological terms.[84] This is true when one considers that the Westphalian international system and regional and global political forces provides the basis for all settlements. Thus the parties' satisfaction, the success of the process, and durability of a settlement depends on how effectively these frameworks can mediate between the zero-sum interests of the disputants, and third parties. Bercovitch has argued that mediation is dependent on timing, intervention occurring in a state of mutual exhaustion.[85] A sense of urgency, along with skilled diplomats who observe a code of secrecy and are able to offer face-saving, represents a fairly standard description of the diplomatic process. Chester Crocker has argued that for a settlement to survive there must be coherent leadership of the implementation process with third parties continually engaged through the processes of negotiation and implementation.[86]

Heraclides has argued that in intractable conflict there are four main obstacles to peace, including the disputants; the state in question; the separatist side; and other states with a stake in the conflict. To this I would also add the nature of the Westphalian international system and the difficulties inherent in its main concepts, which means that disputants tend to view 'sovereignty as indivisible, according to the conventional Westphalia idea'.[87] This gives hardline negotiating positions and the use of military tactics a perceived utility.

The two key concepts often employed by analysts working within the confines of first generation approaches, that of symmetry and ripe moments, seem themselves to be tautological, and both concepts offer few prescriptive possibilities for protracted and intractable forms of conflict. This is borne out by Stedman's work which has noted that from 1900 to 1980, 85 per cent of civil wars were solved by one side winning, with only 15 per cent resulting in a negotiated end.[88] Shearer in turn notes Stedman's argument that such data 'raises basic questions about the ethics and effectiveness of mediation as an international response to civil war'.[89] It is clear that there are limits to consent-based mediation in such conflicts, as Stedman and Shearer indicate, but this tends to be in the context of the disputants' perceptions of international norms (relating in particular to the legal notions of sovereignty, territorial integrity, non-intervention, and self-determination in the context of democratization and human rights).

The state-centric power discourses of the Westphalian international system have appropriated international mediation as a tool to promote international order through a rearrangement of interests; often normative justice at the local level has been compromised in response to the need for regional or global stability. The mediator's role is viewed essentially as facilitating a return of order through trilateral bargaining processes that attempted to find a balance between the negotiators' positions through the use of what is essentially a primitive tool – the carrot and stick.[90] It is expected that other parties with interests in the conflict will exert pressure on the disputants to find a solution in parallel with the mediator and in the interests of the status quo. This means that mediation is a limited tool and disputes that are not amenable to mediation often earn the title 'intractable'. The mediator has to play a balanced role of catalyst and power-broker,[91] a role dependent upon his/her resources. This in turn defines his/her range of tactics, from the facilitation of communication which requires minimal resources but some expertise, to the formulation of proposals, and exerting pressure and providing incentives for concessions. Even so it has been noted that mediation does not tend to alter the long-term climate between the disputants following a solution,[92] primarily because the conflict had not been addressed at its roots. Mediation therefore tends to have difficulty in dealing with intangibles, and the mediation process is severely hampered if the mediator does not possess the influence or resources to back up any bias.[93] It is clear to all that conflicts which contain profound power and resource inequalities are rarely amenable to mediation,[94] primarily because the stronger side will tend to concentrate on its prenegotiation objectives, and the international system itself does not necessarily promote peaceful solutions in intractable conflicts.

The rationalist assumptions underlying first generation approaches tend to deal inadequately with the nature of conflicts in which parties tend to increase their expenditure to attain implausible objectives, rather than admit defeat.[95] As in the Israel/Palestinian conflict, a movement away from inflexible positions occurs in parallel with domestic, regional and global changes which allow all levels of the problem to be addressed, though in an ad hoc manner. The Israelis realized that the *intifada* indicated that they were unable to quell the Palestinian uprising; the Palestinians were strengthened by the uniting forces of the rebellion; and with the end of the cold war Arab–Israeli relations began to soften, partly because the US now had greater access to the region. This complex process was just enough for the US to receive the consent of parties which led to the opening of a negotiating process and a compromise that had actually become plausible for the two sides (though it inevitably favoured the state of Israel). It was in this spirit that Norway was able to facilitate the establishment of the 'Oslo channel' in mid-1992 which led to a Declaration of Principles after eight months of negotiations.[96] In this case high degrees of structural asymmetries of power were partly overcome but not through first generation approaches. In the case of the Oslo Accords, the Norwegian mediators used conflict resolution/facilitation methods to encourage the parties to relax their stereotypes and suspicions of each other, enabling the disputants to address the respective issues of Israeli security and Palestinian recognition.[97] It is notable that since the Oslo Accords, academic debates have come to countenance the synthesis of traditional diplomatic processes with conflict resolution process in particular aimed at officials.[98] However, even with this evolution of first generation approaches, it is clear that even a 'successful' mediation process can very quickly degrade, in particular during the implementation phase, as has occurred with the Oslo Accords, and in Cambodia. Similarly the implementation process in Angola has been fraught with the threat of conflict since the Lusaka protocol in 1994. In El Salvador and Mozambique, implementation is still tentative.[99] Perhaps the archetypal example of mediation in the Westphalian framework was the role of the US in bringing the warring parties to the negotiating table at Dayton in 1995, and then in producing a solution based on its own resources, its own notion of what the solution should be, in the context of strategic interests. While this was 'successful' in the case of Dayton, the issue of Kosovo was ignored, left to a later, failed, mediation attempt at Rambouillet followed by civil war and a highly problematic western humanitarian intervention in 1999.

The problem of power and legitimacy

Within first generation debates, a third party's entry into a conflict environment clearly introduces a series of new dynamics into the conflict environment. In an interstate conflict the disputants' relative power and legal status are perhaps more readily reconciled than in a conflict involving a mixture of state and non-state actors. This line of thinking leads into a discussion of the asymmetric nature of certain types of conflict in the context of the Westphalian international system. For conflicts involving non-state actors, this produces an asymmetry inherent to the frameworks which third parties can apply in order to bring about a solution. As Zartman has acknowledged, internal conflict is always asymmetric – and about two-thirds of internal conflicts have ended in the elimination of one party.[100] Such conflicts are characterized by their intensity and inflexible negotiating positions, and are difficult to end because of the legal and resource asymmetry between disputants.

Before any intervention occurs, the Westphalian framework requires that disputants are faced with either settlement or deadlock, and a long violent campaign. In either case the outcome of non-forcible forms of intervention depends upon the interaction of the third parties' coercive and reward potential and interests with those of the disputants in the context of the state system, as well as the presence of stable conditions on the ground, often provided by peacekeepers. Disputants will tend to believe that they must also apply their own resources to resist pressure from the third party as well as from the opposing party, and that the party which is least able to do this will be forced to compromise more. Within this framework, if a third party can apply a high level of coercive potential and interests the disputants will be forced to conduct three-way negotiations in accordance with their own interests and resources, which will probably lead to a position in line with the third party's interest. These will be derived from three main areas; that of the norms and frameworks of the international system and their preservation (in order to facilitate stability, and provide a basis for future conflict management); the interests of the state or organization backing the process; and any personal interests. It is from the dynamic interaction of the interests and capacities of all parties, their constituencies, and the conceptual frameworks upon which their mindset and negotiating positions are based, that a compromise should emerge based on Westphalian versions of state-centric order as the dominant image of a solution. This notion of a compromise has been reinforced by the supremacy of state, sovereignty and non-intervention, as well as the view of 'international relations' as a competitive chase for limited resources in which the only rational outcomes are based on compromises founded on calculations of relative power and a rearrangement of interests and resources. The normative discourse here is, of course, hidden away behind the minimal role played by international law and humanitarianism, which all parties tend to accept are subservient to the needs of local, regional and global balances of power. Once a solution had been reached, third parties and any related peacekeeping operation would then withdraw in the hope that the new status quo would become self-sustaining.

If such practices in the Westphalian context are conceptually flawed when they occur between states, in a conflict between a recognized government and a local or transborder group without any official status, serious difficulties emerge for third parties and peacekeepers, which then have the unenviable role of avoiding infringing the legitimate status and sovereignty of state groups. 'Successful' peacekeeping forces have generally frozen the post-conflict situation in favour of the dominant actor and it is difficult to open up a channel of communication between the parties without threatening the government's claim to sovereignty. This is often attempted in the context of mediation and negotiation through shuttle talks in which parties do not meet face to face or communicate directly. Though this gives the third party control of the situation, it also tends to reduce the levels of trust that the triad of parties can display in their counterparts. Furthermore, as the sovereign representative controls most of the resources of a recognized government, from funds, military hardware, manpower and intelligence, to the state's seat at the UN and embassies around the world, this imbalance tends to lead the non-state actor into a search for allies, often amongst the states predominant in the regional and global balance of power, leading to a replication of the security dilemma which governs relations in the theory and practice of the Westphalian international system. This often results in the further alienation of both sides, prompting a search for alliances, bringing further interests into the conflict, and the threat of escalation.

This has led to a discussion about approaches to ending conflict that are more likely to succeed in the context of stalemate between the two parties.[101] On the face of it this seems to be a logical suggestion in the Westphalian context, but beneath the surface there are several problematic assumptions being made. Stalemate means power-parity, according to standard realist diplomatic reasoning; this means that both sides are roughly equal and have an equal chance of winning and losing. Furthermore, stalemates have to have been tested through conflict in order to stimulate cooperation with the mediator. Unless the stalemate has been very painful it is unlikely that the parties will want to compromise on paper what they managed to win or retain in open conflict, if the logic of rational self-interest holds, and unless the third party is able to offset losses at the negotiating table with their own resources (as occurred at Camp David in the late 1970s). While a stalemate may provide the mediator with opportunities to find a settlement, it is little more than a reprieve, often controlled, policed or monitored by peacekeepers, from open conflict. Stalemates tend to be protracted, and can exist even while open conflict continues, and therefore do not provide much impetus for a settlement beyond what already exists or has been stimulated by the mediator's own resources. The longer a stalemate continues, the more likely it is that the two sides will attempt to gain the advantage. Even if high costs are incurred, this may (rationally) lead one or other side to deciding that it has invested too much in the conflict to accept a compromise. An addition to this debate has argued that a policy of empowerment[102] may prevent this tendency, but then if it produces parity both sides have an equal chance of success if they revert to violent conflict. Furthermore, empowerment requires that the mediator or related actor has sufficient resources and will (and of course, the ability to measure) to achieve parity, and once again the rational 'paradigm' underlying first generation approaches dictates that even were such an actor willing to do this, it would act in its own interests. Empowerment may therefore serve only to move the conflict into other arenas, and it is also possible that the recipient of empowerment may increase its objectives in response. Furthermore, a stalemate can exist without parity, perpetuating the underlying problem.

Initiation, the process, and success

A major question is whether third party intervention is requested or imposed from the outside. The literature in the field often seems to acknowledge that one or other is possible but that the resulting process is inherently similar. This is probably because most analysts would agree that peacekeeping and mediation must adhere to the dominant norms and structures of the international system and therefore may be seen locally as an imposition, particularly if the disputants are claiming sovereignty for themselves. It is interesting, however, to see that this attempt to 'genericise' two fundamentally different processes merely reflects the attempt to characterize the international system as subject to power politics. Peacekeeping and mediation upon invitation are fundamentally different from when they are imposed in that the latter signifies possible enforcement and coercion while the former indicates the presence of consent and a basic desire of the disputants to settle their conflict. Imposed mediation raises questions related to forcible intervention.

However, on whatever basis third party intervention is founded, representatives of the disputants must have sufficient authority to make decisions on behalf of their constituencies.[103] Often mediators find that negotiators' inability to make concessions reflects the internal political dynamic related to power-seeking and consolidation within the group, and the tendency towards internal fractionation. The fact that mediation requires that interaction take place between strongly positioned representatives is indicative of another aspect of the weakness of the traditional paradigm of mediation. If the disputants are sovereign actors which have the support of the majority of their constituencies (through a democratic process) this clearly would facilitate the process of mediation. Yet if one examines most conflicts which have been the subject of mediation it is clear that more often the negotiators are a mixture of state and non-state actors who rely on the exploitation of nationalism and ethnonationalism, and the use of coercion to prolong their fragile positions. It is often the case (as with Holbrooke's mediation at Dayton in 1995) that mediators are forced to negotiate with actors of dubious 'diplomatic' credentials. According to the mediation literature, however, there must be a party who commands strong support and has a mandate to enter into discussions with the opposing party, and to cooperate with outside actors. Furthermore, the assumption seems to be that negotiators are beholden to the desires of the respective constituencies. Yet negotiators in the Westphalian context often frame their representation of their constituencies' demands in the context of the norms of the international system (particularly those which are already the subject of disputed interpretation, such as sovereignty, intervention, territory, and self-determination) that they feel most suits their cause. Thus the process of conflict management is framed by the interests of the triad of third parties and negotiators, as well as the international system itself, as it has been defined by crucial documents such as the UN Charter, and by precedents set in the past. Negotiators therefore often struggle to frame a compromise with their adversaries which most suits them, and against the limits of the international system itself – in the context of the cold war, it was unthinkable for the official actors in Cyprus or Northern Ireland, Israel, Kashmir or Sri Lanka to accept secession or irredentism.

The argument that a solution is more likely to be found at an early stage before attitudes and behaviour become too hostile, or later when the conflict enters a costly stalemate and the parties are exhausted, is there-fore flawed.[104] In the Westphalian framework of inside/outside binaries it is likely that stalemate and stereotyping have already been phases of the other incarnations of the conflict. Conflict, after all, does not just sud-denly occur. Stereotyping tends to be part of the Westphalian socio-political consciousness, and constitutes a civil level of conflict to which formal approaches to ending conflict cannot respond. However, it has been argued that intervention at an early stage has the advantage that the shorter the initial conflict the less the damage, though it is generally accepted that the second stage of costly stalemate would provide the two sides with a feeling of urgency. But this debate ignores the factors related to the interests of third parties to intervene, often motivated by the intensity of the dispute[105] and its propensity to spread.

Related to this discussion is the general literature on 'ripe moments' for ending conflict, commonly depicted as a 'hurting stalemate' in which disputants recognize that a negotiated settlement provides the only escape from further escalation,[106] or when disputants anticipate future gains from a settlement.[107] This notion is contested[108] and con-ceptually vague at best. It does not explain why some actors maintain failing policies; thus, '[o]nly if we abandon rational-choice assumptions can such behaviour be understood.'[109] Yet, this notion was generally seen as indicating a point when third parties could set about creating a suitable environment for reconciliation and settlement (as classic forms of UN peacekeeping was supposed to do for UN mediation and good offices); this of course led to attempts to create ripe moments – for example, Chester Crocker's attempts to produce hurting stalemates and Henry Kissinger's notion that only a war without victory could produce the will for a settlement.[110]

This illustrates the difficulty of conceptualizing the meaning of non-coercive intervention in the context of an anarchic international system in which the balance of power appears to be the best guarantee of order. The parties may initiate it themselves, though it is more likely that third parties will become involved because the conflict directly or indirectly has an effect on their own interests.[111] Clearly, in the case of peacekeeping forces, consent has normally been required even if one of the disputants was a non-state actor. Princen has argued that the entry of a mediator depends upon how much the disputants need the mediator's input, or upon the danger of escalation.[112] Parties may want to initiate mediation because they hope that the mediator will side with them, or they desire the positive publicity to be gained from initiating the process. They may also be motivated by the desire for a scapegoat on whom to blame any concessions they may make, and it is also likely that they want the mediator to guarantee the eventual settlement, as occurred with the negotiations between Israel and Egypt which were concluded at Camp David.[113] This framework of mediation is plainly an extension of the rational pursuit of interest in an international system of self-help; it is not, however, indicative of a framework which provides long-term, self-sustaining stability, nor which addresses underlying issues relating to identity, representation, historical perceptions and stereotypes, these factors being subsumed by the demarcation of domestic politics.

Extending this description of intervention as an extension of power politics and traditional forms of diplomacy, it is clear that disputants are aware of the fact that whatever the benefits of accepting the presence of a third party, there are certain costs entailed, especially because one of the third parties, strategies may be to form a coalition with one or other side. This may indicate that soliciting a third party might be seen as a provocation or as a sign of weakness by the opposite side.[114] However, accepting a third party entails some obligation on the part of the disputants,[115] though this can be minimal and heavily dependent upon the resources that the third party can bring to bear. This means that the acceptance of a third party entails significant risk, though the literature would have it that peacekeeping and the roles the mediator can then take on are sufficient recompense.

Consequently, initiation is dependent on the attitudes of the parties and the pre-negotiation conditions, the balance of power, the interests of third parties in intervening, and order as it is perceived in the Westphalian context. If the parties want to begin a meaningful process then the mediator may have room for manoeuvre, although, particularly in the cold war environment, the mediator is likely to have been imposed in a conflict situation (which may also have been frozen by external intervention or a peacekeeping). Even if this has occurred with the consent of the disputants the two sides will tend to concentrate on the zero-sum benefits the third party might be able to provide them with. A dynamic will emerge in which the stronger side (either in terms of military resources or in terms if international recognition) would probably adopt an inflexible stance and depend on the weaker side to make concessions, while the weaker side's likely reaction may be to try to form an alliance to strengthen its hand. Both sides will tend to selectively review and appeal to those aspects of the international system which endorse their negotiating positions; particularly in conflicts relating to identity this can concentrate on the existing and somewhat contradictory apparatus of identity relating to self-determination, [territorial] sovereignty, and emerging human rights regimes. This indicates that the mediator would tend to be ineffective if his/her mission were to bring about a settlement unless he/she had a substantial carrot to offer the strong side to persuade it to back down, or to persuade the weaker side to make further concessions. The role of a mediator without these kinds of resources would therefore tend to become one of trying to keep talks alive, perhaps indefinitely in the kind of 'status-quo holding' protracted negotiation (seen in the case of Cyprus, for example), the alternative being a resort to open conflict. In the latter case, if it became apparent that a resort to open conflict was likely other members of the international community might then be persuaded to become involved, either by supporting the existing mediator with more resources of a reward or coercive nature, or by instigating parallel processes on behalf of other states or organizations. In effect, in the Westphalian framework, if a disputant enters negotiations from a position of strength in this environment it will want to translate this into political gain, via a process that does not empower or legitimate the weaker party, and a peacekeeping operation which reinforces the position of the dominant actor.

The issue of impartiality

The debates around impartiality in the Westphalian context underscore the inherent paradox that peaceful forms of conflict management and settlement face in an international environment believed by many, working on a neo-realist, neo-institutionalist, and neoliberal basis, to be characterized by a clash of interests and levels of anarchy which are only curtailed by the balance of power, state-centric order and a level of international society. It is true that a third party must be motivated either by a desire to create peace or by self-interest, rather than some by 'nebulous greater good'.[116] This indicates that the common assumption that third parties should be neutral is flawed on several counts. The disputants will not necessarily require a third party to be neutral if rewards and coercion are applied in line with their interests.

Peacekeeping forces during this period, with the notable exception of ONUC, only survived with their limited means and mandates if they could demonstrate impartiality in their dealings with disputants. This was the only way that they could retain the consent that the mission was inevitably based upon. When a peacekeeping force did begin to move beyond this framework, as in the Congo, or in several post-cold war operations, it became clear that the UN did not have the resources to sustain such positions – that deviating from consent and impartiality undermined its legitimacy and therefore its ability to prevent an escalation of violence.

It is more likely that a mediator will be accepted if he/she is able to influence, protect, or extend the interests of each party in the conflict. This is close to Princen's argument that third parties are invited into a conflict in order to persuade the other side of one's rightful position and to persuade constituencies to accept compromise and concessions.[117] This requires that the third party be trustworthy and have access to leverage over both sides, without alienating either of them. The third party can bargain directly with a disputant to strike a side deal, it can force concessions from one side by making a coalition with the other, or it can make a three-way deal, first with one of the disputants, who then makes a deal with the other. It is apparent, therefore, that impartiality cannot be attained and is not a necessary prerequisite. The coercive mediator acts upon its own interests, as do institutional mediators who operate in a framework of universal norms (i.e. those of dominant sponsor states). In practice, impartiality is implausible, as shown when the government of India became a mediator between the government of Sri Lanka and the Tamils while it was also providing of arms to various Tamil factions.[118] Another example was Milosevic's opposition to a Kosovo mediator during the lead up to NATO intervention in 1999, which he dismissed as a 'ruse' (though he hinted that he would accept a peace 'facilitator').[119] During the same period, the US was developing its approach to the Cyprus problem, prompting the then Defence Minister of Greece to state that he was suspicious of the US role because of the 'history of Cyprus and the roles and attitudes of the mediators in the past'.[120] In the case of Kashmir, there has been little scope for outside intervention by third parties or the UN because of India's stand on intervention.[121]

Conclusion

The first generation of approaches to ending conflict, including peace-keeping, mediation and negotiation identified here are often power-based and hegemonic activities despite their claims of consent, impartiality and neutrality; the level of resources of the third party dictates where the process is based on the procedural/coercive spectrum outlined above (see Figure 2.1). Peacekeeping, mediation and negotiation are derived from traditional forms of diplomatic practice and are, therefore, mainly centred around the activities, in peace and war, of states and their official representatives. They have proven to be far from a panacea for conflict, particularly in cases of conflicts revolving around claims for representation, statehood related to disputed historical possession of territory, identity, and culture. As the state-system allocates territory and rights on the basis of national groups which are self-supporting economically, territorially, and militarily,[122] conflicts which fall outside of these frameworks (constituting the vast majority) or are even caused by the inadequacies of the system, tend to be labelled intractable. In such cases, conflicts have raged unattended for many years (as in Afghanistan and Sudan), and have been cordoned off from world politics by the sovereign state system (which can be used to justify non-intervention even if humanitarian abuses are taking place in a given state), have been subject to methods of management or have been quelled by the use of force while the rest of the international community has looked in the other direction.

International mediation operates in the realms of high diplomacy, concentrating on the state system and the interests of states. This imbalance is also true on a normative level, it being clear that the level of high diplomacy tends to be self-sustaining primarily because states are protecting their interests, through the body of international law which protects states, and the institutions of which they are members. This means that international mediation and associated forms of peacekeeping are essentially monodimensional activities, though they do have an effect directly and indirectly, on other levels of world politics aimed at preserving the status quo in the Westphalian international system. Thus, their primary aim is normally either to provide conditions for and bring about new constitutional arrangement in torn states, to stabilize conflict between states, or far less often to establish a new regional state system consisting of fragments of one or more failed states. Figure 2.1 outlines the role of resources in first generation approaches.

Peacekeeping strategies focus on preventing open violence and monitoring ceasefires and status quos. Negotiation revolves around the

Procedural/ passive
activity

Coercive
activity

Low levels of resources –
mainly diplomatic intervention
backed by consent - based peacekeeping forces

High levels of
resources –
possibly military
intervention

Figure 2.1 Passive/procedural-coercive spectrum of traditional peacekeeping/ peacemaking approaches

zero-sum exchange of concessions in an environment defined by relative power. Mediation strategies revolve around bringing the disputants together, the exercise of coercion or the facilitation of the process of communication, offering incentives and guarantees, and providing a face-saving mechanism. Figure 2.2 outlines the basic framework of first generation approaches.

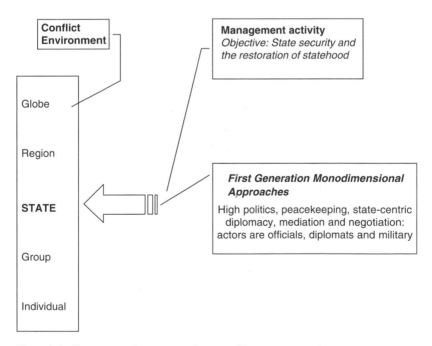

Conflict Environment

Management activity
Objective: State security and the restoration of statehood

Globe

Region

STATE

Group

Individual

First Generation Monodimensional Approaches

High politics, peacekeeping, state-centric diplomacy, mediation and negotiation: actors are officials, diplomats and military

Figure 2.2 First generation approaches: conflict management

Success is defined as spanning the production of a negotiating culture, a ceasefire, or a settlement of a short or long-term nature and is believed to be dependent upon the qualities and resources of the third party, the nature of the dispute and environment, and most importantly, on the will or necessity for agreement. Long term success is generally dependent on external guarantees. Primarily, it is argued, there is a need for the disputants to perceive a relative balance and believe that unilateral action will prove ineffective; secondly, the conflict has not been prolonged to the point of 'intractability' through institutionalization: finally, a third party has the capacity to offer a reward or exert pressure on the disputants to bring them to a settlement.

3
Second Generation: Conflict Resolution Approaches to Ending Conflict

> ...the resolution of any conflict, whether it be intercommunal or international conflict, must be analysed as a situated process located within the structural properties of patterned social systems. The role of conflict resolution or mediation may thus reproduce such continuities or contribute to their problem.[1]

Introduction

This chapter examines the development of the theory and practice of conflict resolution, facilitation and transformation approaches, as well as some of the insights provided by peace research approaches, both as a response to the shortcomings of traditional diplomacy and as an independent approach to conflict. It examines their contribution to, and critique of, peacekeeping and peacemaking in the Westphalian environment. I have given such approaches the appellation of 'second generation' in order to indicate that they lead to a significantly different understanding of conflict and have created a profitable debate about making peace. They provide an important critique of approaches to ending conflict in the Westphalian system and point in a direction beyond that system. Thus, second generation conflict approaches take a radically different view of conflict; the assumption is made that conflicts can be (and ought to be) *resolved* rather than merely managed. Second generation approaches see difficulties in the way first generation approaches attempt to understand and address conflict and therefore propose to address the civil level of conflict, and the structural violence surrounding it. The resolution of conflict, it is argued, can therefore be viewed from a win-win perspective.

The term 'second generation' is used to acknowledge a general debate, within which there are several different approaches, derived from critiques of the socio-political, structural, and psychological, nature of the Westphalian international system. The term is used in order to indicate that such approaches were a response to the inadequacies of the generally defined field of first generation approaches, discussed in Chapter 2, though it is important to note that they are closely related and share a common intellectual heritage. It is used to show that they represent an advancement in the field (though the intellectual effort to enhance the linkages between 'Track I' and 'Track II' diplomacy for example has been difficult), and equally, attempts to show how conflict transformation approaches can lead into wide-ranging peace processes which contribute to peace within the Westphalian international system are problematic.

The argument is examined and critiqued that second generation approaches are able to aid in the development of civil awareness and the reduction of zero-sum views, point to the social, psychological and structural roots of conflict, and may also have an indirect effect on the sphere of traditional diplomacy, contributing to the search for 'peace' within the state system. While these have been key contributions, in part responses to the need for more dynamic approaches to address complex conflicts, there are also conceptual limitations inherent within the body of literature surrounding second generation approaches that need to be discussed in the context of the limitations that the Westphalian system imposes on disputants and on approaches to ending conflict. Where second generation approaches have been important is in their highlighting of human needs and thus human security over state security, structural violence, and the need for new forms of communication to be developed in order for human security in a latent international society, to be realized. This has been crucial, not just in the contribution of new perspectives to peace, but also in providing a conceptual and methodological framework for new types of actors (NGOs, for example) and civil society to become involved in the complex transnational communicational and other transactions that mark the contemporary environment.

The development of second generation approaches

As opposed to first generation approaches, second generation approaches start from an attempt to examine the root causes of conflict based on a discussion of the stimulus for, and the nature of, human

behaviour and constraining structures. There are three main alternatives in this quest for an understanding of the roots of conflict: that human behaviour is derived from genetic factors; that it is a result of socialization; or that human behaviour constitutes an interaction between its inherent characteristics and the social environment.[2] First generation approaches tended to view conflict as inherently objective, relating to national security in a well-defined legal and political framework and intimate that 'intractable' conflicts become so because of the mistaken elevation of subjective issues. Second generation approaches moved the debate towards a more intersubjective view of what constitutes conflict, able to incorporate elements of politics defined by the basic needs of individuals, particularly with respect to their claims for representation, identity, and status as individuals rather than citizens in assimilationist nation or national structures. This in turn has provided a new perspective on debates about security and the role of the state and the individual as actors in world politics. This stimulated a much broader definition of security to come into common usage.

These approaches drew on several strands. Kenneth Boulding coined the term 'conflict resolution' to signify a normative study of resolving conflict.[3] Also significant were Mitrany's ideas on functional integration among countries to create a common interest in peace and Haas's empirical analysis of how this occurred in the case of the European Coal and Steel Community, established in 1951,[4] as well as the early structural concerns of those engaged in a discussion of international inequality. Unofficial diplomacy was becoming increasingly important in international affairs, illustrated by the example of the nuclear physicists from the United States, Great Britain and the Soviet Union, who began to meet to exchange ideas about reducing the likelihood that nuclear weapons would be used.[5] Furthermore, it was apparent that certain types of transnational exchanges were occurring which merited a rethink of the closed nature of the sovereign state. The development of social movements and NGOs illustrated the fact there were areas of the global environment that had not been examined or perhaps even noticed.

There were several stimuli for the emergence of alternative approaches to conflict as a result of several crucial diplomatic dilemmas. Diplomatic practice often allowed settlements based on 'peace without justice' and the application of coercion (even if of a persuasive nature) and often settlements processes occurred only after a devastating conflict had occurred. For example, the 1973 October War led to the start of the peace process in the Middle East which would be partly based on the 'realities' derived from that war; similarly in Cyprus, the first phase of UN-sponsored intercommunal negotiations were based on Greek Cypriot attempts to marginalize the Turkish Cypriots, while after the 1974 Turkish invasion, negotiations were based on 'realities' that appeared to favour the Turkish Cypriot side. Other dilemmas were related to a protection of western-inspired versions of order; airstrikes forced Saddam Hussein to give in to the West several times in the 1990s; NATO bombing forced the Serbs to Dayton late in 1995[6] and again to accept NATO terms over Kosovo in the middle of 1999; nothing was done about the genocide in Rwanda, however. It is also significant that the tradition of conflict management was mainly related to military activity and high-level meetings between official actors and therefore could not be applied to protracted and intractable conflicts over identity and representation, ethno-nationalism, or related territorial claims. When they did attempt to deal with such problems, implementation often failed – as with the Kurdish problem and their proposed state, first mooted at the Treaty of Sèvres.[7]

This indicates another key dilemma related to the emergence of new types of actors with emerging and competing agendas. The elevation of ethnopolitics, and the inclusive and exclusive politics of group representation as a competitor with the state-centric system created areas that traditional diplomacy could not address, as conflicts over ethnicity, language, religion or culture tend to resist efforts toward compromise unless the prize of statehood and sovereignty can be amicably agreed. Because groups and their members engage in constant evaluation of their status vis-à-vis others, this often leads to feelings of victimization, attempts to increase the group's status through legitimate means, or where these fail (either because of opposition or because of conceptual inadequacy), open violence. First generation approaches could do little more than police these conflicts if the international will and funding were there while mediating the disputants' claims for status and territory, as UN involvement in the Cyprus problem has long illustrated.

Second generation approaches developed partly in reaction to the 'balance of power' conflict management techniques associated with positivist Realist approaches, and include conflict resolution and transformation, social, psychological and systems approaches. Though such approaches are partly based on the same realist dichotomy of state and non-state, they place more emphasis on the non-state level and intersubjective factors, and offer a significantly different view of what constitutes conflict. As Galtung argues from a peace research perspective,

Conflict is much more than what meets the naked eye as 'trouble', direct violence. There is also the violence frozen into structures, and the culture that legitimises violence. To transform a conflict between some parties, more than a new architecture for their relationship is needed. The parties have to be transformed so that the conflict is not reproduced forever. There are intra-party aspects to most inter-party conflicts.[8]

Galtung developed a model of conflict, drawn from a line of thinking associated with peace research, applied to both symmetric and asymmetric conflicts within the Westphalian system.[9] In this model conflict can be viewed as a triangle,[10] and elucidates a contradiction, denoting the roots of the conflict and the existence of incompatible goals, attitudes and behaviour. Galtung argued that in a symmetric conflict, the contradiction is defined by the clash of the parties' interests, whereas in an asymmetric conflict, it is defined by the conflict of interests inherent in the parties' relationship. To this can be added the difficulties brought about by the attitudes of the parties' and their perceptions and misperceptions of the self and the other. Behaviour includes cooperation or coercion, but violent conflict behaviour is characterized by threats, and destructive attacks. As Miall and colleagues have pointed out, Galtung makes the subjective/objective distinction (which is also characteristic of the Westphalian environment) in that he argues that attitude can include emotive, cognitive and conative elements, and also objective aspects such as structural relationships and competing material interests.[11] Galtung sees conflict as a dynamic process in which structure, attitudes and behaviour are shifting constantly in the context of each other, in which disputants' interests come into conflict and their relationship becomes oppressive, they develop conflictual behaviour, leading to escalation which may also draw in other parties. Resolving conflict therefore, in Galtung's view, involves transforming the disputants' relationships or the clash of interests that lie at the core of the conflict structure. It is important to note that the distinction between first generation and second generation approaches rests on two different views, also put forward by Galtung, of what constitutes peace: negative peace is characterized by the absence of direct violence and preventing war, while positive peace encompasses the broader issues relating to human security. Conflict resolution therefore refers to addressing underlying causes of conflict while management refers to controlling conflict. What is crucial about second generation approaches, apart from the shift away from rational-actor state-centricity, is the diversity they bring to debates about conflict, opening the way for a multilevel, inter-disciplinary analysis, open to a discussion of the role of subjective issues with a normative undertone.

Another pertinent response to the inherent problems vis-à-vis the conceptualization of conflict offered by first generation approaches lay in Deutsch's work on the issue of how to make conflict productive,[12] and how to differentiate between constructive and destructive conflicts. Deutsch's work concentrated upon the perceptions and cognitions of participants in social interaction with others. He argued that social interactions are guided by participants' perceptions of the other's capacity for awareness, and expectations for participants' conduct. This interaction is based upon existing motives, which are then modified, and generate new motives. This occurs in a social environment, consisting of a family, a group, a community, a nation, and a civilization, which observes its own techniques, symbols, categories, rules and values. This means that social interaction between individuals or groups is composed of many interacting subsystems, which in some instances, however, can act in a unified manner. This illustrates the social psychological aspects of conflict resolution approaches and their inherent conceptualizations of conflict as being a social and perceptual process, spanning the local to the global.

Burton's alternative view of conflict is based on a human needs approach and his resultant vision that conflict outcomes are not determined by power in the long run, as power is difficult to define and conflict viewed as subjective. Burton argues that conflict resolutionists should attempt to understand conflict in terms of universal human needs, which are inexhaustible, and often are not allocated correctly. As these needs are not negotiable and are distinct from interests, their suppression can lead to conflict because their pursuit is said to be an ontological drive common to all.[13] While interests are subject to negotiation, cultural values and universal needs are not, and while they may be suppressed they will always reappear, leading to protracted conflicts. From this perspective coercive approaches to ending conflict are said to 'promote protracted conflict, even after a settlement...'[14]

> The human framework shifts definitions of justice from a normative base to one that reflects behavioural considerations... the definition of justice posits as a basic norm or rule the principle that inherent human needs must be satisfied if law and order is to be sustained and societies are to be stable and non-violent.[15]

This echoes the discussion of human security that preoccupies so many academics and practitioners involved with intergovernmental organizations and the NGO community in the post-cold war world. According to Burton techniques for the resolution of conflict should reflect the needs of the actors within the 'world society'.[16] This theoretical approach has been described as revolutionary[17] and because the root cause of conflict at the conceptual level is deemed to be the suppression of human needs, opportunities for individuals at all levels to communicate with each other in the context of a supportive framework are essential. This type of contact is supposed to increase confidence and trust, leading to a better common understanding. Essentially, this means that a discussion of official matters can take place at a more informal level via a facilitated workshop approach, and civil society discourses can find their way into official debates though, of course, within the constraints of the Westphalian system. This is also indicative, however, of a way beyond that rigid and often exclusionary system.

Initially, conflict resolution approaches were developed through a critique of conflict management processes, in order 'to explain conflict, its origins, and its escalation sometimes by reference to other conflicts, sometimes by analytical means, but within the context of a continuing discussion between the parties'.[18] Conflict, according to Burton, should be approached as a socio-biological problem to be solved, in which the third party must establish conditions in which the disputants attempt first to define and identify their conflict, before solving it. The role of the third party is therefore to make available the necessary knowledge that the two parties will need to draw upon, including references to similar situations in order to show how escalation took place, and demonstrations that both sides probably have the same negative image of each other, based on stereotypes built in the course of the conflict.[19] This problem-solving process endeavours to establish the conditions necessary to de-escalate the conflict and examines the relationship between the parties and the broader goals that they want to achieve in order to reduce negative stereotypes and prejudice that normally characterize conflict environments. In essence, this approach tries to prevent the occurrences in the past relationship between the disputants from dictating their future relationship,[20] introducing a de-escalatory mechanism by focusing on a super-ordinate goal.[21] They can therefore explore each other's fears and hence acknowledge their legitimacy, leading to the possibility of a win-win situation.

In this way, it is argued that enemy images could be deconstructed in the context of a global set of common needs or norms, the suppression of which provides a significant imperative for conflict and which are therefore a serious obstacle to conflict management and a reduction of tensions. Recent work carried out by psychologists and sociologists has focused on reconciliation and the role of third parties in facilitating intercommunal reconciliation processes. According to this literature, reconciliation attempts must first come to grips with the perceptions of victimization prevalent amongst those involved and the process of mourning is viewed as being essential to this healing process. There is also a burgeoning literature by practitioners who are directly involved in intercommunal conflict resolution and training in conflicts environments, although much of it concentrates on the internal dynamics of conflict resolution, rather than its external dynamics.[22]

Burton has been criticized for his approach to human needs and the methods he has developed for resolving conflict. It is unclear whether such needs are biological or a product of socialization, and consequently whether (and how) they can be measured with respect to the stimulus they provide for conflict. Burton does not provide a method through which the existence of needs can be tested, nor whether the satisfaction of basic human needs does lead to a reduction in conflict, though this does seem to be self-evident. Rupesinghe has pointed out that the notion of basic needs and the problem-solving workshop approach are limited in application because of distortions caused by

> faulty communications, difficulties in coping with the asymmetrical power balance in some conflicts, a lack of common cultural ground on the part of actors in the conflict (unlike-minded parties). Furthermore, problem-solving workshops can work among those who share a common language, but tend to be difficult when applied to parties who do not share similar value frames. This can create the problem of not being able to even get to the negotiating table. At other times, problem-solving workshops are not conducted with the active parties to a conflict, or those who can influence the political process. In these instances, successes at the workshop level are unlikely to be transferred in any meaningful way to the conflict.[23]

This also indicates that such approaches may tend to impose dominant Western discourses. Burton does take a universal position with respect to human needs, which implies that any intervention may also take a somewhat acultural and insensitive position. Despite this, Burton's perspective is important insofar as it helps to uncover the many levels of conflict through a human needs spectrum and provides alternative tools not just to understand the basis for social conflict, but also the roots of interstate conflicts and global issues. Indeed, there is still strong support for the universality of the concept of human needs because humans are all the same organism '[h]uman needs are common denominators for all members of humanity at any given time and place since human needs are universal.'[24]

Notwithstanding, conflict is understood from a broad perspective in which individual humans act to satisfy their needs within a collective social context. This has opened up new areas of analysis in the search for a better understanding of conflict, particularly with respect to the role of language and communication. Language is clearly another medium through which conflict and needs find expression and 'the satisfaction of needs depends largely upon language to coordinate social activity in order that those needs may be satisfied'.[25] Cognitive aspects of conflict research, and the concept of misperception, illustrate how significant language can be both as a medium and a root of needs, being the medium through which resolution activities occur but also bound up irrevocably in issues of history and culture, legitimacy and representation – which are themselves implicitly part of the human needs framework. The discussion of the role of language in conflict, in world politics, and in political community becomes more significant in the context of the recent critical turn that some have taken, drawing upon Habermasian discourse ethics and post-conventional morality, as in Linklater's work on cosmopolitan forms of political community and the dialogic community, in Jones's critique of the Oslo Accords via his study on cosmopolitan mediation, and Jabri's work on structuration theory and conflict.[26] The analysis of discourses in conflict has provided an opportunity to understand intersubjective issues in conflict and how they are shaped and reshaped by events and actors, and understandings of those relationships throughout the course of the conflict.

Kreisberg has argued that intractable conflicts involve a clash of group identities and are characterized as multiple, simultaneous conflicts.[27] Similarly, Azar's notion of protracted social conflict has also been a significant contribution to second generation approaches. This conceptualization recognizes the prolonged struggle of communal groups for their basic human needs which tend to be obscured by the state-centric nature of the international system.[28] Azar calls for an end to the traditional internal/external framework for viewing conflicts (which has produced similar divisions within the academic framework for the study of conflict) and to the general focus on overt, rather than covert forms of conflict. He criticizes the European colonial legacy of territorial statehood which he argues has elevated single communal groups in multicommunal post-colonial societies and has led to fragmentation and protracted social conflict.[29] Azar also identified the repression and deprivation of human needs as the root of protracted conflicts,[30] and pointed to the role of structural factors, such as underdevelopment, in instances where social groups try to satisfy their needs through conflict. Thus, Azar equates development with peace.[31] From this, it can be seen how Azar arrived at a position that attempted to merge realist, structuralist, and pluralist approaches into a more multidimensional approach to conflict, and which provided an important additional critique of the many failings of the Westphalian system.

As Tidwell has pointed out, the disputants' understanding of their own histories are significant in that this often indicates the roots of the problem as well as its perceptual nature, as it is through history that stereotypes of the adversary are often perpetuated. Thus, it provides explanations for their motivations.[32] This, ultimately, is a power discourse bound up in the linkages between myth and communication, and the need for group unity in the face of their adversary. It is from this that the roots of nationalism and ethno-nationalism, and the processes through which the Westphalian international system replicates itself, are drawn, which as ideological forces are vital components of the power of authorities in disputed zones. Avruch and Black have proposed a culture-specific methodology, drawing on the integral conflict resolution mechanisms of social groups.[33] Clearly, conflict resolution processes based on one cultural tradition may have difficulty in intervening in another. As Lebaron has pointed out, culturally sensitive processes of conflict resolution have to mediate between different social and normative systems.[34]

Volkan and Harris have found that hidden meanings mark all intercommunal interactions, and that in such cases, the initiation of a process in which problems are mutually scrutinized requires the creation of an atmosphere in which the expression of non-rational responses (i.e. emotions) can occur. This, they have argued, can lead to the recognition of the underlying obstacles to change,[35] though this approach, while touching upon one of the core aspects of conflict, tends to underestimate the hegemonic discourse of state sovereignty.

Most conflicts have been exacerbated or caused by the failure of political, economic, and social institutions to pay sufficient attention to the perceived needs of other communities or minorities. The question of whether these needs are 'universal or relative in a specific context or cultural setting, whether they are different from simple wants or demands, whether they can be hierarchically ranked, whether they are mutable, and whether they are absolute or negotiable' has not adequately been addressed.[36] This has important implications for the development, partly through the insights provided by conflict resolution approaches, of peacekeeping, peacemaking, and peacebuilding, as a humanitarian interventionary practice – as will be discussed in Chapter 5. As Galtung has pointed out, human needs theory can be used to build a priority of issues which should be addressed.[37]

Burton developed his initial approach in his quest to create a 'paradigm shift' in thinking about conflict by drawing on systems theory in which social systems develop and learn through the experiences of their constituent parts, though the systems themselves are more resistant to change than their members. Rapoport developed this idea and argued that the underlying assumptions that are inherent to the system are 'default values' which members of the system will rely on when problems occur. This is termed 'first order learning'. However, the transformation of social systems to deal with conflict requires 'second order learning' which entails an ability to challenge assumptions.[38] Burton and Dukes have developed this idea so that the problem-solving approach could become the means to overcome obstacles which prevent second order learning. In these terms, conflict resolution becomes conflict 'proven-tion' which examines the human and structural dimensions of conflict in order to promote 'conditions that create cooperative relationships'.[39]

In a discussion of various mediation strategies, Bush and Folger have argued that there are four primary objectives, or stories, to be found in mediation.[40] The first is the satisfaction story, in which mediation serves to satisfy human needs through revealing 'the full dimensions of the problem facing the parties'.[41] Mediation is attractive because it is flexible, not adversarial, and seeks to satisfy the needs of the disputants. The second story relates to *social* justice, which emphasizes the role of mediation in the formation of community. This is a crucial contribution through which mediation can help create grassroots organizations that can solve local community problems. It is often at this level that 'intractability' appears to be rooted when viewed through a first generation perspective. A third perspective of mediation is the _transformation_ of both individuals and society, in which people alter their values and beliefs about themselves and others.[42] A fourth perspective (akin to the discussion of first generation in Chapter 2), views mediation as a tool for control and domination by obscuring and hiding conflicts. The authors argue that the transformative approach is the most productive as the goal of transformation engenders moral growth toward both strength and compassion,[43] though, of course, the question still remains as to how far this type of discourse can progress in the context of the imperatives produced by the Westphalian system.

The attempt to develop linkages between the high level and the grass-roots level opened the way for the multidimensional approaches of conflict transformation and peacebuilding to develop. As Miall and colleagues have noted, conflict resolution approaches aim to transform conflict 'into peaceful non-violent process of social and political change' rather than attempt to eliminate conflict;[44] this means that conflict resolution is a never-ending task and also provides a forceful critique of the neatly packaged conflict endings that first generation approaches tried to present – and explains the first generation fall-back position of conflict management *in perpetuity.*

Northrup's work on conflict transformation critiques some of the flawed norms of traditional diplomacy. Northrup argues that conflict transformation is based upon four assumptions found in conflict resolution, which themselves indicate a slightly different conceptualization of conflict. These assumptions indicate that parties to conflict are rational, that misperception constitutes a central cause of conflict, conflict resolution principles can be applied across social settings including labour, international, and interpersonal conflict, and that a high value is placed on peaceful resolution. Northrup argues that parties to a conflict may be rational, but only in their own cultural context; in effect this means that misperception fails as an explanatory tool and constitutes a crucial critique of first generation approaches to intractable conflict which does not acknowledge the tension between the universal and the particular.[45]

Vayrynen has argued that conflict transformation operates at the actor, issue, rule and structural levels. Actor transformation brings about internal or external changes, including the recognition of new parties to the conflict. Issue transformation operates at the level of political agendas and tries to emphasize issues upon which commonality exists. Rule transformation tries to redefine the relationship of the actors according to mutual norms, while structural transformation operates at the level of the structural relationship between the actors.[46]

Conflict transformation approaches have attempted to develop a process through which disputants are able to redefine their conflict, so opening space in which cooperation can occur. The work of Boulding, Curle and Lederach,[47] for example, has examined the possibility of transforming the relationships amongst actors and disputants and has utilized conflict resolution approaches as a method of bringing third parties into the conflict environment who can act as agents of personal and social change. This development in the field has been described by Miall and colleagues as constituting a further track below the Burtonian Track II level. Their suggestion is that this addition to the field should be described as Track III as it has laid increased emphasis on the importance of indigenous actors and resources in the peace process.[48]

Lederach has indicated, through his model on the three levels of leadership in a conflict, the importance of building upwards from the grass roots. At the level of diplomacy, top-level leaders operate in the Westphalian context, while at the mid-level leaders engage in problem-solving workshops, and at the grass roots, local leaders engage in peace commissions.[49] His work on conflict transformation has indicated the need for establishing an infrastructure for a peace constituency, built from within the community, rather than transferred from outside. He argues that a comprehensive approach to peacebuilding should integrate top-level leaders, community leaders, and grassroots actors. This mirrors the multidimensional processes examined in Chapter 5. In Lederach's model the problem-solving approach to conflict resolution and a public, process-oriented approach are combined in order to address the multidimensional nature of protracted social conflicts in the context of the non-linear peacebuilding process. This highlights the possibility of a multisectoral approach to conflict transformation which brings in grass roots, local and NGO actors in order to create a sustainable process.[50]

Lederach has created a three-level system for peacebuilding, including, at the top level a 'top-down' approach including intermediaries or mediators backed by a supporting government or IO, whose goal is to achieve a negotiated settlement. The second level includes problem-solving workshops, conflict resolution training, and the development of peace commissions. The third level includes grassroots bottom-up approaches.[51] Lederach argues that peacebuilding needs to take into consideration

the legitimacy, uniqueness, and interdependency of the needs and resources of the grassroots, middle range, and top level. The same is true when dealing with specific issues and broader systemic concerns in a conflict. More specifically, an integrative, comprehensive approach points toward the functional need for recognition, inclusion, and coordination across all levels and activities. Second, in both of these conceptual approaches, the level with the greatest potential for establishing an infrastructure that can sustain the peacebuilding process over the long term appears to be the middle range. The very nature of contemporary, internal, protracted conflicts suggests the need for theories and approaches keyed to the middle range.

Although such approaches are informed by deeper systemic analysis, they also provide practical initiatives for addressing immediate issues, and, are able to draw on valuable human resources, tap into and take maximum benefit from institutional, cultural, and informal networks that cut across the lines of conflict, and connect the levels of peace activity within the population. These qualities give middle-range actors and subsystem and relationship foci the greatest potential to serve as sources of practical, immediate action and to sustain long-term transformation in the setting.[52]

Lederach suggests that there is an overlap between structural and procedural aspects of peacebuilding in which there is a need to understand systemic issues, the progression of conflict, and the sustainability of its transformation. Conflict transformation operatives in four interdependent dimensions, including the individual dimension of emotional, perceptual, and spiritual aspects of conflict, the relational dimension to maximize communication and mutual understanding, the structural dimension which highlights the underlying causes of conflict and its impact and derivation on and from social structures, and the cultural dimension which refers to the consequences of conflict for the culture patterns of a group, and how culture affects approaches to ending conflict.[53] Thus Lederach has tried to develop second generation approaches by emphasizing the role of middle-range actors which he argues have the greatest potential for constructing an infrastructure for peace through their impact at both the top and the grassroots levels in long-term reconciliation processes.

Rupesinghe argues that,

central to any effective approach is the concept of strategic planning for the elaboration and design of a sustainable peace process and, ultimately, sustainable peace. Designing peace processes involves bringing together a variety of conceptual and organizational elements to help ensure long-term success in peacebuilding.[54]

This also indicates that approaches to ending conflict may be applied simultaneously at several levels. Rupesinghe calls for 'two-track diplomacy' that combines high-level mediation and facilitation approaches, which also focuses on developing a peace constituency for peace 'that spans all communities through community-based development, citizen-based peace groups, the media, business leaders, and others'. He argues that these processes should be complementary, consistent and sustained, with the linkages between them understood. Another necessary element is a wider political framework and relationship of power, which can be used to persuade parties to conflict to enter into ceasefires or negotiations. The US umbrella in the Middle East is one example of this; NATO's involvement in Bosnia is another. Involving outside actors and placing a local conflict in a wider context can decrease the salience of that conflict. For the international community what has emerged most clearly from the violent conflicts in the former Yugoslavia, Cambodia, Liberia, Somalia and elsewhere in that in each case a strategic concept is needed that unites local peacemakers, international organizations, the international non-governmental community and scholars in cooperation towards conflict transformation and war prevention. The scale and complexity of the problems faced are such that the only realistic approach is concerted action involving all levels of the international community, as well as cooperation within the components of that community to maximize the impact of their respective strengths.[55]

Thus, what transpires from this discussion (as is also reflected in the discussion of UN peacemaking/peacekeeping from a more traditional framework) is the development of conflict resolution approaches into a comprehensive and multidimensional approach to conflict transformation and more generally to approaches to ending conflict. However, such approaches still tend to focus on moderating the secessionist or ethno-national challenge to the state by reconstructing states. Despite this anomaly, Lederach, for example, is clear that statist methods of addressing conflict are unworkable.[56]

What this appears to show is that conflict resolution/transformation approaches as methodologies lend themselves, at the very least, to the identification of the core roots of conflict,[57] though the more ambitious claim to aid in the resolution of 'intractable disputes' is more suspect. However, such approaches are able to address aspects of disputes that first generation approaches may actually exacerbate (as has clearly occurred in the case of Cyprus where status and legitimacy has been an all-consuming mantra for over thirty years amongst the disputants). What is more, it appears that NGOs lend themselves to such approaches, in particular because of their local access and humanitarian stimulus, and because much of their legitimacy is derived from the fact that they are independent and they ascribe to certain humanitarian norms which appear to be universal (or at least constitute the 'should' part of debates about global politics from the perspective of a global civil society). However, this assumes that such approaches do not tend to support the most powerful party.[58] As Mitchell has argued, it may be that conflict resolution approaches deny the reality that conflict is an inevitable part of the human condition;[59] the problem with this, however, relates to its impact on those who are not directly involved in a conflict. This sheds doubt upon several assumptions made in the conflict resolution literature, firstly that contact with the 'other' does deconstruct rather than reify conflicts; that funders and organizers are not self-interested; that its effects trickle up to influence official dialogues rather than the reverse (which is probably more likely given the dominance of states); or that the kind of human security discourse which takes place in workshops illustrates how the roots of conflict can be addressed through cooperative means, rather than making participants more aware of the structural violence or injustice they may be undergoing.

Figure 3.1 outlines the overall framework of second generation approaches in the context of the full spectrum of levels that conflict may involve.

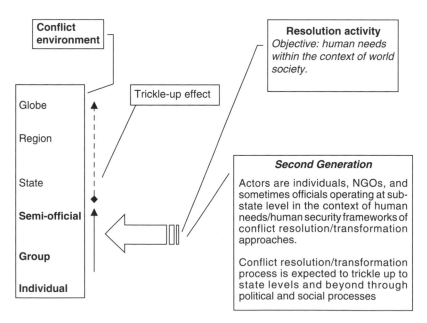

Figure 3.1   Second generation approaches: conflict resolution

A new development in the early post-cold war environment was the broadening of conflict resolution debates and the discussion of conflict transformation, preventive diplomacy and post-conflict peacebuilding, all of which receive attention in later chapters. More recent theoretical developments within the field of conflict resolution/transformation and peace research have seen an attempt to move beyond the binary of subjectivist and objectivist, which reflects the tensions produced by the state in the Westphalian system, and has concentrated on the intersubjective nature of conflict within a framework in which the role of discourse vis-à-vis culture plays a crucial role. As Miall and colleagues have pointed out, this has linked the cultural context of conflict with human needs, in order to develop approaches to address conflict, its resolution and its transformation.[60] Jabri has developed conflict resolution theory in the context of social theory, and views conflict as being reinforced at a social level by dominant discourses and institutions which cannot be addressed via rational negotiations of the more subjective conflict resolution approaches.[61] This illustrates the failings of first generation approaches and the tendency for second generation approaches to fall victim to the trickle-down effect in which the dominant and hegemonic discourse of state-centricity emphasizes strategic concerns related to the internal (rather than external in the case of civil conflicts) integrity of the state. Indeed, such approaches tend to offer the possibility of legitimizing the disunity of the state in a complex federal solution in the minds of officials representing the existing state's interests. Jabri turns to structuration theory to address this problem, which views structure and agency as being mutually dependent and argues that conflict generates hegemonic discourses that clash. Such discourses may be reproduced by third parties, thus perpetuating conflict.[62] As Miall and colleagues have pointed out, this has significant repercussions for the whole debate about third party intervention, including the assumptions normally made about its necessity – often in the guise of the UN – in order to address, manage or resolve conflict.[63] Jabri argues, on the basis of Habermas' concept of communicative action, for an approach that leads to political participation without the threat of dominance.

The key point however, is, that second generation approaches have not yielded what they promised, which was an alternative free of the dominant structures and ideologies of hegemonic states within the Westphalian framework, and that more must be done to achieve this. Much of the rest of this book concentrates on the difficulties emerging in contemporary approaches to ending conflict in the light of this understanding.

Second generation approaches in practice

This section charts some of the crucial practical interventions that have occurred utilizing the insights and processes that second generation approaches have provided.

During the 1970s, interactive problem-solving workshops aimed at internal and international conflicts – such as in Northern Ireland, Cyprus and the Middle East – increasingly came into use. Such workshops involved a convener (often an academic) who facilitated discussions between the disputants who typically were linked to their leadership or were leading members of their community, present or in the future. It was argued that participants might become quasi-mediators upon returning to their community.[64] Burton first applied such techniques in meetings which contributed to the 1966 Manila Peace Agreement between Indonesia, Malaysia and Singapore. Through the Centre for the Analysis of Conflict (CAC) at University College London, he sought to investigate the sources of the conflict. With the cooperation of British Prime Minister Harold Wilson, CAC brought together representatives of the governments of Malaysia, Singapore and Indonesia and began a 'controlled communication' meeting. The parties were asked to explain their conflict in an environment characterized by explanation and analysis, based on an emphasis not on power, but on human needs.[65] Burton then turned his attention to the Cyprus Problem in 1966, which led not to the restart of UN mediation (which had reached an impasse in 1965), but to the start of intercommunal talks under the auspices of the UN Secretary-General's mission of good offices (which was deemed by the parties to be less interventionist than UN mediation had been during 1964–5). Burton's objective was to create a non-threatening atmosphere in which the disputants could mutually analyse their misperceptions about the conflict and each other with the aid of a third party, and then jointly explore functional avenues towards resolution. While such approaches were based on the positivist reasoning that the human needs framework provided, there was also a philosophical and normative undercurrent, which is rarely acknowledged.

Doob also applied conflict resolution techniques in the Horn of Africa, Northern Ireland, and later in Cyprus, and offers a cautionary note in his conclusion that conflict resolution activities can be useful, although risky, but that workshops carry great potential in laying the groundwork for negotiations.[66] Fisher's work on Interactive Conflict Resolution (ICR) also focused on communal and identity conflict defined in racial, religious, cultural, linguistic or ethnic terms; he agreed that human needs form a basis for such conflicts and argued that ICR can play an important pre-mediation role by addressing the subjective elements of conflict.[67] Fisher argued that the third party must be a skilled, impartial intermediary, whose role is to facilitate 'productive confrontation'.

> At the international level, the intervenor typically is a team of conflict resolution specialists with unofficial status and a national or group identification that is neutral or at least balanced. The team needs skills in human relations, group processes, and problem solving as well as knowledge about conflict processes in the context of the international system. A working knowledge of the conflict in question is essential, although a high degree of substantive knowledge can bias the team toward preconceived solutions, thus inhibiting the problem-solving process. The team's identity lays the basis for a respectful, understanding, and trusting relationship between the third party and the parties to the conflict, which is characterised as a helping or consulting relationship. Given that the approach operates from a base of low power, it is primarily through a combination of expertise and rapport with the parties that the intervenor has influence.[68]

Fisher acknowledged the role of the international system in conflict processes, and inferred that power is an important factor in the dynamics of conflict resolution; much of the conflict resolution literature has failed to address the role of the international system in intractable conflicts, and assumed that the lack of direct coercive resources on the part of the third party was counterbalanced by the methodology of conflict resolution and a trickle-up process from the grassroots level. This is, of course, dependent upon the level of democratic processes in the conflict environment.

Kelman, who worked with Burton on the Cyprus Workshops, ran a series of problem-solving workshops with Israeli and Palestinian representatives.[69] In his work on the social-psychological dimensions of conflict, he argued that '[i]nternational or ethnic conflict must be conceived as a process in which collective human needs and fears are acted out in powerful ways. Such conflict is typically driven by non-fulfilment or threats to the fulfilment of basic needs'.[70] According to Kelman, these needs are articulated through identity groups and provide imperatives in international and intergroup conflict. Kelman defined the social-psychological process that promotes conflict as being both normative and perceptual, based on the conflicting norms and images rooted in the collective needs and fears that drive the conflict; this occurs amongst the leadership and the general public and creates 'the escalatory, self-perpetuating dynamic that characterizes (sic) conflict interaction.'[71] Clearly Kelman is right to point out that historical traumas, such as in Kosovo, Cyprus, the former Yugoslavia, Northern Ireland, and the Middle East, provide reference for the development ethno-nationalist and hardline negotiating positions and attitudes among one another (particularly amongst political entrepreneurs). Kelman also agreed that social scientists acting as third parties could facilitate the improvement of communication and understanding as well as problem-solving. The social-psychological nature of this process emphasises social interaction and the dynamics provided by individual and institutional factors in intergroup conflict.[72]

Cohen and Azar's work was conducted between Israel and Egyptian intellectuals.[73] Azar developed a 'problem-solving forum model' for addressing identity-related needs in protracted conflicts, and applied the model to the Falklands conflict, Lebanon, and in Sri Lanka.[74] Similarly, Mitchell called for the development of 'third-party consultancy' as a means of providing conflict resolution services to disputants in a non-directive manner, in an effort to avoid the rigid 'objectivity' of traditional third party approaches.[75] In his view problem-solving exercises contribute to the development of theory about conflict and conflict resolution at three main levels: micro-level theories that examine third-party roles and their impact on the disputants' perceptions, attitudes, and expectations; macro-level theories that examine the sources and dynamics of social conflict and are used to produce proposals; and meso-level theories that examine the framework of workshops and their outcomes. In response to the problems caused by the tension between such workshops and state practice and nationalist or ethno-nationalist discourses, Mitchell has argued that a sort of contingency approach is needed in which conflict resolution activities can be adapted to respond to the stages of a conflict and also coordinated with other approaches.[76] These suggestions, part of a growing recognition that different strategies were required for different aspects and stages of conflicts, have led to the broadening of conflict resolution approaches towards human security based objectives.[77]

Diamond and McDonald suggested expanding the number of recognized tracks in conflict resolution, developing the concept of multitrack diplomacy. Track I describes official government-to-government interaction, while tracks II to IX represent various unofficial activities.[78] According to this approach, Track II involves nongovernmental activities in conflict resolution, while tracks III to IX involve unofficial actors' interactions in areas of business, research, education, peace and environmental activism, religion, and the media. Citizen and unofficial diplomacy therefore incorporates many aspects of civil society. Indeed, the development of a contingency approach to conflict resolution strategies indicates that there are short and long-term strategies which can be applied at various stages in a conflict,[79] allowing a differentiation in the various approaches that can be applied.

The relationship between traditional forms of peacemaking at the official level and conflict resolution approaches has been the subject of much analysis. For some, non-official or Track II methods that precede the more traditional diplomatic approaches may prepare the ground for official negotiations. Negotiations initiated at the Track II level or channel may then be passed to an official negotiating forum. Sometimes, the two work side-by-side in a related or a non-related manner. Perhaps the traditional diplomatic channel reaches an impasse which conflict resolution can help overcome. Yet there has often been no clear relationship between the two processes, raising the possibility that there may be no basis for a connection, as has occurred in the case of Cyprus where conflict resolution and official processes have been disconnected and have had relatively little impact upon each other. In the case of the 1993 negotiations between the Israelis and the PLO representatives conducted in Oslo, conflict resolution approaches and traditional forms of negotiation were interchanged at different stages of the negotiations, though as Jones has argued, facilitation has served to reaffirm the Palestinians' status as non-state rather than sovereign.[80] The argument often used about the Oslo process has been that Tracks I and II are complementary. This is based upon the assumption that the lines between official and unofficial mediation processes have become increasingly blurred and that conflict resolution methodologies can be applied to official processes.[81] This assumes that official processes have not colonized the unofficial level, however.

The Tajikistan Dialogue[82] provides an example in which a wide range of actors were brought together in 1993, after a vicious civil war had erupted following independence from the Soviet Union. A series of meetings resulted which entailed five separate stages,

(a) deciding to engage in dialogue to resolve mutually intolerable problems; (b) coming together to map the elements of the problems and the relationships that perpetuate the problems; (c) uncovering the underlying dynamic of the relationships and beginning to see ways to change them; (d) planning steps together to change the relationships; and (e) devising ways to implement their plan.[83]

This framework forms part of Saunders' notion of a public peace process which offers a detailed explanation of and methodology for civil level conflict resolution style groups involved in creating a sustainable and pluralist public discourse about ending conflict. This provides an interesting and empirically based discussion of the theory behind the process, covering the challenges of conflict and peace, outlining a conceptual framework for peace processes, examining how conflictual relationships can be changed, the role of citizen politics in civil society, relationships across permeable borders, and an outline of the dialogue process Saunders proposes. He argues that peace processes work on multiple levels, emphasize the human level, and require embedding in society in order for them to become sustainable in the long term. This requires that citizens should be able to address the human dimension of their conflict within the parameters of a framework he sets out that would establish an institutional framework to achieve this. A public peace process is

> a sustained political process through which citizens outside government come together in dialogue to design steps for changing conflictual relationships in ways that create capacities to build the practices, processes, and structures of peace. The longer-term goal is to immunize the society against the recurrence of violence.[84]

This framework is specifically for individuals outside government who wish to see their relationships transformed and Saunders argues that such processes can complement, support or energize official processes. This assumes that relationships can be transformed even when state level discourses and practices are locked in conflict-sustaining positions. This is based upon the assumption that civil society processes trickle up to impact upon high level discourses. Saunders describes a five stage dialogue process that may extend over a long period of time, including the decision to engage, mapping and naming problems and relationships, choosing a direction, building scenarios and finally making change happen. In this dialogue, groups begin to recognize the feelings and perceptions of the other[85] in the understanding that peace is never made but is always in the making.[86] As during the Oslo Accords, some of the Tajiks from different factions also participated in the official negotiations. Both examples also illustrate the fact that problem-solving workshops tend to extend themselves into a series of meetings involving similar participants over several months or years. This has occurred with the emergence of conflict resolution groups in Cyprus and the Middle East as well; sometimes the groups are organized by the same conveners and involving the same participants, while it is also common for participants to go on to join other workshops and groups. One general omission in this kind of activity has been that while work on the relationship between opposed groups is focused upon, there has been very little in the way of the exploration of the stereotyping that occurs within the group – particularly in terms of patriarchy and other forms of internal power structures which may then spill over into intergroup dynamics.[87] It may well be mistaken to argue that intergroup conflict stems solely from intergroup dynamics, rather than also from intragroup dynamics. In general, the assumption that the effects of conflict resolution processes are positive and reduce tensions may be flawed, in that it is possible that, for example, exposure to the other in workshops merely confirms prejudices and stereotypes or heightens awareness of recipients of structural violence and strengthens their mutually exclusive desire for security and independence. It is also apparent that the logic of the trickle-up effect in which conflict resolution processes contribute to overall solutions may easily be reversed, leading to national stereotyping and hardline positions constraining civil projects for peace.

However, the institutionalization of conflict resolution practice is extremely important in developing awareness at the civil and semi-official level, and may contribute in a variety of ways to the unofficial level. This may lead to the establishment of long-term peacebuilding and mediation structures at the social level which would complement a constitutional solution. Kreisburg, who has concentrated on the role of identities in giving rise to conflict, gives the example of the coordinated approaches to the ending of the Mozambique civil war (which involved a government and a rebel party, and was therefore clearly intractable in the context of traditional first generation approaches to diplomacy) during the peace process of 1989–92. A Catholic missionary order, the Community of Sant' Egidio, used its links with both the government and the insurgent Resistência Nacional Moçambicano (RENAMO) group, which had been based upon its humanitarian work. Sant' Egidio was able to facilitate negotiations without raising the issue of the status and legitimacy of the disputants. The negotiations were also assisted by an archbishop, a member of the Italian parliament, and representatives of many governments, including the Italian, French, Portuguese, UK and US governments, and representatives of the United Nations. Neighbouring governments also indicated a regional consensus for a settlement by contributing to the process. Humanitarian NGOs were also actively involved and consulted during the negotiations, which increasingly became coordinated at different levels and led to an agreement in Rome on 4 October 1992.[88]

Problem-solving workshops have also been applied in the case of the Moldovan conflict, and have brought together delegates in workshops aimed at identifying their key concerns, and whether they are compatible. This has occurred in cooperation with the OSCE in providing a forum for a settlement of the conflict, including representatives of the Russian and Ukrainian presidents. As Williams has explained,

> No issue, be it small or large, is allowed to be excluded if the parties think it important. A confidential and non-adversarial atmosphere is created. The process seems to work because everything is deniable (there being no publicity); and because there is no pressure from normal political organs or individuals. In short everyone is able to think the unthinkable and create alternatives.[89]

This example is important in that it was made clear to the organizers that their presence was welcomed by the OSCE, and it also appears that the interaction of first and second track processes has been beneficial, though not necessarily decisive. As Williams has argued, in the Moldovan conflict the official Russian and Ukrainian mediators are relatively partial, but 'they and the OSCE representatives who chair the talks between the two sides feel a clear commitment to resolving the conflict as it destabilizes the region and contributes a continuing volatile aspect to their domestic politics'.[90]

The impact of second generation approaches

Second generation approaches have provided an important impetus for change in that where first generation approaches have failed, individuals, social movements, NGOs, and as Hume has pointed out, diplomats and officials, have turned to conflict resolution approaches.[91] The main thrust of this development has been the highlighting of the inadequacies of approaches to making peace in the Westphalian framework. However, conflict resolution approaches still take place within the dynamics provided by that system and the state and the official level creates the limits within which such activities operate. Second generation activities also often take place in environments in which traditional forms of peacekeeping are managing a status quo, in which outside forces are manipulating a 'hurting stalemate' in order to produce a 'ripe moment'. This means that while such activities provide a conceptual glimpse of what lies beyond Westphalia in terms of human rather than state security, in practice they can contribute only in a limited manner. Claims to the 'scientific' nature of such approaches and the prescriptive powers of the human needs framework, as well as to their neutrality are therefore conceptually suspect.

However, the impact of such approaches on high-level diplomacy is inescapable. For example, this has partly resulted in the UN Secretary-General being able to play an enhanced role, based upon his mission of good offices, using facilitation techniques aided by the unique legitimacy of the office. Boutros-Ghali introduced Special Representatives in crisis areas, and developed the use of small groups called Friends of the Secretary-General to provide advice and enhance the linkages between the Secretary-General and interested parties in conflicts. The linkages with regional organizations have been enhanced, as with linkages to NGOs involved with humanitarian and conflict resolution projects. It has also provided increasing levels of peacebuilding assistance for civilian authorities in conflicts, as in Namibia in 1989, and through conducting and monitoring elections in Haiti, El Salvador, South Africa, Cambodia, Mozambique and Angola. In the light of an increasing range of Security Council activity, as in the several fact-finding missions sent to crisis areas in Angola, Bosnia, Somalia, Rwanda, Burundi and Western Sahara, arms and trade embargoes and international tribunals, the UN has played an increasingly dynamic role. In the case of Haiti, the OAS was an equal partner with the United Nations in addressing the crisis through the International Civilian Verification Mission. This was supported by Canada, France, the United States and Venezuela, and led to the 1994 multinational force in Haiti. Regional groups have also played an active role in resolving conflicts in the former Soviet Union. Nine OSCE members constituted the 'Minsk Group' which facilitated negotiations over the future of Nagorno-Karabakh, in which the Secretary-General's mediation is supported by Britain, France, Russia, Germany and the United States (who constitute the 'Friends of Georgia' and the 'Friends of Tajikistan'). Success has been limited, though the intention is clear. Moscow desires a prominent role in dealing with conflicts in the former Soviet republics, and the UN or OSCE has played a role in directing or monitoring Russian peacekeepers. At the same time an ad hoc group of governments has supported negotiation. It is clear that the end of the cold war has led to a significant increase in the application of conflict resolution techniques, mainly because of the intrastate and intractable nature of many of the emergent disputes, and the clear inadequacy of first generation approaches.

Even during the cold war, this trend was evident. For example, the peace treaty between Israel and Egypt and later the agreement in principle between Israel and the Palestinians was developed through the use of a few low-key and secret, exploratory meetings by officials without formal negotiations; there was however a growing development of a conflict resolution culture through non-governmental organizations. As official negotiations began, additional mediation and facilitation efforts by third parties and conflict resolution activity by non-governmental groups gained impetus. In the Egypt–Israel case this led to President Sadat's visit to Jerusalem, and the subsequent Camp David Accords which in turn led to Israel's final withdrawal from the Sinai Peninsula. The Middle East peace process between Israel and the Palestinians has benefited to an extent from Track II diplomacy (though its contribution to the middle level official and the high level official interactions between the Palestinians and the Israelis has led to agreements which Israel has been reluctant to implement), as has been the long development of grass-roots peace movements and NGOs in the area. The international conference in October 1991, convened in Madrid, indicated that there was a regional and global desire for a meaningful peace process, with the Palestinian and Israeli delegations interacting with Presidents Bush and Gorbachev, as well as representatives of the United Nations and the European Community. The subsequent 'Oslo track' soon became an official, albeit secret, diplomatic effort, based on the methodologies that second generation approaches offered, though also susceptible to the foibles of first generation approaches in which states jealously preserve their sovereignty, as can be observed in the subsequent behaviour of Israel.

It is important to note that second generation approaches may often to be undertaken by NGOs and the subsequent contribution of NGOs to civil societies may be critical. As appears to have been the case in Mozambique, for example, NGOs can play an important role in facilitating a tunnel between global and civil society and thus contributing to the resolution of one of the most serious problems of the conflict resolution genre related to the trickle-up (and down) effect; this in effect can also contribute to the diplomatic process of making peace in the realms of official diplomacy. NGOs that conduct humanitarian, devel-

opmental, human rights, and conflict resolution activities contribute to
the objectives which second generation approaches have delineated.
Second generation approaches have provided a human security framework for understanding and responding to conflict which NGOs appear
to respond to. Indeed, conflict resolution/transformation has always
been undertaken by NGO-type independent actors. Second generation
approaches also provide a methodology for NGO activity; they identify
the space they fill and in which they operate. Consequently, it is clear
that the NGO community has potential to aid in the redevelopment of
approaches to ending conflict.[92] This is particularly so in the realm of
civic society because they have access to groups and organizations
which may bear some responsibility for conflict. Here, often applying
the conceptual framework and methodology of conflict resolution,
NGOs may try to undercut nationalist and stereotypes which perpetuate
conflict. Most importantly, NGOs can gain access to conflict environments which other types of more traditional actor cannot. It is the level
of legitimacy that an NGO accrues in its local environment which is
paramount, however, related to the work it does in employing conflict-
resolution models, including bargaining and negotiation, third-party
mediation, and faith-based reconciliation, by attempting to address
economic, social, and political inequities, by creating neutral forums
at which disputants can meet, and through mass education cam-
paigns.[93]

It is important to note that the critique of first generation approaches
and the Westphalian environment implied here, has constituted a part
of a movement in IR itself which had, by the end of the 1980s and into
the 1990s, substantially modified the research agenda of the discipline
in general, and more specifically of peace and conflict studies. This has
seen a shift away from the positivist theories of the dominant realist
school, but also of the liberal-institutionalist, neoliberal, and pluralist
approaches, towards a more critical (or even post-modern) debate including issues such as identity, culture, and an attempt to delegitimate
the linkage between territory, identity and statehood. Thus, the attempts of conflict resolution to bring the individual back into the
discussion of conflict on the basis of human needs, and the attempts
of peace research approaches to examine the structural and cultural
roots of conflict have pointed the way towards a clearer understanding
of conflict, though as will be seen in Chapter 4, there is much more to be
said here.

Conclusion

The 'second generation' of approaches which I have categorized attempted to move beyond the first generation of approaches and their dependence upon the Westphalian system by concentrating on the individual and his/her needs, human security, and structural causes of conflict in a multilevel, interdisciplinary manner. However, within the general discussion of such approaches it is clear that the Westphalian system is still preponderant, and frames, stimulates and delineates all discussions about conflict. Second generation approaches have, however, opened new doors into other challenges to the traditional framework, including both normative and other critical debates about the international system and world politics. As Burton has pointed out, the original realist framework for the analysis of International Relations still persists as there has been little change at the international level. As people are aggressive, so is the state: therefore national defence is the state's priority, to the exclusion of methods of conflict resolution.[94] This, however, obscures the theoretical contribution that such approaches have made, and the manner in which they have helped highlight the tautological deficiencies of the Westphalian system. As Burton states, the traditional methods that have been relied upon may actually be an additional reason why conflicts can become protracted as these methods lead only to temporary settlements.[95]

Methods of conflict resolution have also been criticized because they often did not attempt to find a solution at the elite decision-making level, but rather rely on creating a consensus at lower levels which theoretically then filter up to the decision-makers. Clearly, these approaches are involved in an internal debate about their own inadequacies; this is occurring in a manner which cannot be observed with first generation approaches. First generation approaches have tended to respond to their inadequacies by attempting to mount parallel processes with other actors and mediators, while also (sometimes) encouraging second generation processes. Conflict resolution approaches are, on the other hand, engaged in redefining themselves and branching out into new, critical, areas of enquiry, despite the fact that they have most often occurred in the context of a peacekeeping operation or a conflict involving asymmetric legal identities. This is the mark of a 'progressive' research programme. First generation approaches are constrained by the notion of the state which still dominates officialdom within the international system. Yet second generation approaches to conflict have been somewhat circumscribed in their application by the fact that they are applied within the Westphalian environment, and still carry cultural and other inhibitions.

Second generation approaches seem to have two main areas of potential when viewed in the context of conflict and a local, regional, and global phenomenon impinging, to varying degrees, upon all of these levels through a practical, political, social, political, psychological and normative lens. Peace research opened up the discussion about how conflict can be broadly understood. Conflict resolution could be viewed as a methodology through which citizens are invited to deal with various aspects and dimensions of a conflict in which they are directly or indirectly involved in a non-zero-sum manner, but without any grand intentions of influencing the zero-sum debates which may continue at the official level (though this is a limited, inherently conservative, and contained view of the process). Alternatively, conflict resolution may be viewed as providing a radical (in the context of a comparison with first generation approaches) methodology and epistemology of conflict, which can be utilized in a practical and constructive manner across a broad spectrum of activity, ranging from early warning to peacebuilding, and involving actors ranging from government and international organizations to NGOs and citizens. Boutros-Ghali has argued that making peace in the 'new world order' requires a coordinated strategy which spans preventive diplomacy, peacemaking, peacekeeping/enforcement, and post-conflict peacebuilding as part of a general commitment to a broader notion of peace and security. This involves a long-term commitment to post-settlement environments including disarmament, the repatriation of refugees, the restoration of order, election monitoring, the protection of human rights, reforming and strengthening governmental institutions, and 'promoting formal and informal processes of political participation'.[96] Thus, the process comes to envelop a spectrum of actors from governments to NGOs, academic institutions, parliamentarians, business and professional communities, the media and the public.[97] This potentially leads into a third generation of approaches to ending conflict in which the methodologies of traditional forms of diplomacy, mediation and negotiation, blend with the methodology provided by conflict resolution. The theoretical and methodological impact of conflict resolution approaches has therefore been revolutionary, in that it has prompted official and unofficial actors to take note of new possibilities for the approaches to ending conflict, especially in the light of the necessities of post-cold war conflict and the perceived need for humanitarian intervention and activity in 'subjective' (i.e. non-state[98]) conflicts. They have become a significant part of the neo-liberal toolkit against conflict (especially in the context of the development of contingency approaches to conflict, and the third generation of multidimensional approaches), though as we shall see in the next chapter, some of the claims made, including the identification of human needs, the scientific rather than normative aspects of conflict and its resolution, the impact upon but separation from first generation approaches, the complementary possibilities for official mediation, the claim to neutral facilitation and so on, are problematic. Not least, they have helped develop the rigid Westphalian notions of diplomatic forms of communication, and added a normative aspect upon which much of the more recent critical developments about approaches to ending conflict have been based.

4
Critiquing First and Second Generation Approaches

Introduction

This chapter further develops the critique of the first two generations of approaches to ending conflict in the context of the changing nature of the international system in order to illustrate a progression from mono-dimensional attempts to deal with multidimensional conflicts. This establishes the ground for a discussion in Chapter 5 of attempts to reform and reformulate approaches to ending conflict in the context of the complex emergencies and crises of the post-cold war era.

Approaches to peacemaking and peacekeeping that are derived from traditional state-centric management, diplomacy and conflict reso-lution provide narrow frameworks only capable of addressing a single dimension of conflicts that in their very nature are multidimensional. Traditional peacemaking and peacekeeping are restrictive approaches to ending conflict, however. Conflict resolution approaches, while essen-tially being monodimensional, have recognized and provided impetus for the broadening of approaches in the context of debates about human needs and human security. Both approaches, to varying degrees, rationalize conflict via 'manageable', acultural, frameworks so that they can be reduced to their dominant dynamics, according to each frame-work. First generation approaches are guilty of reductionism and conse-quently undervalue significant aspects of conflict, while second generation approaches allow for a consideration of subjective issues, though their frameworks again tend to restrict this. First and second generation approaches operate by prioritizing the issues that need to be addressed; first generation approaches did this within the Westphalian context whereas second generation approaches expanded this within a structural and human needs context. However, both approaches have been subject to hybridization in order to produce a more multidimensional approach to ending conflict – yet this has meant that two approaches with contradictory epistemologies, ontologies and methodologies have been brought together in an uncomfortable merger between state and human security oriented approaches.

Problems relating to the apparent incompatibility of factors such as justice, identity and individuality, with state-centric constitutional and international forms of organization have been increasingly apparent since the end of the cold war in the context of the changing international system, though such difficulties were recognized long before this.[1] This is somewhat paradoxical in the sense that the general liberation from superpower competition has in many cases highlighted the inequalities pertaining to the distribution of power, rights and resources across the international system, and in the context of international society and an emergent global civil society. Domestic discussions of state security have in many regions and states been replaced with a discussion of economic, political, social, identity, linguistic and environmental rights and stability. This has highlighted the inconsistencies of the practices and structure of the international system and has accentuated claims to territorial sovereignty vis-à-vis security in an environment in which notions of justice have become more significant in practice as well as theory. International society has become more, though not consistently, responsive to the liberation of identity and other pressing problems that can only be handled through much broader normative frameworks than the state and Westphalian notions of sovereignty imply. The implications of this are far-reaching in the context of theorizing about, and the practice of, making peace. This chapter discusses these implications and highlights the particular problems presented by first and second generation approaches in the contemporary search for understanding, explaining and resolving 'intractable' conflicts. It argues that first generation approaches tend to replicate the Westphalian system, with its ordered deficiencies, moderated by the neoliberal stabilization activities of international and regional organizations. Second generation approaches present a critique of first generation approaches, but also often succumb to them, despite their crucial contribution to the elevation of human security discourses. In the post-cold war environment, developments within both generations, drawing upon each other, have attempted to produce more complex and multidimensional frameworks for understanding and managing conflict in response, though these developments have also tended to view state sovereignty as the objective of approaches to ending conflict. This pattern has been repeated throughout the evolution of the debates about conflict and methods of addressing it.

Critiquing first generation approaches

Intractable forms of conflict[2] are rooted in a multiplicity of conflicting and overlapping tensions and are marked by 'self-sustaining patterns of hostility and violence' revolving around 'control of the state's political institutions and/or the search for national autonomy and self-determination.'[3] Such conflicts inevitably involve regional dynamics ('regional security complexes', according to Buzan).[4] Both local and regional dynamics, as well as the structural inconsistencies of the international system over sovereignty, non-intervention, and self-determination mean that it is virtually impossible to address contemporary forms of conflict's underlying issues in the Westphalian framework. The most that can be achieved is a fragile realignment of interests and resources, which then must be implemented and managed in the future,[5] achieved by peacekeeping, mediation or negotiation, and a mixture of high-level, impartial or partial intervention, based on the application of external resources, be they diplomatic or material.

Peacekeeping and peacemaking

The starting point for all attempts to manage conflict during the cold war period was either a crisis or stalemate situation, or installing a post-conflict classic peacekeeping force. Peacekeeping forces were often used to stabilize local environments in order to facilitate peacemaking. Part of the problem during this era was the difficulty in establishing peacekeeping forces in intrastate conflicts, though ONUC, UNIFIL in Lebanon, UNFICYP in Cyprus, UNTAG in Namibia, were examples of UN operations authorized for intrastate conflicts, normally because they were deemed to have international implications. The consent of all parties was generally required, as was illustrated in 1967, when UN Secretary-General U Thant ordered the withdrawal of UNEF I, after President Nasser withdrew Egypt's consent. The ensuing Six Day War illustrated the limitations of traditional consent-based forms of peacekeeping, which not only required consent but also continued cooperation, even if the force achieved little more than freezing the conflict into a post-outbreak status quo. In some instances consent was provided in the long term, as with UNFICYP; despite the Israeli occupation of the Golan Heights, both Israel and Syria have cooperated with UNDOF since its creation in 1974 after the 1973 Yom Kippur War.[6] In many cases peacekeeping has been able to achieve little more than freeze the military situation, though this, in the context of formal negotiations, can be vital. More importantly, this was seen to be crucial in the context of the ideological rivalry and superpower balance of the cold war though it provided little in the way of tools to address the root causes of conflict. UNIFIL provides a good example of this, as it operated in an area of Lebanon not controlled to any degree by the Lebanese government, and was unable to restore Lebanese sovereignty in the south or supervise an Israeli withdrawal. UNFICYP was also conceived partly to prevent a Greco-Turkish struggle weakening the Eastern wing of NATO, and contributed more to this aim that to a solution in Cyprus.

Consequently, peacekeeping was used to placate and refrigerate the conflict environment to allow formal negotiations to take place, though most peacekeeping operations have been protracted, contributing little to a settlement, as seen in Kashmir, Cyprus, the Golan Heights, and southern Lebanon. Peacekeeping was applied to try to keep order in a system that constantly undermined itself by attempting to marginalize as peripheral many actors with the ability to defy the dominant conception of order for which it has been used as a tool. This failing spurred the development of new types of peacekeeping in the post-cold war environment to deal with the many conflicts that flared in Africa, Europe and Latin America as the old order crumbled. Peacekeeping extended itself into humanitarian forms of intervention and governance, driven by a move towards human security rather than state security. This proved to be both vastly expensive and implicitly universalizing – thus, a comparison of UN intervention in Cambodia, Somalia and Bosnia, and non-intervention in Rwanda and until recently in Kosovo, seems to underline the major problems with this approach. As Debrix has pointed out, this move was derived from a blurring of the boundaries between consent and intervention, between peacekeeping and peacemaking.[7] As Paris has also argued, peacekeeping in the international system has begun to run the risk of being exploited to globalize liberal market democracy and thus developing into somewhat naive and counterproductive 'civilizing' missions.[8]

Heraclides has argued that disputants are clearly motivated by the inevitable perception of the rational utility of pursuing armed conflict within the zero-sum Westphalian environment.[9] Consequently, during peacemaking processes, disputants have tended to become entrenched in incompatible positions because the Westphalian foundation of territorial sovereignty makes little provision for conflicting claims over land or representation, as the cases of East Timor, Tibet, Kosovo, Cyprus,

Kashmir, Palestine and Sri Lanka aptly illustrate. These cases also illustrate the fact that claims of the erosion of state sovereignty are undermined by the gap between evolving human rights norms and practices.[10] Yet, confederation and other weakened forms of quasi-state frameworks, or minority status, cannot provide the security guarantees that sovereignty is perceived to provide in the Westphalian framework. Thus, within the peacemaking and peacekeeping process, the question of asymmetry in terms of legitimacy and power tends to predominate in disputants' quests for an empowering solution. In particular, secessionism has become a spectre feared by all states. Peacemaking, predominantly official and state-centric, can be therefore represented as interference and intervention in the internal affairs of states or as according dangerous levels of legitimacy to non-official disputants.[11] This is also a problem for peacekeeping: first generation approaches are dependent upon the question of consent, or inevitably raise the possibility of intervention.

Despite this, such approaches have offered some progress in conflicts; if one examines the current situations in Bosnia, the Middle East and Cyprus it is clear that peacemaking and peacekeeping help to build a negotiation culture which may contribute to the maintenance of stability and status quo, albeit not necessarily self-perpetuating or spectacular. Consequently, the definition of success for first generation approaches has come to span everything from talks for the sake of talks to a solution, or merely the maintenance of a status quo, self-perpetuating or not. It must also be noted that in areas of conflict which were consigned to the scrap-heap of Westphalian intractability, grassroots peace movements often emerged, as in the decade following the 1967 war, for example, when Israel saw the emergence of a peace movement that has became part of the political landscape (though it has not necessarily reduced political polarization).[12]

Functionalist approaches in neo-liberal guise seemed to present a way around the failings of first generation approaches through the development of regional and international organizations and institutions which could represent an international consensus for peacekeeping and peacemaking, but they too are susceptible to the politicization that their state-centric composition entails. If external parties accept the norm of non-intervention entrenched within first generation approaches then little more can be achieved than to erect a *cordon sanitaire*, which will, of course, favour the more powerful – according to first generation approaches this means recognized and thus, legitimate. The recent predicament of the Bosnian Muslims exemplifies this, as does the historical status of the Tamils, Turkish Cypriots and Palestinians. As Heraclides points out, this raises the question of the ethics of intervention and the implications of normative approaches to making peace in which the problem emerges of whether approaches to ending conflict should be based on universal humanitarian norms.[13] In this context making peace moves away from its Westphalian consent basis and enters the fraught territory of intervention, humanitarian or otherwise, as the developments in the 1990s illustrated.

This indicates that Westphalian approaches are imprisoned by the intricacies of potentially fragile status quos. While Mandell has argued that mediation could influence the creation and internalization of new norms for conflict management,[14] this is unlikely if such norms are limited to the local and are not derived from generally accepted and adhered to global or regional dialogue. As Mandell has pointed out, 'bridging cultural differences may prove the greatest mediation challenge of all', as in the case of Syria and Israel where disputants have 'widely different expectations regarding the purpose, process, substantive issues and outcomes of mediated negotiations'[15] within a historical framework of zero-sum perceptions. As Cohen has pointed out, culture as an aspect of mediation appears to be considered as part of the tradition of causal analysis[16] rather than an inherent aspect of the conflict and negotiation environment. It cannot be assumed, as I have underlined above, that the disputants and the third party share the same assumptions or operate within the same framework.[17] It is clear that culture therefore plays an important role in terms of understanding the dissonance of the conflict environment, and therefore must be incorporated into the peace process. However, the diplomatic culture of international relations which underpins traditional first generation approaches tends to assume that norms and rules should be the same, or at least that the dominant party can act to make sure that their version is observed. While this may be the case with respect to the type of process that can occur between states (although in the case of the Egyptian – Israeli negotiations it is clear that even interstate negotiations were subject to cultural dissonance) if they do observe international law and norms, it is certainly not the case with respect to conflicts about identity and representation, which themselves are a challenge to any existing 'international' culture of negotiation.[18] Power-based mediation can do little more than manage short-term strategic interactions:

> To succeed in protracted regional conflicts ... mediation is best conceived of as a norm-generating mechanism for influencing the

longer-term behaviour and capacity of states to develop and intern-alise self-enforcing and co-operative norms. Incentives, rewards, and punishments, seen from this perspective, become integral con-tributions in building new relationships among adversaries rather than simply instruments for constructing new agreements based on narrow self-interest. Furthermore, by adopting a norm-based ap-proach to pacific intervention, mediators become more sensitised to the ways in which disputants signal their intentions to each other and develop rules to manage transactions.[19]

Yet this is unlikely to transpire while mediation is perceived as a mono-dimensional activity, without an impact at non-state levels, in the ap-parent ethical void that traditional diplomacy depicts the international system as comprising. As in the case of Sudan – a protracted conflict over national identity – traditional approaches have not managed to break down polarization and seemingly irreconcilable negotiating positions. There has been much discussion, as in the case of Cyprus or the Middle East, but little of substance tends to emerge, during processes character-ized by the negotiation of hidden agendas which are often unable to move beyond claims for territorial sovereignty.[20]

The concept of 'ripeness' is also problematic, as underlying it is a structural assumption that little can be done to help in a conflict until certain conditions are met – or, even more doubtfully, induced – through the external empowerment of one or other actor. Zartman's requirement of a hurting stalemate to the conflict and a looming catas-trophe in which valid representatives can find a way out seems to imply as much.[21] Perhaps a more plausible framework for ripeness entails the redefinition of disputants' interests because of discontent with the status quo, based on 'new norms facilitating the possibilities for com-promise and the achievement of a durable settlement',[22] because im-plied by this conceptualization are possibilities for external assistance based on a common normative framework, rather than on a power-political framework of empowerment or disempowerment to produce a hurting stalemate. The main difficulty here would be to arrive at a common normative framework for disputants, third parties, and the region.

The shortcomings of peacemaking can also be illustrated by examin-ing the perceptions of the disputants. It is important to note that a basic and rationalist assumption dominates the practice of peacemaking in which a compromise will be made of varying and relative levels of benefit to all the parties concerned, and dependent mainly on their respective access to resources. In the context of the roles the disputants may require of the mediator (of empowerment, as ally, as agent of internationalization, legitimation, coercion or facilitation), what the disputants perceive the mediator as being able to achieve at the various stages of the process, what the mediator 'symbolizes' to them by its presence as a third party, and what they expect the mediator to achieve for them, it is plausible that disputants may view the mediator as a channel through which to continue their conflict at another, possibly less costly level. The question then becomes 'why did they continue to interact with him/her?'. A possible explanation may be that they want to continue the dispute at another, less costly level, or to gain indirect benefits from the process relating to internationalization: the formation of alliances, and time for retrenchment and the search for legitimization. This means that the initiation of peacekeeping or peacemaking should not necessarily be viewed as an indication of a marked deviation in the disputants' pre-negotiation objectives, in that they move from requiring a victory to a compromise, but that the two sides may now pin their hope on using the third party to achieve their initial objectives. Disputants may want to hinder the process of moving towards a settlement, to continue the conflict at another level *through* the process of mediation and the presence of peacekeepers, or avoid making the difficult decisions and concessions associated with a compromise.

The changing environment and first generation approaches

The utilization of first generation approaches during the cold war was largely viewed as being unsuccessful despite the frequent application of external coercion and rewards, and many conflicts remained in a stasis[23] which was often not perceived by antagonists as 'just'. What emerged in the post-cold war world was a focus on much broader peace operations and peacebuilding to stabilize conflicts, more experimental approaches such as peace-enforcement and preventive diplomacy. This is indicative of the failing credibility of first generation approaches in situations where serious conflict has flared up, in particular, in regions where the international community does not have sufficient interests at stake to intervene decisively as it did, eventually, in Bosnia, and as the US has done constantly in the Middle East. Extending this line of thought leads to the supposition that there may well be regions and conflicts that the international community are willing to isolate and stabilise – zones of intractable conflict. The international community is faced with the choice of allowing this to occur or developing more effective approaches to 'intractable' disputes, which are often defined as intractable by the international community itself because of the failure of its efforts to make decisive progress. It is worth noting that this problem forms a circle in which 'intractable' conflict tends to be so because disputants have located their argumentation and bottom-line negotiating positions on what they consider to be legitimate aspects of the international system. Often the role of the third party becomes one of mediating between two (ambiguously) legitimate sets of principles inherent in a flawed international system – for example, self-determination and sovereignty and the continuing controversies over the issue of legitimate intervention, which draw on different approaches to international law and ethics.[24] First generation approaches tend to reproduce the state system with all its deficiencies, and indeed normalizes and legitimates its problems.

With the much-debated post-cold war normative shift toward human security and humanitarianism, it was optimistically thought that the UN could provide a blueprint for a new framework to oversee the activities, external and internal, of states, and potentially those of other, non-state actors in broad operations. This has been viewed as illustrative of the development of a cosmopolitan, global democracy, in which traditional concepts of security are being significantly redefined,[25] motivated by a move from strategy towards the neo-liberal and predominantly western promotion of interdependence, human rights, development and democratization (although strategic debates continue to dominate behaviour in uncertain regions). This has been seen as leading to a potential 'cosmopolis', perhaps carrying neo-colonial implications: certainly the claims of the dominant members of the international community towards a universal normative basis for intervention, often via the UN, raise these fears.[26]

One of the initial post-cold war responses to the inherent problems of traditional diplomacy, peacekeeping, mediation and negotiation is to be found in Boutros-Ghali's proposals for peacebuilding and preventive diplomacy. These proposals recognized the changing context of international relations in the post-cold war world and proposed an avenue through which existing techniques could be developed and enhanced. The concept of preventive diplomacy and post-conflict peacebuilding recognized that the international community could do more to prevent conflict and that 'comprehensive efforts to identify and support structures which tend to consolidate peace and advance a sense of confidence and well-being among people' are needed to provide security for individuals and citizens in cases where states cannot do so alone.[27] Furthermore, the point was also made that under a fully functioning Chapter

VIII of the UN Charter, regional actors could play a significant role. Boutros-Ghali's ideas represented an important change of emphasis and were thought to provide opportunities for the reconfiguring of activities beyond the traditional state-centric approach.

What resulted was an adoption of a new direction, not necessarily any less problematic, and involving the broadening of approaches to ending conflict into less consensual and more societal, local and regional aspects of making peace. This lasted until the disasters of Bosnia and Rwanda, when it became apparent that beneath such operations lay a minefield of distinctly non-relativist normative claims that needed to be resolved by a global common agreement in order to strengthen such operations. It was argued that what was needed was the gradual strengthening of internal and global democratization, facilitated by intergovernmental organizations working with a common goal in mind. Despite the controversy over Walzer's 'democratic peace' proposition,[28] it is clear that democratization does lead to clearer accountability and enhanced recognition for individuals – two factors which seem, from the western, neo-liberal perspective, to be crucial in unlocking the barriers observable in traditional conflict management and resolution approaches, and the relationship between the two. As Held has pointed out, however, the strengthening of democratic institutions can do little to resolve protracted conflicts while democratic relations between states does not exist.[29]

Particularly problematic in the post-cold war environment have been the factors which are the most significant in giving rise to internal conflicts, such as discriminatory political institutions, exclusionary national ideologies, intergroup politics, elite politics,[30] and perhaps more importantly the clash between norms in the international system, such as territorial sovereignty and self-determination. In the case of ethnic conflict – one of the most common forms of internal conflict in the post-cold-war world – there are several schools of thought related to its settlement: ancient hatreds mean that only the coercive intervention of major powers can create a stable balance of power to negate the effects of the security dilemma through 'ethnic unmixing';[31] or that non-coercive intervention can bring the parties to a settlement through hurting stalemates and ripe moments, confidence-building measures, and power-sharing arrangements which should have a eye towards developing democracy, moderation, and liberal institutions.[32] These approaches require the redistribution of political resources.[33] A third approach argues that a just political order needs to be established that promotes democracy and human rights, new norms, democratic political institutions, participatory governance structures, civil society, perhaps utilizing international tribunals, and truth commissions. Disarming, repatriating refugees, building a consensus for peace under the auspices of the UN, and moderate local political leadership also play a role in this method.[34] However, throughout this repertoire run several common themes which deserve examination in themselves. Either identity groups live apart or they come into tension – so separation through sovereignty or constitutional frameworks provides a solution. Of course this ignores the fact that any sort of separation exacerbates a fear of difference. Otherwise, coercive tactics may be used to force and train communities to coexist. Finally, a 'benevolent intervener' such as the UN can import new and universal norms that disputants will eventually accept as their own, given the right safeguards. All such arguments raise the problem of knowing the mind of the other; understanding what goals and standards may become acceptable to them; and the way in which dominant actors create mechanisms through which this can be achieved on their own terms.

This illustrates the problems faced by the quest to find a new conceptual framework for ending conflict, which so far has resulted in little more than a broadening of first generation approaches, and which still requires the application of coercive resources to make a decisive impact, as with UN mediation in Cyprus where legalistic high-level negotiations have made little progress, or Norway's mediation between the Palestinians and the Israelis where agreements were implemented reluctantly if at all, and the dependency on forms of leverage, such as that used by the US in the Camp David negotiations, or used against Yugoslavia over Bosnia and the Kosovo problem. This simply means that disputants become susceptible to the vagaries of great-power intervention, which often tends to be costly, lengthy and counter-productive. Often such intervention just does not materialize, as in the case of Afghanistan, the Sudan, or Algeria. First generation approaches tend to be overpowered by the tension between the relative interests and leverage of sponsor states, third party states and actors and the disputants themselves, situating the practice firmly in the realm of power politics.

First generation approaches, identity and sovereignty

The concept of security for identity groups impinges on many assumptions pertaining to the unit and level of analysis, interests, the shape of the international system, legitimacy therein, legality, sovereignty, territory and borders, and internal political arrangements. The study of ethnicity vis-à-vis IR is interrelated with the emergence of broader definitions of security, the investigation of claims to sovereignty, the increasing emphasis on humanitarianism, and intervention. It has required a turn to sociological and anthropological approaches and has clearly delineated the limitations of the theoretical approaches within the field that overlook identity, the needs of individuals, and substate or subnational groupings.[35] Identity is a vital (inter) subjective aspect of individual and group political perceptions and community, related in particular to cultural, historical, linguistic and religious awareness and perceptions. It provides a basis for intragroup empathy and cooperation as well as intra- and inter-group abrasion. Security in the contemporary environment has transcended by far its previous narrow, state-centric and military connotations, and incorporates identity, societal, developmental, environmental, and status elements as well as state security. First generation approaches have little ability to respond, apart from the utilization of coercive measures in instances of ethnic conflict. Identity issues are particularly threatening when viewed through the strategic prism of the international system, which tends to rationalize identity in terms of cost and benefit by fixing it to territory.[36]

This results in the rationalization of normative and cultural issues into a self-legitimating obscurity. Yet ethnic actors have shown throughout this century that they can have significant impact on international order and disorder. This dichotomy can currently be observed in the two main and conflicting perspectives of ethnic conflict: either it is seen as a threat to order, undermining sovereignty and the legitimacy of states, or it is seen as a poor indictment of oppressive constitutions and the norms of Westphalia, requiring reappraisal through the lens of humanitarianism, justice and self-determination.[37] Both approaches require different methods for ending these sorts of conflict.

The positivist work of so-called ethnic realists[38] indicates that the application of the rhetoric and framework of political realism to ethnic groups leads to the surmise that they perceive the international system and their own objectives vis-à-vis all other actors in the way that state-centric actors are thought to do vis-à-vis the location of their state in relation to other states in the international system. Thus, the self-help rhetoric of neo-realism produces forces of disorder within an international system in which states are clearly not the only significant actors. While this may be the case, it is not because of the reductionist, rational, self-interested and biological framework provided by realism, but because, as a theory of conflict management, it creates security dilemmas (and therefore self-fulfilling prophecies) which must rationally be responded to by the escalation of conflict to negate threats, and by the attainment of statehood, in which security is thought ultimately to lie. The point here is that ethnic groups, often hard-pressed by state actors who fear secession or other forms of division, tend to view the international system through a prism in which security can only be provided by independence or autonomous guarantees, and modified by the notion that sovereignty is irrefutably the ultimate guarantee of status in the eyes of the international community. Thus, ethnic groups become caught up in wider systemic struggles related to recognition, legitimacy and statehood; and in doing so incur the wrath of states who feel that their integrity is being threatened. Ethnic groups and minorities are therefore often trapped in a metaphorical and physical 'no man's land' in which they are caught in the cross-fire between irate states and those who seek to endorse the sanctity of sovereignty and statehood, those that fear minorities or oppress them, and ethnic entrepreneurs who exploit such tensions for personal advancement and ultimately to gain more autonomy or even statehood for their group.[39] The logic of the security dilemma[40] arises from the separation these approaches create between units whose cohesion depends on national, ethnic, or multiethnic identity arrangements, with clear implications for the efficacy of first generation approaches to making peace. Identity politics, as Kaldor has pointed out, impact on the local and the global – and thus require diverse responses.[41]

Within multiethnic states, or states which are troubled, failing and have succumbed to high levels of civil violence, state-centric morality tends to apply in that borders are drawn around interest groups.[42] This is particularly problematic, if one of the interest groups has a set of perceived borders that pass around another group outside their state. Much then depends on this group, and its relative control of local and regional resources. For example, the Kurds of Turkey and Iraq do not present the states of Turkey or Iraq with an overwhelming threat, but Turkey's inclusion of the Turkish Cypriots in their perceived area of interest (and vice versa) has exerted a stranglehold on the ability of the Republic of Cyprus to function internationally, and on the viability of any power-sharing arrangements which the Cypriot parties might agree to. The same has also been true of India's influence over Sri Lanka and Syria's influence over Lebanon. This is indicative of the fact that all types of interest groups could pose a threat to the Westphalian conception of a state, even with the modification provided by the UN system. States cannot completely accept the principle of national self-determination, for example, even if it was on this basis that they became independent and autonomous, as this would undercut their own legitimacy.

Consequently, ethnic groups are often seen as by states 'Trojan horses',[43] leading to a self-fulfilling prophecy based on the pursuit power and domination. This contradiction can even be found within states; Turkey's attitude to UN involvement in Cyprus, which is predicated on the creation of a federal state, has long constricted its stand on its own Kurdish issue, which it argues is not actually an issue at all. Turkey's support of UN involvement in Cyprus in terms of a federal state is in itself ambiguous. What this means is that first generation approaches fail in many conflicts because the structural asymmetry between state and non-state actors make compromise unlikely.[44]

The case of the Turkish Cypriot community illustrates why such groups will often turn to sovereignty if they perceive direct threats to their security from majority groups, as they increasingly have done since intercommunal violence first flared up in Cyprus in 1963. It also illustrates how such groups tend to try to form alliances with more powerful actors (in this case Turkey) in order to overturn the internal balance of power. Often third actors will exploit the conflict for their own ends, as have Turkey and Greece vis-à-vis Cyprus and Greco-Turkish enmity.[45] Here the notion of security is wrapped up in the requirement of the hardline leadership to have the right of continued Turkish military protection; given the length of time that the Turkish Cypriot community has had practical independence, albeit under Turkey's wing, they have managed to organize themselves along the lines of a state; all they now require is legal sovereignty which will provide them with the legal right of non-intervention. Subsequently, they would also avoid the fragile status of being defined as a minority.[46] The international community has backed the rebuilding of the republic of Cyprus in a less monolithic form with little success. Ethnic claims to sovereignty have won through in the Cyprus case in that thirty years of negotiations have not brought significant progress to the reconstitution of the state. However, the Cyprus case does tend to show that there is the possibility that the EU as a regional organization can promote a normative, legal, social and political structure which may undermine traditional security dilemmas, and replace them with an imperative for interdependence, profit and cooperation, while identity is still elevated beyond traditional nation-state confines. This would be dependent on the hardline Turkish Cypriot leadership moderating its rhetoric, adopting EU norms and structures, and realigning its focus away from Turkey, something which their leadership has categorically rejected.[47]

For the Palestinians their alliances with Arab states have been both productive and counter productive; the Arab states proved too weak to defeat Israel, and Egypt, for example, made a separate peace through the Camp David accords, seemingly valuing its relationship with the US and peace with Israel more than the Palestinian cause.[48] Whatever the regional dynamics, it is evident that the result is often that ethnic groups and minorities are forced into a vicious spiral of escalation giving rise to the organization of political, bureaucratic subgroups, which apply military resistance (terrorism, etc.) in order to territorialize themselves. The Palestinian leader, Yasser Arafat, and the Palestinian Authority reacted to the difficulties which emerged in the peace process in the Middle East by reviving his threat (mooted in 1988) to declare a separate sovereignty.[49] This was a move calculated to show the Israelis and the rest of the world that the PA was an organized political entity which could claim independent control over its territory and population and can therefore exercise an independent right of decision-making and a legal right to security and non-intervention. This was seen as an indirect challenge to Israeli sovereignty, but particularly its security. Israel, in the face of international pressure, accepted autonomy as a compromise between internal hawks and doves, and between sovereignty and human rights, though it is increasingly under pressure to accept the sovereign claims of Arafat.

Clearly, in the case of the dissolution of the former Yugoslavia, and in the example of the struggle of the Kosovo Albanians or the East Timorese for independence, ethnic identity, security and territory, are driving issues. The perceived lack of security on the part of identity groups tends to prompt movements to emerge with the aim of organizing a coherent political and military machine that can be used to challenge the existing state framework, along with the long-term goal of attaining security through sovereignty, which provides an international legal personality and the right to act autonomously. Regardless of whether this merely replicates the security dilemma from the international system through states to identity groups, causing a spiral of conflict, ethnic groups (or more precisely, hardline subgroups) perceive this as being the only mechanism the international system allows them to attain security. This has caused the ethnic Albanians of Kosovo, for example, to organize and respond to Serbian domination, and their call for statehood. In turn, the knowledge that this territory could be lost through secession caused the Yugoslav government to use the language of non-intervention and sovereignty, after having used the apparatus of internal repression for the previous decade and force to retain their territorial integrity. The response of the international community was to conduct coercive-style negotiations which appeared to favour the Kosovo Albanian community[50] through the application of the threat of force against the Federal Republic of Yugoslavia if they did not negotiate in 'good faith'.[51] It is clear that the international system lacks a formal framework through which to deal with security dilemmas at the ethnic or identity group level, and predictably the Kosovo Albanians accepted the peace plan produced at Rambouillet while the Federal Republic of Yugoslavia did not on the grounds that it violated their sovereignty.[52] NATO was called into action in an attempt to provide security for the Kosovo Albanians, although the bombardment of Serbian targets also provided Milosevic with an excuse to speed up his policy of ethnic cleansing in retaliation. Yet, this normatively based intervention carried serious implications for the international system, which both the British prime minister and the American president referred to constantly in their subsequent briefings.[53]

What occurred in the case of Kosovo is that the West decided that the norm of intervention should be expanded to provide punishment (although not necessarily effective assistance to the Kosovo Albanians or the KLA) against the Serbs for attempted genocide and contravention of human rights (though without the agreement of the UN Security Council); this action was based on the elevation of normative considerations backed by the dominant West.[54] Yet the West has also been cautious about over-extending itself lest other actors are able to respond with an alternative or a more traditional set of principles based on the elevation of the nation-state. (This latter is probably a more efficient, though not necessarily just, set of principles in terms of zero-sum gain, as the Kosovo intervention seems to indicate). After the Holocaust and several other acts of genocide (as in 1994 in Rwanda, for example), the post-cold war era has seen a selective number of interventions at both a military, diplomatic, and socio-economic levels, to win the hearts and minds of the recipients in the old manner of imperialism and realism, but also for reasons intrinsic to the elevation of humanity. Kosovo has been the latest and perhaps one of the most brutal European reminders that ethnic groups are dependent on the toleration of their host state, and that first generation approaches are not sufficient. NATO intervention led to the Serb leadership expanding their operations against the Albanian minority in retaliation, and there existed a general lack of comprehension on the part of the Serbian people as to why NATO would defy the laws of sovereignty and intervene against them on the side of a rebel group which in their eyes was trying to secede. It also illustrates that while ethnic security is a *theoretical* no man's land, the refugees that began to stream out of Kosovo after the NATO attacks and President

Milosovic's escalation of the conflict also found themselves unwanted in the regional environment. Although NATO would have preferred the refugees to be located in neighbouring countries until they could return, Montenegro and Macedonia initially tried to avoid admitting them on the grounds that they did not have the resources to deal with them, and that their presence might destabilize their political infrastructures.[55] As refugees, the Kosovo Albanians found themselves moving from a theoretical no man's land to a practical one, just as in Cyprus where the estimated 200 000 refugees across the island find themselves, a quarter of a century after the conflict, still without access to homes and properties, or also as with the Palestinian refugees still located in camps in Jordan. The relative reluctance of the West to take preventive action before the referendum which was held over the future of the disputed territory of East Timor, and the subsequent violence carried out by Indonesian-backed militias and members of the Indonesian army against the East Timorese population illustrate the problems of identity and making peace in state-centric systems, and the difficulties of applying outside intervention in an even-handed manner.

In Northern Ireland, the progress made with the Good Friday Accords (though very problematic in implementation) indicates that identity and human rights may have become elevated over traditional sovereign concerns, and also indirectly that the EU membership of both the UK and Eire has been important in underlining the common interests of both sides. This has been prompted partly by the elevation of normative issues after the end of the cold war (in itself an important part of the unravelling of the Northern Ireland situation), which the British government has professed to be part of its decision-making processes.[56]

In contrast, the history of Sri Lanka, since its independence from Britain, has been one of a struggle between several ethnic groups and the regional power of India, for some say in the constitution and reconstitution of the state.[57] Sri Lanka seems to provide a more traditional perspective of a post-colonial intractable conflict in which the forces and norms of regionalization and civil society peacebuilding are lacking. The Sinhalese and the Tamils have been engaged in a struggle for autonomy and the control of the institutions of the state; once again the security of distinct ethnic groups is at stake. Security has been linked in the perception of the Tamils to the notion of statehood and therefore secession. In their view statehood carries with it international legitimacy, and therefore the promise of long-term survival and security, even if the norm of sovereignty and non-intervention often means that small states are susceptible in the extreme to the whims of regional powers, as

Sri Lanka has been with India, and as Cyprus has been with Turkey and Greece. In the case of the Tamils, as in all other cases, this constitutes a leap of faith, in that to become a state the objections, backed by military force and legal arguments, of the host state and regional power must be overcome.[58] India itself is dogged by similar problems, in Kashmir and in Nagaland for example, where diverse groups clash over their claims for sovereignty, territory and power, and any third party intervention runs into the difficulty of recognition and the undermining of sovereignty. Thus, India's 'mediation' and intervention in Sri Lanka has tended to be highly coercive, based on its projection of military power.

The case of East Timor illustrates the inherent tension between human security and state security. The attempts of the Indonesian army and of former President Suharto to eradicate secessionist sentiment in East Timor through a long campaign going back to 1975 failed, despite the fact that the Indonesian military has exploited the full range or legal and illicit strategies. Yet Indonesia changed tack in mid-1999 and seemed willing to accede to the separatists' demands and even countenance the possibility of more than mere autonomy, despite the fact that the Indonesian military had invested a quarter of a century of effort there.[59] However, after the East Timorese vote for independence in the referendum which took place in August,[60] the violence which emerged was indicative of the tension between state and ethnic group.

In the cases of the Tamil Separatist movement of Sri Lanka, the East Timorese, and the Kurds of Turkey, it is apparent that identity concerns have led to attempts to receive autonomy and statehood, and also to draw international attention (particularly in the West) to their problems. During the cold war such problems were far less high profile, mainly because of the importance of regional powers in the cold war balance; since the cold war ended, these groups seem to have come closer to gaining a modicum of international support and it has become much harder for Indonesia and Turkey for example, to justify their repressive measures. Yet it is apparent that regional powers are still able to reduce the consequences of the internationalization of conflicts over sovereignty, as the case of China and the diminishing international support of Taiwan, or the example of Tibet, indicates. The Kurds of Turkey and Iraq in particular do not represent a challenge only to a state and its sovereignty, but to a regional order of sovereign states; perhaps it is the sheer scale of the challenge that they represent to the regional order which has resulted in the glaring exception made on the part of western normative views as to their status.

While the above examples represent only a diverse selection of cases with different characteristics, it is possible to observe some general trends emerging, both in the conflicting norms of the international system vis-à-vis identity and approaches to ending conflict, and within those groups themselves. Peace efforts come to revolve around the need to achieve a situation in which the group can legally demand a status that entails the right of non-intervention against other actors. Ethnic groups perceive a lack of political and practical security in their status as a minority (which merely passes the responsibility for their welfare to their host state), and consequently full-blown sovereignty becomes their objective if the host state is perceived to be resorting to heavy-handed tactics as a consequence of external interference, and/or fear of fragmentation. However, there are transitional stages which they must follow, normally entailing a campaign of violence against their regional or local oppressors as well as a programme of attention seeking, aimed at slowly accruing international recognition of the righteousness of their cause; often this entails attempting to discredit their host state.

As Heraclides has pointed out most studies on conflicts that involve in particular a state and an insurgent party during the post-Second World War era illustrate the fact that the result is usually the outright military victory of one side, with only around one quarter reaching negotiated settlements.[61] In about 15 per cent of the internal wars ending with a military victory, violence often re-emerged.[62] Such conflicts often led, through external intervention to the situation becoming frozen, with both sides waiting for a future opportunity of victory. The disputants convince themselves that there is no alternative other than their own zero-sum view, as occurred in Kosovo, Cyprus, Kashmir, Irian Jaya (West Papua), or Krajina, in which neither side could accept the potential legitimation of their loss of territory (which a solution would imply). The Westphalian norm became paramount, and first generation approaches are structured to operate in that context. Conflicts at the substate level (while not ignoring their regional impact) tend to present incontrovertible evidence of the fallacy of this position, as does the existence of forms of quasi sovereignty during this era and before. However, the notion of indivisibility was often used to justify hardline stands against secessionism, and the use of force on behalf of governments. This was believed to be crucial in preventing internal balkanization, with which so many multiethnic states such as India and Pakistan, Myanmar, Ethiopia and the Russian Federation have been threatened.

Identity groups view security from a broad viewpoint, spanning linguistic rights, development, access to resources, facilities and opportunities, and more traditional notions of security. This may tend to promote oppressive regimes and assimilation and can easily become a self-perpetuating cycle where mutual distrust leads to conflict and separation, de facto or not. Minority rights, however, tend to be acceptable to states as they are generally patrolled by the state in question.[63] Yet, it is increasingly clear that the state's internal and external legitimacy (as opposed to legality) depends to a certain extent on how it treats its own minorities, interest and identity groups. Thus, the notion of security is also linked to the problem of international intervention and when, and under what conditions, it is just. Clearly, the claims of states, minorities and groups within states and across state lines might benefit from being mediated according to an applicably normative universality – yet in practice enunciations of this (see Chapters VI and VII of the UN Charter, for example) it tends to be highly selective. Increasingly, 'humanitarian intervention' has entered the lexicon of the international system in the same way that self-determination did in the 1900s, though both are still heavily contested concepts.[64] But since the genocide in Rwanda, a consensus has grown in favour of intervention despite the apparent sanctity of sovereignty:

> In Kosovo a group of states intervened without seeking authority from the United Nations Security Council. In East Timor the council has now authorised intervention, but only after obtaining an invitation from Indonesia . . . As in Rwanda five years ago, the international community stands accused of doing too little, too late.[65]

> Neither of these precedents is satisfactory as a model for the new millennium. Just as we have learnt that the world cannot stand aside when gross and systematic violations of human rights are taking place, we have also learnt that, if it is to enjoy the sustained support of the world's peoples, intervention must be based on legitimate and universal principles . . .[66]

Crucially, Secretary-General Kofi Annan argues that there are two types of sovereignty extant in global politics:

> State sovereignty, in its most basic sense, is being redefined – not least by the forces of globalisation and international co-operation. States are now widely understood to be instruments at the service of their peoples, and not vice versa. At the same time individual sovereignty – by which I mean the fundamental freedom of each individual,

enshrined in the charter of the UN and subsequent international treaties – has been enhanced by a renewed and spreading consciousness of individual rights...[67]

Individual sovereignty relates directly to identity, conflicts with state sovereignty, and highlights the concept of humanitarian intervention which Annan defines as spanning the use of force, peacekeeping, humanitarian assistance, rehabilitation and reconstruction. He argues that it is derived from a broader definition of national interest in which the collective interest *is* the national interest and in cases where forceful intervention does become necessary, the UN should be able to find common ground to uphold the principles of the Charter in the long term.[68] This constitutes what Annan regards as a developing international norm in favour of intervention and has crucial implications for the way previously weak groups perceive their status and rights in world politics. However, the concept of humanitarian intervention is a projection of the status quo thinking that underlines first generation approaches where the status quo is no longer just preserved, but is reconstructed. As will be seen in the next chapter this raises all kinds of problems related to its supposedly universal normative basis.

Reconciling state sovereignty with ethnic identity is consequently extremely difficult. Three decades of peacekeeping and international mediation by the UN and other actors in the Cyprus problem have failed to do so; many years of mediation in the case of the Palestinians and Israel may only make progress if both sides agree to reduce the linkage between territorial sovereignty and security; US mediation in the case of Kosovo, and formerly in the case of Bosnia, could only hope to succeed by threatening to use force against the Serbs,[69] and also by installing elaborate constitutional frameworks and arrangements, the like of which did not succeed for Cyprus in 1960, and are proving extremely problematic to implement in the case of the Good Friday agreements in 1998 over the status of Northern Ireland, or with the 1995 Dayton agreement. When security, justice and legitimacy are perceived to arise from the identity group there is little room for compromise with or by states. It can therefore be assumed that the reason why ethnic conflict, for example, was immediately seen as such a threat to stability at the end of the cold war was because of the threat it posed to the post-Second World War order, based on the hierarchy of the permanent Security Council members and the sanctity of the principles of sovereignty, non-intervention and the inflexible territorial control of states. This problem is indicative of the need for a basis from which all states and other actors can approach a range of security issues, as the logic of state-centricism provides a serious impediment to compromise and concessions in anything other than a zero-sum manner, which has been transposed from interstate to communal relations. This discourse consequently provides only fragile solutions in which citizens tend to be treated as means rather than ends in the race for territorial sovereignty.

Critiquing second generation approaches

Second generation approaches have provided an important critique of the failings of first generation approaches. This has occurred from the point of view of the structures that give rise to conflict, human needs, and the need to create sustainable peace processes that involve civil society and a wider range of actors. These have provided a way forward but are still subject to the problems brought about by the overbearing nature of the sovereign state. In practice activities derived from these approaches have been a victim of territorial sovereignty and zero-sum thinking, partly because they have often occurred in the context of a peacekeeping operation and a stalemate situation. They are dependent upon the main forces influencing the local and regional environment. However, from a theoretical point of view second generation approaches have been important in prompting a shift away from reliance on state security as the goal of peace processes and the order that they recreate, to versions of human security. However, Duffield has been very critical of what he has described as a western 'human development' model, which he argues has resulted in approaches to ending conflict which verge on social engineering, and which have provided a cheap alternative for the West to do very little.[70] Conflict resolution approaches have tended to reflect western thought and values, while assuming that they were universal.[71] The imposition of externally based conflict resolution models has often been the result of ignorance about locally based mechanisms (as was apparent during western intervention in Somalia in the early 1990s when the UN set up various negotiating forums in a western diplomatic style, while the Somali clans actually already had their own socio-cultural apparatus for conflict management[72]) and privileges a hegemonic discourse based on rational negotiation.[73] Furthermore, there is the problem, as Jeong has recently noted, that conflict resolution processes may be exploited or serve indirectly as 'an instrument of bureaucratic control' rather than of emancipation.[74]

What has occurred has been a tendency to look for linkages between conflict resolution approaches, such as workshops, unofficial diplomacy and other forms of facilitation, and high-level diplomacy, something that has led to an uncomfortable merger between different epistemologies, ontologies and methodologies, working on the premise that while conflict resolution approaches may influence official debates, they are immune to the rhetoric contained in official debates. This has been proven not to be the case in practice.

Conflict resolution approaches have traditionally seen conflict as a subjective phenomenon dependent on altering disputants' negative stereotypes and understanding of each other through facilitation and problem-solving techniques. The problem-solving workshop is based on the assumption that conflict is a subjective, social process,[75] and much analysis has been conducted on how such workshops can be run and can aid disputants in understanding their conflicts, but little has been said of the indirect results of the workshops other than in terms of success or failure at the citizen level and in the realms of diplomacy. It is precisely because theorists argue that conflict is essentially a matter of the perception, attitudes, values and behaviour of disputants that this oversight constitutes a significant flaw in the whole conflict resolution package as it is currently practised, both by scholars and by external, possibly state-backed, institutions, or at the official, semi-official and professional levels. The indirect effects of the alternative understandings of conflict fostered by conflict resolution approaches lie in the participants' perceived understanding of their role and the role of facilitators, but also in the changing relationship between participants and their own community in wider understanding of identity and human security as opposed to state security.

This is also affected by the level of politicization that the conduct of the workshops receives from the political establishment and constituencies of both communities about participants intentions and perceptions vis-à-vis workshops, and also perceptions of the other communities' exploitation of such workshops at both the unit and system level. It is a fallacy to argue that because such workshops may not rely on officials directly related to any negotiating process in a conflict, that the culture, the establishment and conduct that Track II diplomacy creates does not in turn affect the whole culture of political debate. In other words, there is an observable linkage between conflict resolution practices and high diplomacy (ironically, this is as most practitioners hope). However, the linkage is often expressed via the negative perceptions that official hardliners hold and may use such processes to stir up; in this case workshop participants may become divided or victimized, in some cases by their own communities. This can extend to verbal and even physical violence; yet participants are not prepared or equipped to deal with such contradictions by the workshops themselves, as practitioners tend to assume that because they do not perceive themselves to be directly linked with mainstream political debates within a conflict environment there will be no reaction and they will not be perceived as a threat by officials. Yet it must not be forgotten that in intractable conflicts, ethnopolitics or hardline rhetoric emotion flourishes, and this is often utilized by political elites to mass support behind their hardline policies, which include militarization and the search for legitimation through political and military alliances in the region and in the context of the international system and traditional diplomacy. State actors tend to hope that conflict resolution activities will bring 'rebels' into line; non-state actors hope it will aid them in accruing legitimacy. Any semblance of a crack in subgroup unity and the homogeneity of objectives tends to be ruthlessly dealt with in order to preserve the unity of the state and, by implication, the Westphalian system. The effects of unofficial or citizen diplomacy which trickle up in the long term to influence official debates are probably counteracted by official debates which trickle down to conflict resolution process, as seems to have occurred in several instances with workshops run in Cyprus, Israel and Northern Ireland, for example.

In Cyprus, workshops bringing together both communities have taken place since the late 1960s with negligible impact upon the two communities' ethno-national stereotyping or official negotiating positions. Indeed, many participants have found that the workshops have confirmed their stereotypes as well as making them the target of structural violence (such as being passed over for promotion) or intracommunal abuse.[76] Indeed, when official political tensions increase, as occurred several times in the 1990s, conflict resolution activities were physically blocked or attendance dropped. However, such activities have introduced a more diverse discourse into the conflict environment, though nationalists often dismiss them as being a product of US or European (being the principle organisers and funders[77]) attempts to persuade one or other side to compromise. Suspicion even among moderates of Track II processes runs very high. For example, the Greek Cypriot side tends to view anything which promotes friendships between the two communities as desirable if it contradicts the hardline thesis of the Turkish Cypriot leadership that the two communities cannot live together by virtue of their ethnicity, historical and culture consciousness, which have been tainted by the communities' imbalance of numbers. For this reason, the Turkish Cypriot leadership frowns on bicommunal events as they may promote friendship, undermining the leadership's hardline position of complete separation. The Greek Cypriot leadership does not like that fact that conflict resolution workshops base their understanding on the perceptual level of conflict, rather than on international norms of just and international law. Obviously, conflict resolution processes impact upon very sensitive areas; yet their practice in Cyprus has shown a certain insensitivity to such complex issues. Greek Cypriot participants have often become divided from their own community and have found it difficult to make the necessary contributions to bring about changes because they have been identified as traitors, or are seen as being misled by third parties (often perceived as state-backed and self-interested); the Turkish Cypriots have actually been prevented by their administrations on numerous occasions from taking part in conflict resolution workshops. The net result has been that such workshops have been the source of tensions and have become heavily politicized in certain circumstances. One solution to this put forward has been to provide such processes with the official stamps of approval of both administrations, but this has proven impracticable both because of the all-pervasiveness of the sovereignty and recognition issues, and also because this would locate such workshops in the mainstream political debates (which would of course be counterproductive).[78]

The actual conduct of conflict resolution may itself be divisive within communities involved in external conflicts, leading to a division between moderates and hardliners in which moderates are often seen to betray the morality and norms of each community – each of which aspires to become part of the state system. This conflict between alternative views of 'peace' and its relation to justice vis-à-vis statehood is seen as somewhat less significant in traditional mediation approaches, which are located in a Hobbesian international system. In Track II workshops, peace and justice are perceived as the objective of participants and practitioners alike. However, what tends to occur in practice is that citizens' discussions of their needs, and their views of the conflict become ensnared by the traditional political discourse, which is characterized as intractable because of its concentration on legalistic approaches, strategic security and resources. Thus, the issues of the dispute come to be characterized by 'trigger-words' that become the objects and vehicles of endlessly circular and inconclusive discussions, not to mention negotiations. The sensitivity of conflict resolution practitioners and participants alike illustrate the direct linkages between Track I and Track II. The fact that facilitators often ban the use of trigger-words, or try to avoid their use through their deconstruction, often means that participants begin to build a picture of the facilitator's agenda, just as negotiators do with mediators in the realms of high politics. This inevitably leads to the participants holding views of conflict resolution processes against the backdrop of their wider (international and global) belief system. The point is that official and non-official disputants have belief systems that operate at many different and potentially irreconcilable levels, from the local to the regional and global – but also the 'international' in the context of the traditional interstate system. The motives, understanding and misperceptions of funders and facilitators all become subject to a wider speculation among participants and their communities alike: here traditional international perspectives dominate.[79] It is also possible that conflict resolution approaches, by introducing a human security perspective of a conflict to participants, serves to enhance their sense of injustice and even harden their views of the other.

What this demonstrates is that Track II diplomacy is actually much more closely interlinked with what its own practitioners perceive to be separate – Track I diplomacy – and consequently that forces are at play which are akin to the more pernicious forces characteristic of political realism. Conflict resolution proponents argue that the hope is that at some point Tracks I and II will merge, although Ryan has argued that there is also a possibility that the two tracks will just continue unconnected.[80] As was seen in Chapter 3, many of those working in the field have moved towards peacebuilding and contingency approaches which have attempted to broaden the scope of facilitation and mediation (and to a certain extent peacekeeping) processes, though still utilizing the human needs approach as its basis. This has occurred particularly in the context of ethnic conflicts and has increasingly been applied, directly or indirectly, in the context of UN peace operations, and in the discourses of officials. However, this has assumed that high-level and citizen approaches can be complementary. Yet, as I have pointed out, they operate with different world-views, creating tension between the notions of state security and human security. Their different methodologies may be applicable at both levels, but only if there is complete cooperation and commitment to peace, which in the context of the dynamics of the territorial system is unlikely, as the long-drawn-out and periodic violent collapses of the process of implementation of agreements in the Middle East have demonstrated.

This indicates that it cannot be automatically assumed that conflict resolution practitioners and participants are separate and immune from so-called high politics. Tracks I and II exist in the same reflexive and mutually constituted environment and are therefore victims of the same shortcomings. Unless this understanding is incorporated it may be, as Jabri has pointed out, that conflict resolution as a response to conflict will be influenced by and reproduce the social continuities which constitute social and political systems.[81]

If located in a binary system and an isolated environment, conflict resolution processes can be potentially divisive, and can threaten political elites who may utilize them for their own ends; the result is that participants are left dislocated. This argument may well seem to fall into line with those of the so-called ethnic-realists[82] who have tended to characterize ethnic conflict and conflict techniques through the lens of power politics, and therefore concentrate on state rebuilding. Such approaches, however, tend to make the mistake of overlooking the role of human needs and the individual/citizen by characterizing the main basis of conflict as revolving around security which can be solved through the extension of the Westphalian system of sovereignty.[83]

The definition of human needs, the assumption that the suppression of such needs leads to an inevitable backlash, and the argument that such needs are actually inexhaustible tends to disconnect aspects of conflict from the environment in which actors are located and to underestimate the reach of non-ethical states and actors. The argument that human needs are ontological tends to imply that individuals have certainly a greater level of agency in international structures than many would find to be acceptable. In other words, it seems to be a mistake to regard the perceptions and potential effectiveness of participants in their conflict environment as a one-way street in which the spillover effects of conflict resolution processes impinge positively on the conflict itself. This seems to be merely repeating the somewhat facile argument that the international/national divide is clear-cut and watertight. Thus, while the theoretical basis behind conflict resolution approaches tends to argue against the overall importance of the state as the sole actor in conflict, the practice of conflict resolution at least illustrates the overwhelming weight of 'official' diplomacy as compared to citizen diplomacy. This is especially borne out by the examination of conflicts in which one of the actors is a non-state actor. Asymmetric negotiations between the state and non-state representatives remain relatively unaffected by Track II processes, although Track II processes operate only on the approval of the Track I process or official actors, otherwise participants run the risk of being alienated from their local communities. What this illustrates is that there is perceived by the participants in Track I diplomacy to be a much greater linkage between Track I and Track II, to the possible detriment of hardline negotiating positions adopted at the official level, than participants in Track II process themselves perceive. This point is extremely important as it underlines the fact that the 'holy grail' of conflict resolution might not be as unlikely as it has come to be seen by many commentators: in other words that Track II does have a direct effect on Track I. The negative side of this is of course that the opposite also holds true – those involved in Track II immediately become much more susceptible to the vagaries of official approaches, and the associated dangers that may go with becoming so directly involved in sensitive political debates in societies that are split, and are not beyond envisioning the use of force both on internal 'dissenters' and external opposition.[84]

What makes the practice of conflict resolution more tenuous is the apparent tendency of practitioners to treat participants as if they were guinea pigs in 'conflict resolution experimentation' believed to be of such limited scope.[85] In essence, conflict resolution approaches are again detached from the wider conflict environment in an attempt to prevent citizen diplomacy from succumbing to the standard politicization which tends to take place in ethno-political, substate or intractable conflicts. The conflict resolutionists would tend to argue that this separation is necessary if citizen diplomacy is to reduce stereotyping and contribute to an overall settlement; yet how can such approaches contribute to an overall settlement if they are indeed de-linked from the socio-political environment at all the levels at which protracted conflict is extant? It seems somewhat tautologous to argue that linkages only operate in certain directions. Much local and regional conflict tends to be predicated on the imperfections and anomalies thrown up by the state system itself. Much of the theorizing which takes place in IR tends either to use a power-politics framework in which it is the pursuit of power that creates conflict and its method of management, or tends to criticize the role of the state in de-emphasizing the potential role of other actors at other levels. This seems to ignore the fact that disputants' perceptions of their situation are often framed with respect to their shifting identities and the ethno-political dialogues within their groups, but also with respect to their understanding of the international system as they perceive it.

A further difficulty theory lies not only in the fact that ethnopolitics within constituencies often tends to mirror the realms of Realpolitik, but in the more critical point that, whether or not political realism aids the understanding of conflict and should provide a framework for its management, it is important to recognize that official political debates of an internal nature, and intragroup debates, tend to be framed in the language of Realpolitik, which is often the most acceptable conceptual framework for such groups because of its deceptively simple, rational, approach to security issues.

Yet practitioners and subjects alike have tended to become engaged in their search for an understanding which may become divorced from the overall political conflict environment and may tend to ignore the impact of workshops in terms of the individual and subgroup polarization that it can cause. Furthermore, despite their believed conceptual isolation from traditional politics, conflict resolution workshops do not avoid the intense politicization inherent in intractable conflict; external sponsors of such processes, as well as practitioners and subjects or participants, tend to be swept along by such undercurrents. The general focus on the local conflict environment and the perceptions of citizens implies that they are agents in the conflict environment: yet often the result of conflict resolution approaches is a narrow definition of the conflict itself which ignores the very levels it seeks to have an impact upon – the official level. Clearly, there is the strong possibility that participants have a lesser agency with respect to the directives thrust upon them by the regional conflict environment; however, official actors in this environment may consider the level of their potential input to be significant and may take measures either to suppress or remove it. What is clear here is that participants are powerless when official diplomacy intervenes at their level – short of resorting to sub-group conflict.[86] Furthermore, this indicates that the official level is clearly influenced by citizen diplomacy.

Research on conflict resolution tends to focus on its internal dynamics – how such groups work – rather than on its external dynamics. Obviously, the linkage between high politics and citizen diplomacy is a major grey area that most practitioners respond to by making a leap of faith in the hope that the alteration of enemy images and perceptions at the local level of key citizen groups will eventually filter up into the political debates taking place at the official level between the disputants themselves. However, the impact of conflict resolution workshops is not merely linked either with individuals' perceptions and understanding of conflict, nor merely with the realms of high politics, but with the whole social fabric of groups, communities, states, and regions in conflict. The dynamics of neutral, outsider academics operating at the one level at which they are free to do so in conflict situations are every bit as significant as are those third-party mediators operating in the realm of high politics, and as are, by extension, the indirect, unintended, and often ignored consequences of their actions. As a consequence, the activities of conflict resolution participants and practitioners produce a 'ripple effect' throughout the entire conflict environment, and if the official actors in the conflict disprove of the outcome of such activities, participants and practitioners can suffer consequences for which they are not prepared – either with respect to physical harm, or alienation, and psychological displacement.

This somewhat contradictory perspective on conflict, and the methodology which is derived from it for resolving conflicts, has been argued to remove the critical difficulties inherent in first generation approaches, crippled by the intensity of disputes, the lack of resources, and the type of issues at stake for the disputants.[87] This Gordian knot can, according to the conflict resolution perspective, be untied by a bottom up approach and the trickle-up effect. However, it appears that conflict resolution techniques are crippled by the same logic that provides a barrier for first generation approaches. Difficulties relating to the third parties' resources, the level of which relates to how dynamic its role is, the perceptions of the parties, their devious objectives, and the impact of the interests inherent in the wider global and regional environment, and the role of relative legitimacy and status, continue to play an important role.[88]

Conflict resolution approaches inevitably find themselves situated, as Jabri has argued, within the grand debate of agency versus structure, as has been alluded to above.[89] It seems somewhat problematic to place the emphasis solely on the individual, as most conflict resolutionists do, given the fact that the local regional and global environments are wrapped up in an interlocking web of regimes, norms and transactions in which individuals find themselves situated and which limits or determines their search for security and identity. The common perception of actors who are involved in conflict resolution workshops, or in mainstream political debates is that legitimacy lies in 'official' political activities. There is a great reluctance to question this. Conflict resolution activities do acquire a certain legitimacy, based on their emphasis on the needs and will of individuals, but their legitimacy is also very dependent on the levels of 'official' recognition that they have acquired. This issue is very complex, mainly because as with traditional approaches to IR, the individual is regarded as separate from, but (somewhat confusingly) dependent on, high-level political actors; yet an examination of conflict environments tends to illustrate how closely the two are interlinked and how second generation approaches may have fallen victim to their own methodological near-sightedness, as with first generation approaches, in the context of the Westphalian international system. For both the Palestinians and Israelis, and the different factions in Northern Ireland, for example, the dialogue which takes place at the domestic level, both official and non-official, is tainted by the systemic competition that the notion of the 'Westphalian imaginary' has produced: as a consequence, those involved with second generation approaches cannot but take account of this. Second generation approaches promote human security as the conceptual basis for order – yet this competes with state security within the Westphalian framework, which assumes that human security can only be offered within the context of a stable state and states-system.

It is also apparent that, as with first generation approaches, the notion of culture is not sufficiently examined. While traditional diplomacy makes an implicit assumption that the 'culture of diplomacy' in the international system will overcome the wider problem of culture, second generation approaches, while recognizing the sensitivities that go along with culture, tend to be firmly based on western norms of communication and needs. The human needs paradigm is essentially acultural. As Rogers and Ramsbotham have pointed out, one of the key challenges facing peace research is the development of 'a fully global and cross-cultural venture'.[90] As Tidwell has pointed out, 'it would seem obvious, for example, that in cultures in which to speak directly about a conflict is regarded as inappropriate, many Western methods would simply not work.'[91] Clapham has made a similar argument, based upon research in Rwanda, about the assumptions of applying a stand-ardized model of conflict resolution to conflicts involving parties with different norms and values, revolving around the common establish-ment of Western style neo-liberal democracies.[92] Shearer has argued that certain types of conflict are simply not amenable to consent-based strategies such as conflict resolution. Using the illustration of Sierra Leone, he suggests that in conflicts revolving around the warlord phe-nomenon, it may be more pertinent to promote a better understanding of the role of military force.[93]

Conflict transformation approaches have consequently tried to broaden conflict resolution debates both from the point of view of levels of analysis, and that of the time-frame of commitment. This movement has been based upon the very problematic assumption that there is a linkage between the two methodologies and objectives of traditional and conflict resolution approaches. This has generally occurred within the already existing positivist framework, though the normative and structural implications of human security have been partly addressed. This normative understanding has resulted in its attempts to create constructive non-violent solutions to conflict, and to encourage the establishment of cooperative and just societies. The purpose of conflict transformation therefore, is social change, but this of course occurs within the wider systemic framework of state sovereignty and therefore runs the risk of becoming either a victim of the sovereign discourse, or part of its exclusionary position.

Other recent efforts have attempted to move beyond dominant positivist frameworks. Jabri's work has been critical of the positivist and rationalist framework used for understanding conflict. She has argued that violent conflict is 'a deeply embedded continuity reinforced through dominant discursive and institutional frameworks'.[94] Neither the first generation (which she describes as objectivist or rational actor/ bargaining) approach nor the second (which she describes as subjectivist, communications/problem-solving) provides either a plausible understanding of the roots of conflict, or a methodology through which to address it. Both accounts of conflict tend to be individualistic and ignore the role of structure. Jabri transposes Giddens's structurationist theory into the debates around conflict analysis in order to bring together both individualist and structuralist approaches. Her subsequent argument indicates that conflict gives rise to hegemonic discourses relegating subjective forms of representation and creating a 'confrontational interaction with another assumed/constructed monolithic entity'. This leads to the reproduction of monolithic entities through the activities of third parties, and may 'reproduce the exclusionist, violent discourses and practices which perpetuate it'.[95] Jabri has thus attempted to overcome the division between the emphasis of peace research on structural aspects of conflict, and conflict resolutions' subjective understanding of conflict. This has important consequences for the implied critique of the entire environment (i.e. the Westphalian environment) in that both the disputants, and the structures that define and redefine them and their conflicts, should be incorporated into any understanding of conflict and approaches to redress it. Perhaps more importantly, this approach assumes that 'peace' itself can be defined in Habermasean terms: as communication free from power discourses and deception. This is a significant step beyond the first generation definition (reinforcing statecentric order) and the second generation interpretation (meeting human needs), though it presents a conundrum to peacemakers about exactly how to achieve this in a practical sense without falling into the pitfalls inherent in both first and second generation methodologies and frameworks for understanding conflict.

As Hoffman has pointed out, 'identities are socially and historically constructed...and...are central to the dynamics and causes of conflict'.[96] The role of the third party within conflict resolution approaches to conflict is therefore to facilitate a better understanding of these issues, without becoming directly involved in the conflict itself. Yet, with a framework which privileges certain types of actors with legitimacy, recognition and sovereignty, it is difficult to see how this can occur amidst the deep social, legal, economic and political asymmetries inherent in many conflicts. This merely seems to return us to the debates surrounding first generation approaches. Indeed, as Jones has pointed out, Burton's human needs framework hints at social engineering in its attempts to fulfil them and arrive at a normatively legitimate world society,[97] which reduces the level of agency that actors in conflicts may have. Thus, the socio-biological and psychological debates that have formed the basis for conflict resolution approaches locate them in a somewhat suspect scientific framework, which, in opposition to first generation approaches, both overestimate the role of individuals while reducing their agency, and under-estimate the dominance of the rational state-centric discourse.

These critiques underline the fact that the literature on second generation attempts to reduce conflict to simple and manageable models, which themselves may constitute part of the reason for the continuation and very existence of conflict in the first instance. The danger has been that they may fall victim to the insensitivities of the general application of models and frameworks to ending conflict exported from the outside, which themselves are often viewed by internal actors as methods through which the other can be normalized or marginalized. The issues of identity, culture, and structural forces in the environment have tended to be analysed in a positivist framework that de-emphasizes their significance in the face of more traditional discussions over territorial sovereignty and powersharing arrangements. Generally, second generation approaches opened a new pathway for approaches to ending conflict to follow, and provided a critique of first generation approaches, but failed to move very far down this path because of the all-encompassing restriction of the Westphalian system. As human security issues became an accepted part of the landscape of the international system after the end of the cold war, new tensions began to emerge. This has brought into question modernity's conception of the elements of the international system as ontologically given and fixed, and raises the problem of how to sensitize the practice, objectives, and language of making peace to the wider intersubjective, self-fulfilling, and structural pitfalls that await it.[98] This begs the question of whether second generation approaches can successfully lead to internal political reform and prevent a 'revolution' from upsetting the status quo.[99] Giving the overwhelming weight of the Westphalian states-system, it seems unlikely that non-state actors or social movements can find the required resources through such processes aimed at minimal reformism and that mass violence will remain a possibility.[100]

Conclusion

Both first and second generation approaches to conflict are monodimensional. They have fallen into the trap of basing a theoretical framework on only one aspect of the international system, states or individuals, and have therefore found themselves unable to respond to other factors over which conflict can emerge. It is this that has led to the conceptualization of certain types of conflict as 'intractable' – in particular conflicts that involve a linkage between identity and territory which challenge the still predominant nation-state framework in many parts of the world, with the possible exception of the so-called 'postmodern' states of the west. This chapter has illustrated the inherent weakness of both approaches when placed against a broad and nonreductionist characterization of the forces and trends within world politics, as well as at a local and regional levels. First generation approaches have tended to replicate conflict, while second generation approaches have opened up avenues by which to respond to this danger, though they too tend to become ensnared in the sovereignty trap derived from the Westphalian system. One response has been to unite both approaches, though this juxtaposes different epistemologies, ontologies and of course, methodologies, in the context of the structural asymmetries of the international system and the individual's role therein.

The problem with both generations is that approaches to ending conflict serve 'the task of historical and cultural reproduction in times of crisis'[101] in favour of dominant actors and their discourses. This means that they reproduce the frameworks that underpin the sociopolitical and international systems which its proponents are constituting and are constituted by. This means that before any intervention takes place there needs to be a critical understanding of what is being reproduced: why, and whether, it is normatively desirable to do so. First generation approaches assume that this need not take place, as preserving the status quo is the dominant objective, which in itself is seen to provide all, or most, of states' internal and external requirements. Second generation approaches, and their emphasis on subjectivity, structure, and human needs move beyond this, hint at normative insights, and offer some hope for future progression. However, the overwhelming weight of the Westphalian discourse has hindered the second generation 'bottom-up' discourse, often nudging it towards forms of social engineering. The approaches differ in that the first generation approaches serve to openly reproduce the international system whereas the second generation challenge and reform it – though later transformation approaches seem to represent a compromise in these goals.[102] First generation approaches endorse exclusionary practices; second generation attempt to move beyond this, but with great difficulty given the hegemony of statehood and sovereignty. First generation approaches and their application during the cold war and beyond have been predicated on the preservation of a statecentric order against which there is so much pressure that the resources expended to preserve it have been vast – but may never be enough. Both peacekeeping and peacemaking approaches have been aimed at the preservation and reinforcement of a state system based on certain, western-oriented, universal values. Yet, despite this, identity and culture have been disregarded as crucial to the formation and reformation of political community, and deviations from national and international norms has been viewed as pathological and in need of subordination if order is to be maintained.[103] The emphasis on consent and intervention has too readily assumed that all actors carry the same image of order in their mind, and the move towards non-consensual operations has illustrated the assumed universal basis of peace and order. Problems such as these, as well as the lack or misapplication of material resources, has produced a tautological practice of making peace, mono-dimensional in its nature, and unable to address significant aspects of conflict, justice or human security, without a significant reconfiguration of the international system. Thus, first generation approaches have in practice attempted to 'normalize' the international system, and have co-opted second generation approaches, according to material, territorial and strategic issues, and in many cases have resulted in producing an order delinked from justice and sustainability.

5
A Third Generation of Multidimensional Approaches to Ending Conflict

... in its work at the field level, the United Nations has already started to embrace a new holistic sense of security. Its efforts to reduce poverty and promote development and democratization – including electoral assistance and civil education – have gradually become more comprehensive and more integrated. All of those efforts may be described as preventive peace-building, since they attack the root causes of conflict.[1]

Introduction

This chapter examines the development of multidimensional approaches to ending conflict, including UN peace operations, and the roles of intragovernmental organizations and NGOs in addressing the local, regional and global issues that create and impinge upon 'intractable' conflicts in the post-cold war era of global dislocation. It assesses the potential for future developments (and back-sliding), particularly as it seems that such approaches are becoming increasingly interventionary in nature as a result of the legitimization of claims for human security. It also examines recent theoretical developments and addresses the problem of whether attempts to create multidimensional approaches may continue to recreate exclusionary structures in the international system, or provide a basis for the development and acceptance of alternative types of political community in which tools for making peace play a crucial role in the creation and recreation of sustainable orders.

The attempt to produce 'manageable' frameworks through which to address and rationalize conflict have failed because conflict cannot be reduced to its dominant dynamics without undervaluing significant aspects pertaining in particular to representation and identity, or by mediating the exclusionary binaries created by the operation of the Westphalian system. The development of third generation approaches has aimed at the creation of multidimensional processes including diverse actors, issues, norms and frameworks for understanding and organisation, not just in systemic and strategic terms, but also at a normative level. Thus, the ad hoc or coodinated development of a global, regional and local political framework for making peace, through economic, political and social concurrence on common norms (part of the growing interdependence of political communities) might be viewed as a significant departure from previous approaches to making peace, which sought to fit the conflict to the process and the outcome within the states-system. However, this presupposes that there is a universally agreed normative and cultural basis for peace and the order that approaches to ending conflict replicate, and that interventionary practices will be properly supported by all actors with the requisite resources. In contrast, while approaches to ending conflict have become more interventionary in some cases, they generally still operate on the basis of consent, if at all. Thus, making peace appears to be a selective practice, based on hegemony, on confused and contradictory norms that claim a contested universality, and lacking the necessary resources to make it effective and sustainable. The Westphalian states-system promotes a universalizing foundation for these activities. International economic considerations, the role of the Security Council in decision-making, the contradictions between the notions of human security, state security, sovereignty, self-determination, and non-intervention, provide mixed signals about the sort of order that is projected by approaches to ending conflict.

This has increasingly become controversial in the post-cold war environment, though there has been little creative discourse at the policy level. The documentation released by the last two Secretaries-General has been read as calling merely for adjustments to the international system, rather than for radical change – which is what their subtexts actually imply. The UN as a universal system is faced with developing a universal framework for making peace and for intervention, or becoming operationally, if not normatively, bankrupt. The various approaches discussed so far in this book are faced with a similar dilemma, especially if they are not to be seen as methodological tools for the imposition of 'peace' in a status quo that favours the West, and the system which it has created and exported.

This implies that (inter) subjectivization of making peace and perspectives on conflict needs to occur at the official level, in the context of shifts in the international system which are both a product of the end of the cold war, and the growing critiques of the structures of diplomacy, sovereignty, intervention and approaches to ending conflict. Approaches to ending conflict should engage with the need for a just global order to be mutually constructed and refined in order to retain its legitimacy.[2] Yet, as this chapter illustrates, the development of third generation approaches to ending conflict generally remain within the context of the Westphalian system. This provides only a limited context for the sorts of changes required to facilitate reflexivity in diplomatic processes, emancipation from the structures that reproduce conflict, non-exclusionary forms of community and broad mutual security. As Jabri has argued, conflict

> derives from the ontological relationship between agency and structure, where war as a human action is a product of human decision made within the context of structural social relations... [t]he argument is that violent conflict is itself structured through the actions of agency situated in the relation to discursive and institutional continuities which both enable war's occurrence and legitimate it as a form of human behavior.[3]

Because conflict can therefore be defined in terms of self-perpetuating inclusion and exclusion, approaches to making peace can only contribute if they can gain access from within such systems and their continuities:

> [s]ystems of inclusion and exclusion generate a 'normative' discourse concerned with justifications of such formations, a 'sociological' discourse centred around the workings and maintenance of systems of inclusion and exclusion, and 'praxeological' questions related to the practical implications of such systems...[4]

Such constraints against change may be provided by the 'sovereign' practice of making peace, derived from the traditional international system of Westphalian states, which continues to condition diplomatic discourse about international and intrastate conflict. This system coexists uncomfortably with changing discourses in civil and international society, and a discussion of non-exlusionary political communities. While national imagined communities are still important, the tandem forces of the local and the global are squeezing the national state from above and below. Consequently, it is becoming more plausible to view the role of conflict management in the international system as one of mediation between the global and the local and the still predominant international state system (through which many official actors still view conflict). Approaches to making peace need to find a practical and theoretical basis on which to promote human security beyond the level of rhetoric without being seen as interventionary in a negative sense (via a new colonizing practice), in order to promote pluralism, wide participation and justice in world politics and its constituent communties. Contemporary approaches are found to be lacking here, aiming mainly at fine-tuning a 'balance' in world politics which creates order, rather than responding to the deeper-rooted issues that cause conflict.

New possibilities in the 1990s

Because first and second generation approaches have been seen as too narrowly defined, this prompted the view that approaches to ending conflict should engage with several relatively distinct levels in world politics at once, because conflict is constituted in varying combinations by issues at all levels. Figure 5.1 illustrates the shift that has occurred since the dominating bipolar structure of the cold war broke down whereby world politics became far less exclusionary with legitimacy and authority beginning to flow from multiple actors in a greater diversity of directions. The state is still the dominant actor but not exclusively so and through this shift new opportunities for making peace seemed to arise, which seemed far more able to address the roots of conflict in a comprehensive manner, and avoid the constraining interests of strategic actors in a system of binaries.

The dominant forces emanating from the state were, under the framework of traditional diplomacy, to prevent regional, global and substate conflict, providing the state and intergovernmental organizations with the pivotal role of managing conflict. Increasingly, however, alternative (and fluid) types of dominant forces/issues from below and above affect the ability of the state to operate in this role. Binaries and exclusionary positions have begun to lose their conceptual legitimacy in the face of emerging normative issues in the post-cold war environment. Any legitimacy they possessed in the past was derived from their ability to preserve a status quo as a shield against regional and global war. In the West at least, this is seen as less significant, thus opening up the conceptual space for a discourse about a third generation approach to making peace. As arguments emerged pertaining to the need for more compre-

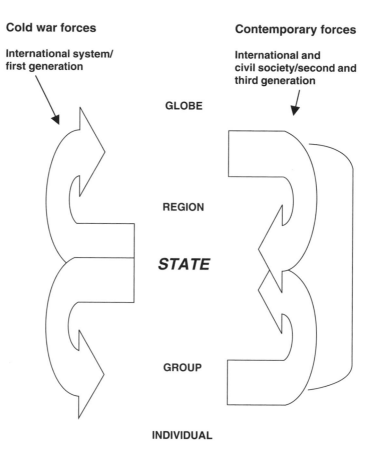

Cold war forces

International system/
first generation

Contemporary forces

International and
civil society/second and
third generation

GLOBE

REGION

STATE

GROUP

INDIVIDUAL

Figure 5.1   Making peace and (re)creating order in world politics

hensive frameworks, this was mirrored by the development of the role of peacekeeping forces, which increasingly became directly and indirectly involved in civil affairs, administration, democratization and human rights. In the context of peacemaking and conflict resolution, parallel efforts emerged at the regional and local levels, often sponsored by intergovernmental organizations, including official and unofficial actors. This was combined through the discussion of peacebuilding[5] and a comprehensive discussion of ending conflict – a third generation of approaches – which, it was believed would be more suitable to addressing the complex 'third kind' of identity conflicts and complex emergencies which emerged after the collapse of the Soviet Union. Projecting human security and neo-liberal forms of democracy increasingly became a motivating factor in the context of an explosion of media interest in conflicts in previously remote areas.[6]

The basis of making peace in and between political communities

Such changes necessitated a rethinking of the original formulation of approaches to ending conflict as being to attain or retain a status quo and involved both a practical and a normative aspect. The practical aspect involved the attempt to bring in diverse actors at different levels to address the roots of the conflict, including subjective issues. Within the Westphalian system the normative aspect of order was clearly defined within states as being significant, but was far less so beyond state borders. During the twentieth century there were a number of institutional attempts to introduce a semblance of society through reciprocal sovereignty and international law. Though these were to a large extent stillborn during the cold war period, there was a debate in the context of the UN which purported to present a universal basis for order, peace and security – through a somewhat feudally conceived Security Council. Jones has argued that universalism does exist in the area of the ethical interaction of the community of sovereign states, a process which is supplemented by intergovernmental institutions, taking place in the context of mutually agreed and self-imposed rules and regulations pertaining to the use of force, peaceful settlement, and non-intervention. Jones argues that the principles derived from these interactions are 'universally endorsed in the international system'[7] via such treaties as the Locarno arbitration agreements of 1925,[8] the Kellogg-Briand Pact of 1928,[9] the UN Charter, the Declaration by the General Assembly in 1970 on the Principles of International Law concerning Friendly Relations and Co-operation among States,[10] and the 1987 General Assembly Declaration on the Enhancement of the Effectiveness of the Principle of Refraining from the Threat of Force in International Relations. The latter declaration expressed the General Assembly's 'deep concern at the continued existence of situations of conflict and tension' and that 'the obligation to refrain from the threat of or use of force is universal and binding'.[11] This is important insofar as it begs the next question, which is on what basis can intervention occur?

In this context it is important to examine how approaches to ending conflict may emphasize or import universal or particularist norms in conflict environments. Frost has argued for the existence of a settled body of norms pertaining to sovereignty, international law, domestic politics and modernization, including the preservation of the society of sovereign states, that peace is a settled norm, collective security arrangements, the preferability of democratic institutions, and the protection of human rights by both states and the international system.[12] This argument is predicated on the grounds that international order requires the preservation of the system and society of states,[13] in which states achieve the limitation of violence following a common code. Yet this entire framework fails if it cannot manage the problem of 'which people, are entitled to live, in what area, under what state?'[14] New claims for both sovereignty and human security require a new basis for making peace. Consequently, there has been 'growing concern and more effective activity by regional and global intergovernmental organisations (IGOs) and international non-governmental organisation (INGOs) – akin to an 'international civic society' – in safeguarding human rights and endangered minority groups...'[15] This assumes that there is a universal basis for making peace which seems to indicate that, as with first generation approaches, such efforts continue to equate state security with human security in some instances.

It is, however, plausible to argue for a pattern of similarities between global and civil norms, or between the universal and the local,[16] though there is a main difference in terms of when these norms are universal and when particular. While it is important to note that globalization has brought about a global dislocation underlining in particular the politics of exclusivity, it has also underlined the potential of a more cosmopolitical approach to the construction of the international system and approaches to maintaining that system through approaches to ending conflict. Both cosmopolitan and communitarian approaches agree that a single framework of legitimate politics can emerge; contention lies in whether this will be a single world community (a cosmopolis) or an association of communities.[17] The latter means that the sequence of kin, tribe, city, state, does not have to be extended to 'globe' and produce a universal normative structure; this structure could be produced through a 'practical association' between political communities,[18] based on common social justice. As Brown has argued, community therefore makes sense locally rather than globally,[19] and '[t]he goal would be an association of socially just communities which was, itself, constructed on socially just lines'.[20] Thus a 'plurality of morally autonomous, just communities relating to each other in a framework of peace and law'[21] has been the objective of approaches to making peace in the post-cold war environment. This means that the normative basis of making peace is unlikely to hinge upon a single global view which could then be used as a basis for action, but should rather hinge upon human security at the local level through a system in which human security is not reduced if communities transgress political, legal, social, ethnic or environmental cartographies. Yet this seems impossibly complex, and raises the problem of whether approaches to ending conflict should be consent-based and status quo-oriented (as with most first generation approaches), interventionary as a cosmopolitan view might imply, or attempt a compromise between the two. In this case, normative principles may be compromised by a need for 'pragmatism' in response to conflict, though pragmatism might not be a universal norm in itself. Clearly, however, approaches to ending conflict are increasingly open to the accusation that they operate in order to sustain a global hegemonic order, something that fits uncomfortably with the alternative cartographies that exist in world politics, particularly from a human security perspective.

One of the most significant insights that the examination of first and second generation activities in protracted conflict illustrates is related to the inadequacy of state-oriented methods of conflict management, settlement and resolution, particularly in dealing with identity issues/representation, which most intractable conflicts (protracted social conflicts to use Azar's term or international social conflicts to use Miall and colleagues' sophistication of it[22]) revolve around.[23] At an epistemological level, such cases illustrate the weaknesses of state-based approaches, and the over-simplification of conflict that tends to occur.[24] However, second generation approaches, by positing the possibility of win-win scenarios through a concentration on individual needs in a world society, and the identification of structural causes of conflict, moved theorizing about ending conflict away from the conceptual binaries which have dogged it and introduced a norm of inclusivity and integration. By implication they saw human beings as 'ends in themselves' in international society. Thus the deconstruction of stereotyping, the building of peace constituencies, and conflict resolution's linkages with the official sphere of politics became areas of debate. In the context of identity conflict, this seemed to provide a way forward, and the language of human needs and human security, and local conflict resolution and peacebuilding activities found their way into actual practice. It is debatable whether the import of the discourse of conflict resolution into institutional and state peace processes can progress far while Westphalian norms of sovereignty remain dominant, and while conflict resolution approaches themselves fail to address the practical and philosophical issues they raise. However, increasingly it has been recognized that what is required is a concerted policy of norm building coupled with a strengthening of external and internal democracy and sustainable development. The development of a political community in which there is a commitment to ethical principles, non-state actors are activated, and there is universal inclusion (though not imposed), are crucial components of this picture.[25] The difficulty lies, however, in the possibility of sufficient agreement on a mutual normative basis; thus local injustice merely replicates international injustice in a self-perpetuating cycle. Even multidimensional approaches to ending conflict seem to locate political communities as integral to the cartographies of states, which are in their nature territorial and sovereign, as they endeavour to export a neo-liberal democratic order.

The increasing importance of unofficial actors

The growing 'subcontracting' of wider peacebuilding activities and the institutionalization of actors working in the realms of human security, often directly using second generation discourses in their response to conflict, has occurred partly in the guise of NGOs and their involvement at the civil and semi-official level. This has emerged in the context of a global civil society, responding at a transnational level to specific issue areas which involve local and global identities, ethics and norms. A context has also been provided by the argument that 'various intermediaries and approaches generally need to be combined to be effective'.[26] The human security framework has enabled NGOs and other unofficial actors to play roles at alternative levels of conflict, mirroring the understanding provided by conflict resolution approaches, though it is also clear that the resources NGOs sometimes bring into conflicts may in effect be used to extend the conflict (a form of devious objectives outlined in Chapter 4).

NGOs have become a vital part of the emerging multilevel and multidimensional approaches. The international community's response to the complex emergencies that emerged with the end of the cold war has involved a turn to various types of NGOs to provide humanitarian aid as well as early warning, preventive peacebuilding, conflict resolution and reconciliation projects. It is the space between officialdom, state and human security, that NGOs have begun to fill; perhaps no other actor has this potential in world politics. As Natsios has argued the emergence of numerous centres of power ranging from the civil to the global has in part prompted this turn,[27] particularly as NGOs have access to local civil societies and their authority structures. Traditional tools of conflict management are becoming defunct as isolated approaches and this, along with the financial and logistical imperatives to subcontract, has prompted the international community to turn to

NGOs for assistance in preventing, managing and resolving conflict and the humanitarian, social, and development issues that surround conflict.[28] In some cases, NGOs may now substitute for local government, and often refuse to allow sovereignty to be used as a barrier to their activities. The increasing legitimization of NGOs at the local, state, regional and global levels, means that their agendas are more widely propagated; it also means that civil society has a linkage with a formative global civil society[29] as NGOs are legitimized in international organizations like the UN. NGOs are relatively unencumbered by sovereign concerns and therefore are themselves relatively free of claims to sovereignty, enabling them to work in normative frameworks that may not be tainted by official and systemic interests, though of course they do carry their own interests and imperatives and are open to cooption by states.

Humanitarian law provides a legal context in which NGOs operate, and was first brought into prominence with the Geneva Conventions of 1949, which provided protection for war victims, and then through the Nuremberg Principles which sought to protect victims from genocide and racial killings, though the principle of non-intervention was a decided obstacle to any sort of enforcement. It was not until UN resolution 688 in which the Security Council requested access for humanitarian organizations in Iraq in the context of Operation Provide Comfort that humanitarian intervention went beyond this.[30] In Bosnia, Security Council Resolution 808 also established an international tribunal to try those suspected of committing crimes against humanity, reaffirming the reprioritization of human rights in world politics. In this context, as Willets has pointed out, the status of international NGOs has shifted and clarified as shown in their encroachment on the UN General Assembly, and indeed in the Security Council (often through the use of Rule 39) since the ICRC became an observer in 1990.[31] Willets also points out that the 'strongest evidence that NGO rights have become established . . . is the way in which NGOs can often gain access to intergovernmental proceedings even when the political climate turns against them . . .'.[32] This has developed to the extent that international NGOs may now have become a third category of subject in international law, along with states and international organizations.[33]

When the West responded against the Iraqi invasion of Kuwait in favour of Kuwaiti sovereignty and the subsequent crisis of the Kurdish population of northern Iraq emerged, the result was UN Security Council resolution 688 of 5 April 1991 which, though passed by a narrow margin, brought human security to the fore – above that of state security perhaps for the first time. This resolution insisted that Iraq allowed humanitarian intervention to assist the Kurdish population. For the first time at the national level, the rule of law was not allowed to reinforce majority rule and assimilation and at the international level, sovereignty, in itself an obstacle for humanitarian intervention, was relegated. Usually, the rule of law meant that humanitarian intervention and the access of official third parties in conflict environments could often legitimately be limited, or alternatively must be based upon the use of illegal coercion, or replaced by the normative rhetoric of humanitarian intervention at the state level (as in the case of Bosnia). However, in the case of resolution 688, active humanitarian intervention involved a number of NGOs coordinated both with the US and with the UN.[34] This illustrated the developing role that NGOs have played in humanitarian intervention, a role made possible by a series of UN General Assembly resolutions which called for access for humanitarian assistance where it was required.[35] These called for humanitarian assistance to victims of emergencies and natural disasters, for access for accredited agencies, the establishment of relief corridors, and the establishment of the UN Department of Humanitarian Affairs to coordinate humanitarian intervention (though bound by the rules of sovereignty).[36] The fact that NGOs have become part of this again illustrates that there is increasingly a normative discourse in both local and international politics, relating to the wider existence of political communities in terms of human security. Though problematic in terms of the rule of law and political interests, humanitarian intervention is clearly increasing on an official, but especially on an unofficial level.

NGOs derive their legitimacy at both the local and the global level and they tend to engage in projects relating to human security rather than state security in situations where the state is often perceived, from inside or outside, to have failed its population. This human security ethos highlights the gap between humanitarian issues and state practice. As the UN Secretary-General has pointed out, NGOs provide access to a global civil society which they themselves have been instrumental in highlighting and promoting. At the same time they aid in preserving local values within the wider human security context which has emerged in the post-cold war environment. Yet the tension in debates about human rights, which has tended to lead to the propagation of western norms, underlines the structural and economic inequalities between north and south, and other non-democratic inconsistencies in world politics.[37] Thus, the discussion of human rights norms and regimes, and the associated development of humanitarian intervention, impinges upon the discussion of the universal and the local, and the desirability of western forms of intervention which are sustained by global power hierarchies. Such hierarchies have, despite their professed interests in human rights, recently been responsible for refusing to call what happened in Rwanda genocide until after the event, and for supporting third world countries like Indonesia where gross violations have occurred; this means that monitoring is not merely required for those involved in conflicts but also for those not involved directly. Thus the scene has been set for NGOs to begin to intervene unofficially on the basis of providing general humanitarian services and monitoring from the outside, and for the establishment of local NGOs within conflict environments in the context of such humanitarian regimes. This in turn has, at the expense of sovereignty and possibly traditional notions of 'order', led to NGOs becoming important contributors in the context of a new security agenda in which NGOs are now involved in humanitarian interventions and peace operations as a matter of course, as 'subcontractors' to official actors. Problems of coordination, have however, plagued this relationship – especially with the military.

Diamond and McDonald have distinguished nine types of actors involved at the civil level including governments, professional organizations, the business community, churches, media, private citizens, training and educational institutes, activists and funding organizations.[38] These actors contribute to making peace in the context of NGOs, the UN and its linkages with regional organizations. High-level diplomacy, unofficial diplomacy, and forms of citizen-based diplomacy contribute to more three-dimensional responses to conflict paralleling the multiplicity and variety of actors involved in generating conflict. For example, when official peace talks fail, private individuals can try to break the impasse, as was the case in Namibia, human rights abuses can be monitored at the grassroots level, while international institutions like the World Bank can provide incentives, and grassroots groups can form peace coalitions to bring the various parties to the negotiating table. The argument in favour of NGOs indicates that they are able to aid in the creation of the general conditions which enhance peacebuilding, promoting peace constituencies, including cross-cutting segments of people from different sectors of civil society involved in the development of sustainable peace.[39]

An important question relates to the goals of NGOs and the question of impartiality in the context of their objectives. As in first generation approaches, the asymmetry of the legal environment in which conflict occurs means that even impartiality can be perceived as evidence of bias.

For example, if a legally constituted government still exists it will regard any assistance given to non-state actors or rebels as evidence of bias; paradoxically in situations where a government no longer exists and the state has collapsed it may be easier to play a neutral role, although of course asymmetries still exist between competing actors or warlords who may thus tend to see the roles of NGOs and mediators alike as biased.

Despite this, NGOs offer the flexibility, expertise, rapid responses, and commitment in local environments to respond to rapidly emerging signs of trouble. In such situations they provide essential services and aid, and have the capacity to inform the public both at the national and global levels in order to mobilize opinion.[40] While the erosion of regional and local self-help capacities, and state sovereignty, and the possibility that NGOs may actually aid one of the disputants indirectly have been put forward as criticisms of NGO activity in complex emergencies,[41] the role of NGOs in conflict resolution and prevention is undeniably vital to the emerging practices of making peace. NGOs can try to empower parties to deal with conflict constructively, monitor and lobby for human rights and the protection of minorities, and enact capacity-building and protective measure for disadvantaged or endangered groups. NGOs, consequently, play an important role in the creation of 'peace-constituencies'.[42] Humanitarian NGOs may be manipulable in conflict environments by disputants, as Abiew and Keating have argued,[43] yet this is an indirect offshoot of their concern with normative issues like justice and human rights. This is far less likely to be coloured by interests that overlook such rights than are state-centric activities and this is why NGOs often attain local and global legitimacy. The problem is to retain the advantages of their unofficial status without incurring the wrath of sovereign actors which fear interventionary practices becoming institutionalized upon their territory. This indicates a contradiction (noted by Boutros-Ghalis in *Agenda for Peace*) in that the international system of sovereignty has often been used as a cover for humanitarian abuses and oppression by states, which international organizations and international law have been unable to respond to in a convincing manner because of the framework of non-intervention. Similarly, the rule of law in the local environment has often been used to impose ethnic, religious and linguistic constraints, presenting NGOs with a dilemma about which framework should take precedence as a basis for their activities. Obviously, the legal and normative structures of non-intervention have been influential, although increasingly a normative view of the international society has taken precedence when human security has been threatened – even by states. Kofi Annan has also emphasized the importance of the private sector in peacebuilding and consultations between the UN Security Council and NGOs have increased, though as Griffin has noted, such relationships have been sporadic and problematic.[44] Thus, the environment in which NGOs operate is complex and confused. Early-warning signs were not translated into action in Somalia, Bosnia and Rwanda, nor recently in Kosovo or East Timor, until it was too late.

There has been an increase in the number of NGOs, (though this tends to be dominated by agendas from the North) and frameworks have emerged for NGO access and participation at the global level, as well as at the governmental level, though often NGO activity has again been curtailed by state-imposed limits. Within the UN, for example, there is evidence that there exists a deepening society of global NGOs. Yet, states only provisionally accept NGOs' contributions to UN conference processes as many governments refuse to see their claims to ultimate sovereignty over issues within their sphere of interest eroded by NGOs. While the support of civil society is generally considered an important contribution to peaceful social transformation, it has been argued that 'this concept often was equalled with the support of the NGOs in developing societies by Western donors which, without a sufficiently social basis, only created a fragmented and artificial society'.[45]

The failures in Somalia and in Bosnia illustrate how the neo-liberal humanitarian discourse can produce paradoxical methods and ends for peace projects. Grand schemes of rehabilitation, and reconstruction of failed or failing states in the international system, can easily fall victim to actors who see such normative projects as a threat to their own projects (for example, the plethora of nationalist and tribal leaders in both Somalia and Bosnia).[46] In Bosnia, Security Council Resolution 771 of 13 August 1992 called for humanitarian organizations to have unimpeded access, but humanitarian assistance was rapidly politicized and might even have prolonged the conflict. In Somalia, the mandate of the force included the role of helping to create conditions for the strengthening of civil society and humanitarian relief operations.[47] The Secretary-General's Special Representative, Ahmed Sahnoun, attempted to bring in NGOs in order to facilitate this in order to involve local groups in the peace process. However as the mission was essentially a military enforcement one, which due to China's objection did not have a human rights component, this marginalized local human rights groups.[48] NGOs were also drawn into the protection rackets that sprang up around the relief efforts. In Haiti, the joint UN–OAS International

Civilian Mission (MICIVIH) also suffered from the fact that there was no clear mandate guiding a relationship with local human rights NGOs.[49] In Rwanda, links between the UN Human Rights Field Operation (HRFOR) and local human rights NGOs were also somewhat tenuous and in Liberia, links between the UN Observer Mission (UNOMIL) and NGOs were often blocked by the institutionalized violence which took place against human rights NGOs.[50] Clearly where human rights regimes spring up, the local rule of law must democratize; in instances where this has not happened human security concerns suffer and approaches to ending conflict tend to become marginalized by state security concerns, which does little to bring an end to conflict.

In the case of East Timor, human rights NGOs played a crucial role throughout the many permutations of the conflict over the years, which kept the issue on the agenda of the UN, and in the public eye. International, national, and local NGOs influenced the discourse about human rights in this case during the last two decades through a persistent campaign against former President Suharto's regime, lobbying the UN, regional states and the US.[51] While the activities of the many NGOs involved tended not to be consistent with each other they were united that human rights violations should not be ignored despite the sovereignty of, and great power interests in, Indonesia. However, it took changes in the political climate in Jakarta before the human rights discourse could enter the official discourse, though when that change occurred the NGO community had already created the basis for such a discourse. Indonesia changed tack in mid-1999 and seemed willing to accede to the separatists' demands and even countenance the possibility of more than mere autonomy, despite the fact that the Indonesian military had invested a quarter of a century there.[52] However, after the East Timorese vote for independence in the referendum which took place in August 1999,[53] the violence which ensued was indicative of the tension between sovereignty and human rights, and of the failing nature of preventive diplomacy.

There are other problems here. NGOs from the West are now recipients of large amounts of state funding, and can have a significant impact on the economy of the state and region in which such funding is directed – as was seen in Cambodia and in Somalia. Many NGOs do not acknowledge the fact that they have a political role, while others do not acknowledge the fact that their work may serve to prolong conflict. There is the clear problem of the provision of resources to enhance human security, which may then be redirected towards the conflict itself. It may well be that it is the monitoring function of NGOs at civil, state, regional, global and related institutional levels that will become key to human security in a democratizing global context.[54]

Because the turn to human security has undermined state claims of sovereignty, making peace in humanitarian guise has increasingly become a form of intervention within the sovereign territory of states. As Ramsbotham and Woodhouse have pointed out, the human security context has meant that in some cases, NGOs have stopped recognizing sovereignty altogether, as occurred in the case of Médecins Sans Frontières' many operations in Afghanistan, Kurdistan, El Salvador and many others places.[55] This, however, as Somalia, Bosnia, Rwanda and Kosovo have so emphatically illustrated, has often been highly problematic. (In Kosovo for instance, the humanitarian norm appeared to lead to a contradictory situation where intervention to aid the Kosovo Albanians led to the violation of the human rights of ordinary Serbs not involved in the ethnic cleansing, in order to punish those who were.)

Clearly, NGOs should not be seen as a panacea. Ultimately, it might be said that the NGO community and its independent humanitarian and monitoring capacity is symptomatic of the elevation of democratic and cosmopolitan norms, at least within the dominant perception of the West. Clearly this means that human rights issues have been reprioritized, but it does not mean that the western hegemonic and neo-liberal discourse about human rights and the rule of law regimes and norms is the last word on the issue. NGOs can both exploit and be exploited, and there are many examples where NGOs have contributed to the institutionalization of conflict through their humanitarian activities, sometimes at the behest of states. There are large parts of the planet where such norms and regimes are alien, and individuals are unwilling to be (re)colonized by such western discourses. The UN Office for the Coordinator for Humanitarian Affairs, formed to coordinate the roles of such actors, faces a major challenge in overcoming these obstacles. Yet, one cannot escape from the fact that if approaches to ending conflict are to become more inclusive then local 'cosmopolitans' (as Kaldor calls them) need to be consulted and included.[56]

Regional approaches to ending conflict

Regional approaches to conflict resolution have become attractive because actors near to a conflict suffer most from its destabilizing consequences and may be better placed to understand its dynamics, though they may also have more interests at stake. The argument has been that local conflicts are more likely to be comprehensively addressed in a regional context than in the more complex global contexts that carry broader agendas and interests,[57] though it is the interplay of the local, regional and global which ultimately provides a network of opportunities, resources and obstacles for the resolution of conflict.[58] Yet it is also the interaction of these environments that often produces the constraints which have reduced peacekeeping and peacemaking to managing activities and obscured the normative issues at stake. Regional organizations may replicate conflicts and are bound by the same tensions which hinder international organizations and recreate the binaries of statehood and sovereignty.

In the post-cold war environment, the UN began to utilize subsidiary organizations under Chapter VIII of the Charter in order to relieve its financial and logistical burden, but also to provide consultation, diplomatic and operational support, and to allow for co-deployment and joint missions. Under Article 52(2) members states and the regional organizations of which they are members are expected to aid in the settlement of local disputes, though without impairing the role of the UN. Article 53(1) allows the Security Council to authorize enforcement action by regional actors, many of which have formal or informal arrangements with the UN as an umbrella organization, or observer status, and have been involved in peacekeeping, peacemaking and peacebuilding acitivities. These include the Organization of African Unity (OAU), the Economic Community of West African States (ECOWAS), Association of South East Asian Nations (ASEAN), the Commonwealth of Independent States (CIS), the Islamic Conference (OIC), and the League of Arab States (LAS), as well as NATO, the OSCE and the EU.

The Organization for Security and Cooperation in Europe (OSCE) provides the best example in that member states have accepted a common set of norms affecting the human dimension of security providing the foundations for the creation of conflict management institutions such as the High Commissioner on National Minorities (HCNM), the Long Term Missions, and the Office for Democratic Institutions and Human Rights. This preventive security regime, focused on national minorities, has wide geographical coverage, and is based on a normative system of sovereignty and minority rights, and the recognition that human security outweighs state sovereignty.[59] As Adler has argued, the OSCE is a 'security community-building institution', which in the former communist countries of the OSCE region, has promoted the association of international legitimacy with democracy and the accountability of states regarding their citizens.[60] This has both promoted the pursuit of justice at the citizen level, and the development of an international community of states and regions that have clear aspirations to move beyond traditional interstate diplomacy. For example, the OSCE has worked at the strategic level in Bosnia and Herzegovina, in cooperation with SFOR (Stabilization Force) and IFOR (International Force) towards the ends of regional and local stabilization. In Albania it played a leading role in the June 1997 elections in cooperation with the Multi-National Protection Force, members of the Council of Europe, and the European Union. It has also been involved in human rights monitoring in Croatia, and has worked closely with the UN Transitional Authority in Eastern Slavonia. In Estonia, Latvia, Moldova, Macedonia, and Ukraine, it has worked on human rights and democracy building issues in conjunction with the Council of Europe. In Georgia and Tajikistan the OSCE and the UN coordinate their activities on similar issues.[61] The OSCE has involved itself in activities normally associated with NGOs which concur with the Helsinki norms on democracy, basic rights and the rule of law, and has particularly significant links with NGOs specializing in conflict – peacemaking, prevention and management, mediation and confidence-building efforts.[62] It has developed a multidimensional approach, from grassroots to high diplomacy, through formal and informal channels and coordination networks.[63]

In Africa the Organization of African Unity (OAU) (which in 1993 established a Mechanism for Conflict Prevention, Management and Resolution (MCPMR) to provide assistance to states affected by war),[64] the Economic Community of West African States (ECOWAS) (which has been involved in conflicts in Liberia and West Africa), the South African Development Community (SADC), and the British Commonwealth are all developing along similar lines. Similarly, the Organization of American States (OAS) (whose member states undertook to act against violations of democracy, through the Santiago Commitment (1991), and have worked with the UN Secretary-General's Unit for the Promotion of Democracy in Central America) has established machinery to protect human rights, support democracies threatened by military coups and monitor elections.[65] In Asia the Association of South-East Asian Nations (ASEAN) has been involved in regulating interstate disputes and its Regional Forum has tried to build consensus on security issues and has cooperated with the UN as umbrella for Track II initiatives.[66] However, most of these organizations are caught up in the inevitable tension that such activities create with the principle of non-intervention, although one solution has been to address conflicts which are defined as in danger of spilling across state boundaries, so upholding the norm of non-intervention.

As Miall has pointed out, the coverage of regional organizations is not comprehensive – the Middle East provides an example where no organization has managed to provide a forum for regional conflict resolution.[67] Yet it is obvious that such organizations have the advantage of proximity, and familiarity with regional conflict environments and with the social, cultural, political and economic issues and norms which pervade it. Though this advantage is often diluted by regional hegemons (take the example of India and SAARC[68]), they provide an essential part of the global fabric of peacebuilding networks, despite their top-down construction. Yet, as Paris has pointed out, they mainly concentrate on exporting economic and democratic liberalization, thus replicating a western version of peace and order.[69] This is illustrated by one key area of concern, that UN authority over multilateral peace operations may be dissipated by the trend towards regionalization, though as has been pointed out by Griffin,

> regionalization has coincided with a growing awareness of the need of holistic approaches to conflict management approaches that incorporate aspects of preventive diplomacy, peacemaking, peacekeeping, humanitarian assistance, peacebuilding and development and necessitate the involvement of the UN as the only multilateral body with mandates in all areas.[70]

Global approaches: peace operations

Operation Desert Storm is a key disembarcation point for our understanding of the changing approaches to ending conflict. As Zolo has pointed out, the contradictory understanding of this 'coming of age' of the UN as an assertion of principles and sovereignty or a hegemonic struggle for oil was indicative of the tension between 'doing nothing' and 'doing something' which, it is argued, led to a movement towards interventionary activities based upon absolute hegemony[71] in terms of interests and norms.

Along with the outsourcing of peacebuilding functions, monitoring and preventive approaches to NGOs and regional actors, the post-cold war environment has seen the emergence of two main approaches: multidimensional peace operations (which incorporated traditional peacekeeping with humanitarian components and democratization); and briefly of quasi-enforcement operations. The former has been the primary approach, and as in Cambodia and initially at least in the former Yugoslavia, the UN has tried to gain the consent of involved actors. However, this increasingly multidimensional approach has exacerbated the tension between disputants' 'sovereignty', and the interests of the organization and of its member states.

The shift from classic peacekeeping operations such as UNDOF and UNEF, which involved the interposition of a peacekeeping force between the disputants after a ceasefire with the consent of the parties, to multifunctional operations such as UNTAG, ONUSAL, and UNTAC, entailed the implementation, again dependent upon consent, of complex multidimensional peace agreements.[72] These new approaches to peacekeeping have been seen as vital contributions, in that such 'operations were deployed as part of negotiated political solutions and the responsibilities of peacekeepers included non-military tasks such as disarmament, demobilization and reintegration of former combatants, resettlement of refugees, police training and supervision, election monitoring and other transitional administrative tasks.'[73] This led to the linkage of peacekeeping with peacebuilding, which has seen a blurring between the tradition functions of the UN, one which is reflected in the peacebuilding literature:

> The concepts of peacemaking, peacekeeping and peacebuilding, now considered central to the UN, are not even mentioned in the UN Charter. Yet it is clear that the drafters of the Charter had in mind an organization empowered to engage activities along the entire continuum of conflict management and resolution, ranging through preventive emergency to long-term responses and from economic and social to political and military engagement. It was only with the demise of Cold War, however, the UN peacekeeping operations began to link their hitherto limited peacekeeping activities explicitly to the full range of activities envisaged in the Charter.[74]

Indicative of this post-cold war change were the concepts offered in *Agenda for Peace* in which peacemaking, peacekeeping and peacebuilding were presented as separate activities. Kofi Annan has pointed out that this is a somewhat artificial division,[75] arguing that peacebuilding activities need to be located outside of a post-conflict chronology, as activities dealing with national institutions, elections, human rights, development, reintegration and rehabilitation should complement and orient prexisting humanitarian and development activities.[76] This is part of what has been described as the role of international and transnational organizations in development of a norm of 'conflict-culture with its focus on preventive diplomacy, early warning and improved

negotiation capacities'.[77] Adler argues that such transnational institutions help diffuse the norms and knowledge required to settle conflict
peacefully: thus such institutions play a 'critical role in the social construction of... communities'.[78] Until the setbacks in Bosnia-Herzegovina
and Somalia, these concepts seemed to be in the process of becoming
institutionalized on civil, state and international levels. For example,
the UN Observer Mission in El Salvador (ONUSAL)[79] operated in the
realm of human rights, verified the San José agreement, the ceasefire
between the government and the guerrilla resistance movement (the
FLMN), monitored the maintenance of public order, and observed
elections held in March 1994. The UN became involved in efforts to
address the roots of the conflict that had led to the civil war through the
expansion of ONUSAL's mandate and the inclusion of a police component to monitor public order. There seemed to be great faith in the ability
of the UN to aid in the prevention of human rights abuses on the part of
the people of El Salvador[80] and the UN played a crucial role in initiating
the development of a peaceful civil society and undercutting old divisions. This formed part of a much broader peace operation in Central
America. The UN operation in Angola, on the other hand, was not so
impressive and due to the fact that the international community was
unwilling to provide the UN with the necessary resources, the UN
Angola Verification Missions (UNAVEM I, II and III) found it difficult
to approach the levels of activity which were attained in El Salvador,
particularly with respect to human rights, reconciliation and development.[81]

UNTAG was the first example of the wider peacekeeping that blurred
old conceptual boundaries,[82] though its location in a diverse cultural
cartography proved a major challenge. It was reasonably successful in
facilitating the transition of Namibia's independence from South Africa,
an operation based on wide local, regional, and global consent.[83] One of
the most important aspects of this new approach, which laid out the
parameters for later missions, was that rebel forces were now to be
regarded as 'proto-political parties' with equal status to governments.[84]

This was followed by the UN operation in Cambodia, which involved
a vast operation to implement a settlement while also dealing with the
conflict over the legitimacy of the incumbent regime.[85] The Paris Conference on Cambodia, held in August 1989, had indicated the need for a
ceasefire and the withdrawal of foreign forces, a transitional administration and internationally supervised elections. It also called for guarantees of Cambodia's neutrality, sovereignty and territorial integrity, but
most importantly it indicated the need for international support for

rehabilitation and reconstruction.[86] UNTAC was assigned to supervise these requirements and also to oversee human rights, and to develop and implement a human rights education programme in an attempt to ensure an environment conducive to free and fair general elections. Clearly it was to be the most multidimensional operation ever, though its military component was its largest by far. Shortly after the establishment of UNTAC[87] the UN was mandated by the Security Council to develop and implement a human rights education programme, to take corrective action and 'co-ordinate the international programme for Cambodia's rehabilitation and reconstruction'.[88] UNTAC proved that the UN could at least lessen intractable conflict amongst the most hardline and entrenched of opponents, provided that it received the backing of the international community and had access to civil society. Despite the vast scope of the mandate of UNTAC, the UN found itself dependent upon local high-level consent and falling back on 'dialogue, persuasion, negotiation and diplomacy'[89] in the face of the non-compliance of the local protagonists. The UN was involved in the administration of the state with direct control of foreign affairs, defence, finance, public security and information, but seemingly lacked sensitivity to the host culture and the cooperation of local officials.[90] It found itself unable to sustain local law and order, and therefore could not produce the conditions required for undisputably free and fair elections in May 1993. However, in June 1993 the Security Council declared that the elections had been free and fair despite complaints from some political parties, an attempted bloodless coup, and a secessionist attempt. By 1997, another attempted coup threw all that had been achieved into doubt.

The UN operations in Somalia and in the Former Yugoslavia illustrated the difficulties of grand schemes of rehabilitation and reconstruction of failed or failing states in the international system. The integration of wider functions in peacekeeping mandates was somewhat compromised by the trend towards quasi-enforcement in the case of UNOSOM II, which was based on Security Council Resolution 814 of 26 March 1993, authorizing it to use force to deliver aid. This provided an early sign of the dangers of this new approach as it extended itself into increasingly interventionary territory, though within the rubric of the New World Order announced by US President Bush in 1990.[91] The UN operation in Somalia was, fresh from the Gulf War, an attempt at the realization of this order in the name of humanitarianism – though with the proviso of rebuilding an anarchic state without the consent of local actors. Debrix argues that Somalia was exploited by the UN in order to set an example for the international community, despite the fact that there were humanitarian crises developing elsewhere in the Sudan, Liberia, and Tibet.[92] Further, statelessness was implicitly seen as a threat to the international community.[93] A peacekeeping force designed to aid in the humanitarian tasks arrived in Somalia in April 1992, led by Mohammed Sahnoun whose task was to mediate a compromise between clan leaders and allow humanitarian assistance via the UN and NGOs to begin.[94] By November 1992 it was clear that Somalia was descending further into crisis and that the peacekeeping force was desperately in need of help. The US then intervened to enforce humanitarian assistance through Operation Restore Hope in December 1992, and in doing so stepped into to the clan struggle involving Mohammed Aideed, among others, who was soon identified as an obstacle to the success of the mission. At the same time, the UN Secretary-General continued trying to start negotiations between the tribal leaders, leading to an agreement in principle in January 1993, and UNITAF worked on bringing tribal elders together, establishing a police force, and disarmament. In March, the leading warlords and tribal representatives signed a commitment to complete disarmament and the establishment of a transitional system of governance. In early May UNOSOM II took over and on 5 June suffered its first casualties when a party of Pakistani UN troops was attacked. This increasingly drew the force into a bloody battle with Aideed, resulting in US casualities in Mogadishu. In October 1993, President Clinton announced the eventual withdrawal of US troops and the experiment was at an end. Somalia had shown that, conceptually, peace operations as in Cambodia, and intervention as in the Persian Gulf War did not necessarily blend to produce a 'New World Order', and that such operations needed local support and commitment if they were not to be seen as neo-colonial impositions, undercutting local (and often illicit) interests and insensitive to the needs and norms of local cultures. However, the UN attempt to mediate a solution led to the National Reconciliation conference in Addis Ababa, though this attempt to create a two-track peace process completely ignored the conflict resolution mechanisms of the Somalis themselves, in favour of western models.[95]

The partnership between ECOWAS and the UN in Liberia was indicative of the burden-sharing that Boutros-Ghali wanted to promote, while retaining overall UN responsibility for peace and security. After the failure of the ECOMOG intervention in August 1990, a new peace plan was agreed with the aid of the UN and the OAS. UNOMIL was established to monitor and verify the implementation of the Cotonou Agreement,[96] and in December the function of 'social reconstruction' was included in the mandate;[97] however this was jeopardised by the cavalier approach of ECOMOG to its functions and the UN was unable to make an impact in social reconstruction, though the situation did improve gradually.

The role of UNAMIR in Rwanda was to oversee the disengagement and reintegration of the armed forces into society, then to supervise and monitor a demilitarized zone, and to ensure the appropriate environment for elections to take place.[98] However, within a few months, ethnic violence escalated and came to a head after the presidents of Rwanda and Burundi were killed in a plane crash in April 1994. The Security Council at this time was simultaneously involved in Bosnia, Somalia and Iraq and resources were overstretched. The US review of peacekeeping had also resulted in Presidential Decision Directive 25 (3 May 1994), which expressed US reluctance to take more risks in, or carry the burden of, UN peacekeeping operations. Thus, the escalation in Rwanda was not met with sufficient will by the international community – rather a fear to avoid the excesses of 'mission creep' in yet another location. The failure of the UN to even acknowledge or respond to the genocide that occurred saw independent French and Belgian intervention.[99] By April, the Security Council was faced with a choice between massive reinforcement of UNAMIR, reducing it to a small group focusing on mediating a ceasefire, or withdrawal. The Security Council chose to reduce the force and avoid an escalation of involvement,[100] despite the fact that the Secretary-General had warned of UN passivity in the face of genocide.

The UN's involvement in the former Yugoslavia also highlighted the fast-appearing cracks in the new approach to peace operations. It was indicative of the international community's inability to address the issue of minority rights and secession,[101] aptly illustrated by the course of events during the dissolution of Yugoslavia, the secession of Slovenia and Croatia in June 1991 because of Serbian nationalism, the civil war in Croatia and then Bosnia Herzegovina leading to the latter's referendum which confirmed its desire for independence in March 1992. This was followed by its recognition by the then EC, and ultimately NATO intervention (to rescue a failing UN peace operation) against the Serbs over Bosnia.[102] By September 1991, the UN had imposed an arms embargo and in February 1992 the United Nations Protection Force (UNPROFOR) was mandated for Croatia.[103] UNPROFOR was to help broker a ceasefire and address immediate humanitarian issues, and Security Council Resolution 749 authorized the full deployment of UNPROFOR in three UN

Protected Areas.[104] The UN peace operation in Croatia, based on the so-called Vance Plan, defined the operation as an interim arrangement to create the conditions required for the negotiation of an overall settlement of the Yugoslav crisis. Its key elements included the withdrawal of the Yugoslav army (JNA) from Croatia, the demilitarization of the UN Protected Areas, and the continued functioning, on an interim basis, of local authorities and police under UNPROFOR supervision. In this context the local authorities were bound to ensure the full protection of human rights and UNPROFOR was to provide support for humanitarian organizations and facilitate the return of displaced persons to their homes in the UN Protected Areas. In May 1992, Croatia was admitted to full UN membership and in August 1992, after the conflict had spread, the forces' mandate was expanded to include Bosnia (notably its headquarters had been established in Sarajevo) and UNPROFOR II was empowered to 'use all measures necessary to deliver humanitarian assistance'.[105] However, the significance of the UN's role did not have a clear impact until the creation of a no-fly zone over the safe areas through Operation Deny Flight in April 1993.[106] Given the inability of the UN either to provide the conditions for a settlement or to prevent humanitarian abuses, the strategy became increasingly interventionary, resulting initially in the role of NATO in policing the no-fly zones over Bosnia and the safe areas. As atrocities mounted, this strategy gained the upper hand. After the infamous bombing of the Sarajevo market place in February 1994, NATO demanded that Serb artillery around the city be removed, and late that year bombed Serb positions to force their compliance. With NATO bombing' against the Serbs escalating, and a Croatian offensive against the Serbs in the former Croatian Krajina region, the Serbs accepted a ceasefire mediated by Richard Holbrooke in October 1995 which was to lead to the Dayton Peace Agreements later that year. The NATO force, IFOR (Implementation Force) was sanctioned to take over from the UN by these agreements. Later called SFOR (Stabilization Force), it was mandated to guarantee the return and transfer of displaced populations in Bosnia, the creation of a police force, and the establishment of reasonable living conditions. Clearly, the new framework of human security for dealing with conflict had led to practical demands which the UN was unable to meet alone, leading to the forcible intervention of NATO. Ultimately the involvement of the international community led to the creation of new states, boundaries, and an attempt to restructure the political institutions of the affected territories according to the perceptions and assumptions of the international community. It is yet to be seen whether this approach will provide a sustainable local and regional environment, though while the presence of SFOR continues there is at least an absence of overt violence. What was learned, however, was that for multidimensional operations to work in this kind of environment, force might have to be used as a basis for the rebuilding of a peaceable society and its institutions. This line of thinking led to the intervention of NATO over Kosovo, and underlined the contradictions produced by 'humanitarian intervention', the massive resources required for multidimensional peace operations, and the fact that once a solution is in place its long-term survival is far from guaranteed in an environment where territorial sovereignty and ethnonationalism provides local actors with their *raison d'être*.

UN intervention in Bosnia was seen as an opportunity to test the new possibilities for peace in the post-cold war environment. Clearly the boundaries between standard approaches to peacekeeping, mediation, conflict resolution, sovereignty and statehood were being blurred, particularly in the peacebuilding approach of the UN Secretary-General. As Debrix has pointed out, 'peacemaking', as used by the Secretary-General during the conflict, referred to the move beyond peacekeeping in which a range of strategies, including force, could also now be used to achieve 'peace'. This meant that the concept of consent was increasingly ambiguous as the approaches applied became increasingly interventionary as a result of the zeal of the international community to operate at the humanitarian level led to a need to take ever more decisive action.[107] *Agenda for Peace* had defined peacemaking as a continuation of peacekeeping and a form of intervention aimed at bringing disputants to a solution.[108] This meant that the different roles that could be taken within a conflict situation were now blurred, as was the distinction between consensual third party roles and intervention. In the *Supplement to an Agenda for Peace*, the Secretary-General introduced the idea of multifunctional peacekeeping, which Debrix argues was an attempt to justify the failed missions in both Somalia and Bosnia.[109] In his view the new multifunctional and multipurpose UN, through the use of safe areas, tried to simulate its own ideological universe in Bosnia with insufficient resources and became ensnared in its belief that such simulations were in fact reality as the Serbs ruthlessly attacked them, starting with Bihac in 1994.[110]

The case of Yugoslavia also had important implications for the relationship between the UN and regional organizations, particularly with respect to the issues of recognition of states and cooperation in peacekeeping, peacemaking and peacebuilding. From the start, on both issues, both the EU and the UN were undecided as to the nature of their relationship with respect to both and therefore often seemed to operate against the interests of the other. Economides and Taylor have suggested that in such cases the UN Security Council must take the leadership role which would both reflect and enhance its authority, though this assumes that its authority and its ability to apply resources would indeed be more effective at the local and regional level.[111] The case of Yugoslavia illustrates that the UN Security Council's authority was undermined by its own tendency to pass ambitions resolutions in response to worsening violence that it could not uphold because of a lack of resources.

The case of UN involvement in Macedonia is also pertinent. In response to the danger posed by the collapse of the former Yugoslavia, the UN introduced UNPREDEP, the first preventive peacekeeping operation, in Macedonia in January 1995.[112] It was a small force designed to prevent Milosevic from bringing Macedonia into the conflict. At the same time, a UN Special Representative attached to the force undertook a number of projects with local political parties and social groups to encourage the development of civil society. The OSCE was also invited by the government to participate in and monitor the internal political and regional situation. This led to the discussion of education and employment policies, citizenship and local government, and the establishment of problem-solving workshops and conflict resolution projects. Despite the ethnic tension still extant, this provided a clear example of a multidimensional approach to conflict.[113] Italian intervention in Albania (Operation Alba) occurred on the basis of a UN mandate and provided a similar example that halted the violence and opened the way for elections.[114] Again, the Personal Representative of the OSCE Chair-in-Office was involved in mediating between Albanian politicians, together with the Italian NGO, Comunita di Sant'Egidio, which helped mediate an agreement with respect to a transitional government. Though Albanian politics remained volatile, intervention pre-empted further violence.[115]

In Kosovo this emerging norm of intervention on a multidimensional level was tested even further, under Chapter VII of the UN Charter.[116] The fact that the warning signs of an explosion in Kosovo had existed for more than a decade since the rights of the Albanian community were reduced raised many questions about the whole notion of preventive diplomacy, pre-emption and early warning, as well as significant questions about intervention itself, and the response once conflict has broken out or been brought to a ceasefire. As a consequence of the asymmetry promoted by the international system and first generation approaches, the Albanian side was forced into the internationalization of their plight. The establishment of a 'shadow state' policy and their non-participation in Serbian elections was indicative of their desire to escape the domination of the Serbian side, which predictably hid behind the rhetoric of sovereignty, treating the conflict as an internal matter. The oversight of the Kosovo Albanians at Dayton led to their embrace of militancy, as advocated by the Kosovo Liberation Army with the support of the majority of the community. This led to a decisive intervention on the part of NATO, of dubious legality in terms of traditional international law, and which achieved the goal of aiding the Albanian community which had endured much hardship. However, it also underlined a certain hypocrisy in the international community's 'universal norm' of humanitarianism, emphasized its divisions and underlined how humanitarian intervention may assist one community at the expense of another, which may not necessarily support the policies of its leadership wholeheartedly. After the fighting stopped, the machinery of peacebuilding went into action, but in a locale now ethnically cleansed and in which there was little hope of promoting the norms of cooperation and multi-ethnicity. However, in mid-1999, a comprehensive framework for Kosovo became the focus of UNMIK (UN Interim Administration Mission in Kosovo), which was to operate on the basis of four pillars: a UN-led civilian administration, humanitarian assistance led by UNHCR, an OCSE-led democratization process, and reconstruction run by the EU.

In East Timor, intervention occurred only after a period where it was gradually becoming very clear that violence would escalate. It is important to note that Indonesia had finally decided to give up its claim to the territory and to hold a referendum, but the manner in which the territories' new status was to come about did little to reinforce pluralism and multi-ethnicity.[117]

In Sierra Leone, after a peacekeeping force was authorized to aid in the pacification of the country by the government, the UN was again soon forced to play an active role in the face of increasing violence, some of which targeted the UN troops.[118] This resulted in the initial 6000 troops being reinforced with another 5000 in order to facilitate the revision of peacekeeping attempted by Kofi Annan, and his belief in acting decisively and engaging force with force, thus underlining the dilemmas produced by the blurring between peacekeeping and intervention in the name of a universal notion and cause of peace.[119] Again, the UN was unable to achieve a credible response because of a lack of support, capacity and political will in the Security Council.

Since the genocide in Rwanda in 1994 the need for intervention at a humanitarian level, and the need for more dynamic frameworks of, and for, making peace has been widely proclaimed. The changing role of UN peace operations pertaining to military and non-military activities – to the creation of 'security space' in which NGOs, mediators at official and grassroots levels, UN civil agencies and aid agencies can operate and create humanitarian space – is partly indicative of this. However, the objectives of most third parties are still chained to conceptions of the international system, rather than to the international society or global/ local civil society in instances where zero-sum conceptions of territory and sovereignty still predominate. This means that attempts to create security, humanitarian and political space are weakened by the continued equation of political community and territorial sovereignty, albeit democratic and pluralistic; yet clearly a sustainable peace process, and mechanism for facilitating this must be created in order to lead to a sustainable peace.[120]

The traditional diplomatic tools for peacemaking that are built into the UN Charter have begun to evolve towards a third generation approach, for example, in the context of the Department of Political Affairs where the UN has been able to develop (with the consent of respective governments) its involvement the fields of good governance, human rights and economic and social development, as tools of peacemaking, prevention and peacebuilding. These coordinated activities involve the High Commision for Human Rights, Department of Peacekeeping Operations, UN High Commission for Refugees, UN Development Programme and the World Bank. However, these activities are still normally dependent upon the consent of the disputants (though this increasingly depends on the legitimacy of their positions in the eyes of the international community). As has been noted elsewhere, the development of the UN's future role depends partly on how it copes with the conflicting forces of fragmentation, regionalization and globalization.[121] There has been a shift towards a slightly greater normative authority for the UN, but with respect to intrastate conflict there is still a significant gap between conflict prevention and the capacity of the UN to respond to conflict. The reform process established by Secretary-General Kofi Annan has, however, tended to reflect a wider normative agenda,[122] though, as Knight has argued, there is a general belief in the west that the UN Charter is,

a body of rules that underwrite the authority of the international community. It reflects the minimal agreement within that community about the social values and principles that govern it, about the right way of doing things. It provides legitimacy for the actions of the organisation and its members...[123]

Developing this standard position, it can be argued that UN approaches to ending conflict have gradually encompassed regional actors, states, NGOs and local constituencies in an effort to become more effective. However, as outlined above, the UN's post-cold war experience has been very mixed partly due to problems emanating from the Security Council (and not least the heavy politicization the UN has received in US domestic politics), but mainly due to the question of consent and commitment on the part of the disputants, and the imposition of financial constraints which seriously undermines the liberal universalist ethos of the UN and sheds doubt on the intentions of its main actors. Peace is not something than can be installed complete, but must be built into the fabric of local communities, regional structures, international society and world politics. However, the overall structure that the UN provides for this is still caught between the ambiguity of an international prevention regime in the context of state sovereignty and non-intervention, and of course with the scale of the conflicts in which the UN system is itself involved. The norm of prevention and resolution has entered the lexicon of many aspects of human interaction: international financial institutions such as the International Monetary Fund and the World Bank now link financial assistance to the establishment of the conditions of 'good governance'. However, while several regional organizations are in principle committed to prevention and resolution, the conditions of local and regional politics and political culture tend to influence implementation.

One outcome has been reflected in Mohammed Sahnoun's proposal for a new institution which would integrate and mobilize third parties at all levels in order to deal with conflict.[124] This envisages local and regional actors applying their preventive and peacemaking resources within a global framework which itself is constituted by the interaction of distinct political communities.[125] This respects the fact that traditional forms of sovereign statehood, political community and international political relations have been transformed by processes which have resulted in a highly complex order in which the states-system is increasingly in tension with, and embedded in, the regional and global political networks that are part of the emerging international society, and in itself demands a re-articulation of the practices of making peace within the new discourses that are emerging.

This touches upon one of the most controversial areas of approaches to ending conflict – the problem of how multiple approaches are coordinated. It is presupposed first that they should be coordinated, and second that this would not entail a neo-colonial agenda, but, given the depth of the problems that forms of international-social conflicts cause for the stability, operation, and progression of the international and national system of politics, this is an area which needs careful attention. Some have argued that there is a need for long-term, coordinated (though not systematically imposed) strategies, which in turn need to be funded, planned, timed and implemented at a variety of levels and in a variety of dimensions. The international system is supposed to provide inherent coordination; the fact that it does not has led to serious weaknesses in dealing with conflict, and to the possibility that such conflicts could upset regional stability, or even global stability, as in the cold war period. Yet there is also the possibility that approaches to conflict are reifying an inherently unstable order. This can be seen in the mainstream attempt to synthesize different actors working at multiple levels via different rationalist methodologies, and to include a discussion of preventive regimes and post-conflict approaches to peacebuilding. Thus, both the conceptual frameworks, scope and chronology of approaches to conflict has been expanded. Obviously, in this emerging third generation approach, this has meant that making peace (see, for example, Dayton in 1995, and numerous UN peacekeeping operations in the 1990s) has become far more interventionary when viewed within the more traditional mainstream state-centric framework. Yet, these difficulties in making this a credible development are inherent in Kofi Annan's reactions during and since the events in Sierra Leone. His increasing frustration has been evident in his calls for tougher mandates and more capacity for enforcement.[126]

Theorizing a third generation approach to ending conflict

Boutros-Ghali's *Agenda for Peace* was an attempt to engage with a shift in the international system and the need to address the issue of new approaches to conflict to create and preserve a new 'order' based on universal ideals, supposedly encapsulated within the UN Charter.[127] *Agenda* presented a far broader definition of security than had hitherto been common in the diplomatic arena and discussed early warning systems and preventive diplomacy, peacemaking, peacekeeping and peacebuilding, as well as peace enforcement operations, to become engaged in addressing the 'deepest causes of social injustice and political oppression.' Though this was an expansion of the first generation divide between peacekeeping and peacemaking, these were seen as separate functions, operating in a chronological continuum relating to the life-cycle of conflict.[128] Boutros-Ghali argues that it is,

> possible to discern an increasingly common moral perception that spans the world's nations and peoples, and which is finding expression in international laws, many owing their genesis to the work of the Organization.[129]

In *Agenda*, a tightrope is walked between concepts which seem to call for a reduction of sovereignty and those which imply a right of intervention (relating in particular to humanitarian problems).[130] Boutros-Ghali pointed out that the tension between sovereignty and self-determination must be resolved in the context of democratization at all levels in order to deal with the roots of conflict.[131] It is clear that he lays the blame for the general failure of what I have described in Chapter 2 as first generation approaches during the cold war at the feet of states which did not see fit to respect the UN Charter, and because of the fact that third parties generally did not possess much in the way of resources for leverage.[132] Thus, what was required in his eyes was a coordinated strategy[133] that spanned preventive diplomacy, peacemaking, peacekeeping/enforcement, and post-conflict peacebuilding as part of a general commitment to a broader notion of peace and security. This involved a long-term commitment to post-settlement environments including disarmament, the repatriation of refugees, the restoration of order, election monitoring, the protection of human rights, reforming and strengthening governmental institutions, and 'promoting formal and informal processes of political participation'.[134] Thus, the peace process theoretically comes to envelop a spectrum of actors from governments to NGOs, academic institutions, parliamentarians, business and professional communities, the media and the public.[135] This leads into a third generation in which the methodologies of traditional forms of diplomacy, mediation and negotiation blend with the methodology provided by conflict resolution and an ethical/normative dimension pertaining to justice and not merely the replication of the status quo as a core objective of making peace. The somewhat uncertain discussion of international trusteeship, perhaps under the auspices of the UN, is also part of this development. However, in the *Supplement to An Agenda for Peace*, the Secretary-General noted the shortfall between the objectives that *Agenda* had outlined, and the ability of the UN to achieve them.[136]

This broadening of the debate is mirrored at the theoretical level, though this was reversed in practice by PDD-25, which was used to prevent several deployments.[137] However, Kofi Annan continued to concentrate on developing UN peace operations, arguing for a multi-disciplinary approach based upon a combination of 'coercive induce-ment' and 'induced' consent, requiring more resources, clearer international commitment and the ability for the UN to take decisive enforcement action.[138] The so-called Brahimi report outlines how the UN sees the development of peace operations in order to 'make the UN truly credible as a force for peace'.[139] The report outlines how peace-keepers and peacebuilders are inseperable partners in the quest to create a sustainable peace,[140] and calls for rapid responses, broad and inte-grated approaches to achieving this, still based upon consent and im-partiality, but with the potential for enforcement if necessary.[141]

There has been a tendency in those working within both the first generation and the second generation of approaches to expand the levels and actors involved, most notably seen in Chopra's peace-main-tainance approach, Lederach's peacebuilding approach, also developed by Rupesinghe, Mitchell's typology of the roles and functions of exter-nal peacemakers, in the work of Galtung, Vayrynen, Osler, and many others. Lund has argued for the organization of a preventive regime with the common consent of actors from diverse regions and from all levels and perspectives, encompassing traditional diplomatic interests, citizen interests, global and regional political, economic, cultural and identity interests.[142] Mitchell has supported the idea that a more comprehensive framework is needed with his typology of micro-level theories, which examines third-party roles and disputants' perceptions, attitudes and expectations; macro-level theories, which examine the roots and dy-namics of social conflict; and meso-level theories, which examine the framework of conflict resolution approaches. This typology provides a framework for a contingency approach in which activities adapt and to the conflict environment and are coordinated.[143] This raises the contro-versial question of whether preventive and peacebuilding approaches are plausible within the current international system in what Ramsbo-tham has described as the UN's 'standard operating procedure'.[144]

However, this line of thought is predicated upon the requirement that approaches to ending conflict must address the local, regional and global system via an integrative approach where all levels of activity operate in concert, rather than in opposition from both the bottom up and from the top down. This, however, requires that a set of common norms need to be established which all parties involved at whatever level are aware of and accept. Furthermore, this implies that there exists a global normative context in which approaches to ending conflict can operate without conflict among the various parties involved over their motives, processes and objectives. From this, we can also see that making peace has the potential to become far more interventionary, given the requisite resources, as general agreement on the above means that action could be taken to address conflicts heedless of infringements of state sovereignty. Thus, it is the question of the normative basis of, and the assumptions that lie behind the recent developments in peace operations which are most problematic, closely followed by financial and logistical constraints. When the UN becomes involved in a conflict, either through good offices, mediation or one of the various forms of peacekeeping, its dominant members are projecting a neo-liberal, normative, and sovereign discourse onto that environment on the assumption that the conflict can be redressed in this manner and that 'order' can be 'restored'. 'Others' may ultimately be colonized by a flawed Westphalian system.[145]

Lund has assessed what he describes as a new climate for preventive action and ending conflict as follows:

> respect for human and minority rights is more widely accepted as a norm for judging nations; and the inclination to eschew the use of force to resolve conflicts is more in vogue. This sense of a value congruence was reflected in the 1992 UN Security Council summit, which showed 'an unprecedented recommitment, at the highest political levels, to the Purposes and Principles of the [UN] Charter.' The spreading values are now written more firmly into recent statements by several regional organizations: the 1990 Paris Charter of the OSCE, the 1990 Santiago declaration of the OAS, and the 1993 Cairo summit document of the OAU.[146]

On the basis of these developments, Lund seeks to establish a framework that reflects the changing nature of the international environment. He moves from the traditional list of factors around which third parties operate – timing, international support and moderate leadership – to 'multifaceted action' which he defines as the 'extent to which third parties, acting in coordination, employ not one but several diverse instruments'[147] This is a crucial addition to the more traditional theoretical and methodological approaches to ending conflict as it requires that monolithic views of politics, conflict, representation, security and human rights are discarded. Lund develops the idea of a stratified, multilateral regime with clearly defined organizational dynamics and normative principles. While this once again raises the problem of universalism and the imposition of a dominant cultural, political and economic system, Lund also argues that such a regime would be approached 'incrementally in the short run to accommodate present political realities and capabilities of the actors in various regions'.[148] This means that once again, normative principles are made subservient to practicability in the short term, on the positivist basis that interests of dominant actors must be assuaged. The paradox of such approaches is that the long term never becomes the short term. The implication of this is that the role of such interests in creating conflict must be assumed. The practical/normative trap, which Keohane referred to in his 1988 paper on international institutions[149] is the inevitable result of institutionalizing conflict management and resolution within a positivist framework. In contrast, promoting integral conflict resolution mechanisms in a normative framework of international and global civil society indicates that both conflict and its resolution should not be regarded as artificial overlays on situations of order and disorder, but an integral part of the fabric of global, regional and local interactions.

Lund argues that a vertical division of labour is required so that problems which can be handled by a lower level of government or organization should be delegated to that level, and more serious problems handled at higher levels.

> The vertical division of labor in preventive diplomacy would be achieved by pushing explicit direct responsibility and accountability downward – wherever possible and not all at once, but increasingly over time, as the capabilities at those levels permit – to the parties to the conflict themselves and to sub-regional and regional actors. At the same time, extra-local and extra-regional states and the United Nations would provide appropriate facilitative, technical, political, and (if necessary) military support.[150]

This, of course, requires that there are actors at the various levels equipped to manage, prevent and resolve conflicts, something that has emerged only since the end of the cold war. However, Lund argues that at the intercommunal and intergroup level of disputes within existing states, the political institutions of those states should act as the first means of prevention.[151] This implies that such actors are not actually contributing to the conflict. In this case, Lund argues, responsibility shifts to subregional or regional organizations (ROs).

At what Lund describes as the second level of prevention – the regional arena – the capacity of ROs to aid in the peaceful resolution of conflicts that arise within and between member states is also crucial. Within the parameters of the UN Charter, ROs can promote democracy, monitor human rights, and establish preventive observer missions. At the third level – the global arena – Lund argues that the UN Security Council and Secretary-General can concentrate on large-scale crises: conflicts that local and regional third parties have failed to prevent, and 'the creation of backup peace enforcement forces for possible deployment into new local and regional conflicts in those instances when regional military resources are inadequate to the demands of those conflicts'.[152]

What is also significant is the development of a public–private relationship.[153] This is constituted by relationships between official actors at the various levels and conflict resolution NGOs, or those NGOs involved in the various aspects of civil society by virtue of their transnational contacts, local legitimacy, and subsequent access to disputants and actors in civil society and identity groups. It is through such actors and the humanitarian nature of their functions that peacebuilding and peacemaking can become an integral part of society. Indeed, Lund calls for their participation in preventive diplomacy, 'to become a matter of deliberate multilateral policy – and thus, perhaps, a reason for greater government funding of NGOs'.[154]

Stedman has criticized the discussion of preventive diplomacy, along with Vayrynen.[155] Both have been critical of the claims that have been made for preventive diplomacy, arguing that it is costly, complex, and may even trigger conflict. Stedman argues that only the threat of forcible intervention can work, and that preventive diplomacy may hinder political change. Vayrynen's somewhat more sensitive discussion points out that preventive diplomacy cannot occur where major powers tend to pursue 'hands-off' forms of diplomacy – this has meant that the focus has tended to be on preventing conflict escalation after the conflict has begun.[156] Lund has responded to Stedman's critique of his work by pointing out that early warning has had some practical effects in the international environment, for example in the case of US warnings preventing Milosevic from spreading conflict until the end of 1997.[157] This debate underlines the difficulties of developing a more proactive and multilevel, multi-chronological approach to ending conflict while still using the framework of Westphalian diplomacy for intervening in conflict. Preventive diplomacy requires the identification of the cause of the conflict and sensitivity to the underlying assumptions which perpetuate it. This is something that is lacking to various degrees in the strictly Westphalian frameworks applied in this debate.

Chopra has argued that there must be a harmonization of efforts, but they must also reflect the unique environment of each conflict environment and the exercise of the political authority of the international community.[158] Peace maintenance involves a mechanism whereby the UN, regional organizations, member states, and local actors could take control of government in the event of a complete collapse. This could control or monitor the instruments of administration, the judicial system, police, and armed forces; it could act in partnership with local authorities; or it could provide an international standard for the development of local governmental structures.[159] Therefore the mechanism would need highly developed facilities for control of all aspects of a conflict environment, including, government, administration, humanitarian issues, prosecution, and coercive force. It is here that Chopra makes the problematic assertion, which plagues third generation approaches, that such coordinated activities and intervention imply that there is a common, perhaps even universal, basis for such action agreed by the vast majority of the world's actors, states, organizations, governments, administrations and communities. This raises the question of why finding the requisite resources for such operations is so difficult and takes us back to the problematic debate of the universal versus the relative normative basis for such action and the possibility that such mechanisms would be viewed as neo-colonial. However, Chopra's framework has attempted to integrate preventive diplomacy, peacemaking, peacekeeping, and peacebuilding, and highlights the direction in which approaches to ending conflict has moved since the end of the cold war with the experiences of the UN's missions in Namibia, Cambodia, Mozambique, Somalia, the former Yugoslavia, Western Sahara and El Salvador. Chopra counters the accusation of neo-colonialism by arguing that resources are channelled into the local environment rather than removed. This is an important observation, though it does not take into account the normal quid pro quo of conditions attached to the inflow of resources and the normative and practical expectations attached, nor the fact that they may may end up perpetuating the conflict.

Lederach's contribution to the debate can be found in the vertical model he offers for peacebuilding. It includes three main levels, including the official level consisting of mediation and negotiation, the middle level consisting of workshops, training and peace commissions, and the grassroots level. He brings all of these levels together and calls for approaches that go beyond traditional statist diplomacy in their search for an enduring reconciliation sustained by networks and mechanisms that promote justice and address the root causes of conflict. Lederach concentrates on the importance of middle range leaders and the need to address both broader systemic and subsystemic issues.[160] He argues that an integrative and comprehensive analysis is imperative to take into consideration

> the legitimacy, uniqueness, and interdependency of the needs and resources of the grassroots, middle range, and top level. The same is true when dealing with specific issues and broader systemic concerns in a conflict. More specifically, an integrative, comprehensive approach points toward the functional need for recognition, inclusion, and coordination across all levels and activities.[161]

This, Lederach proposes, offers the key to conflict transformation. Building peace is a long-term project in which the conflict is transformed into a dynamic, peaceful relationship which regenerates itself.[162] Lederach then moves from the structural and practical aspects of peace to four interdependent dimensions which he identifies, including the personal, the relational, the structural and the cultural.[163] These various elements need to be coordinated, though Lederach argues that the establishment of a master plan developed by a 'peace authority' could well be counterproductive.[164] However, coordination is required if there is to be

> effective implementation of a comprehensive peacebuilding strategy and in the building of an infrastructure for peace. Coordination facilitates the cross-fertilization of the various elements, levels of work, and activities across the progression of conflict in a given setting. Armed conflicts in deeply divided societies represent complex, long-term challenges; if these challenges are to be met, a multiplicity of roles and functions, approaches and activities must be brought into play. Peacebuilding efforts and initiatives must have points of contact and be coordinated if the constructive transformation of a conflict is to be sustained. This calls for not only an understanding, of the larger challenge but also an acknowledgment of the need for a multiplicity of roles, for multiple levels of activity, and for diverse strategies and approaches, each with a distinctive contribution to make.[165]

This attempt to redevelop analytical and practical frameworks is sensitized to the somewhat problematic and exclusionary frameworks that have generally been the products of order-producing activities during the emergence of the three generations of activity outlined here. Yet, this contribution still lacks a discussion of the basis upon which making peace and therefore international society does, and should, rest, assuming that these activities may not imply radical structural change or major shifts in priorities in the international system. While Lederach does take a position upon the normative requirements of conflict transformation, this is a preliminary position only.

As Ramsbotham has argued, the 'liberal universalist assumptions' behind UN peace operations have not conclusively been shown to have failed outright – though peace operations based upon them shows them to be clearly inadequate.[166] Clearly there is some room for a discussion here about the assumptions and practicalities of creating positive peace: the alternatives are stark – to do nothing or to impose a negative peace. The importance of these approaches, outlined above, and particularly in Lederach's model, is that issues associated with human security, societal security, and culture are gradually being incorporated. The next step is to realize just how radical and far-reaching the implications of this project are.

Conclusion

Attempts to reconceptualize approaches to ending conflict represent in part an evolutionary process (to which the post-Versailles idealism, the development of peace research, the existence and development of functional institutions, and the pluralist discourse, have all contributed). However, it has only been in the post-cold war era that the potential for the harmonization of these activities in tandem with the emergence of a normative aspect to the conduct of international relations has become clearer. This has been based upon an attempt to merge the quite different methodologies, epistemologies, and ontologies of first and second generation approaches into an integrated and multidimensional approach. The potential to utilize the emergence of global and regional norms in order to strengthen a global project of sustainable endings to conflict, to create multidimensional peace operations on the basis of clear interests and norms, apparently provided a window of opportunity for the unravelling of many of the Cold-War's most intractable of disputes. Conflicts could now be discussed in the context of local, regional and global debates, no longer epitomized as clearly by the clash of interests that the world of Realpolitik knew so well. Third generation approaches, depicted in Figure 5.2, are multilevel, multidi-

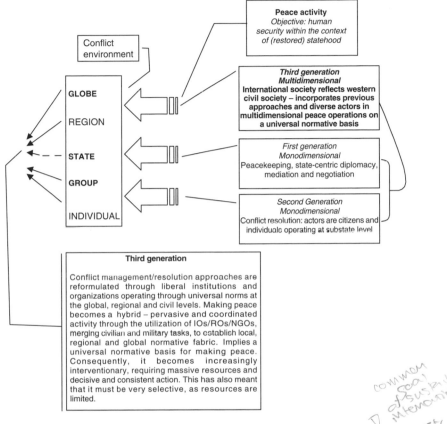

Figure 5.2   Third generation approaches

mensional operations based on the coordination of local, regional, state-centric and global projects aimed at the 'common' goal of a sustainable international society. Yet, this experiment in ending conflict has served to emphasise gaping problems in the foundations and concepts of the shifting international system (as well as the implementation of these new approaches) that it has tried to reinforce.

Third generation approaches have attempted to create a hybrid of traditional diplomatic approaches, conflict resolution approaches, state security and human security, and has seen states, international organizations, regional organizations and NGOs endeavour to contribute to the ending of conflict. It resulted in the multidimensional missions of the early 1990s which attempted to blend the military tasks of ending or preventing violence with civilian roles in responding to human security issues. This in turn has led to a reaction against the massive cost and philosophical basis of such operations as they became increasingly interventionary, often on humanitarian grounds. This has underlined the highly inconsistent nature of making peace, as well as significant flaws in its claims, and in the international system.

How can the international system mediate claims for peace, justice and statehood? A clear clash between state interests and the normative path has recently emerged, which emphasises the inconsistencies of the international system. Clearly, a fresh balance between identity, security, and political structures must be found – a balance that third generation approaches attempt to locate in the development of reciprocal norms and regimes[167] related to liberal international and regional institutions, political and economic interdependence and transparency, and democratization – and the elevation of the sovereignty of the individual and the practical reciprocity of sovereignty.[168] This still leaves the problem of community as an inclusive or exclusive framework, however. Peace efforts must attempt to decrease the exclusiveness of the communities in which they take place. Yet, what has tended to occur since the end of the cold war is that peace operations have aimed at the reconstitution of states and their frameworks. From Cambodia to Somalia and Yugoslavia, the official focus guiding peace operations was the creation and recreation of Westphalian states in order to democratize or solve humanitarian problems. In former Yugoslavia, in Kosovo and in East Timor, the focus was on creating new states or greater autonomy, but ones that were ultimately based on ethnic majoritarianism. This tendency emphasizes the fact that states underpin the international system, conceptually and physically, as well as the key organizations through which peace operations occur, and the end result is the replication of that system. The implications of this are discussed in the final chapter.

6
Conclusion: Rethinking Approaches to Ending Conflict

Quis custodiet ipsos custodes?[1]

Introduction

The hybridization of the monodimensional approaches that character-ized first and second generation approaches to ending conflict has led to the development of multidimensional third generation approaches op-erating from the global to the local in an effort to produce inclusive structures and settlements. This has led to the merging of top-down and bottom-up approaches in an attempt to replace particularism with cosmopolitanism. This reframing has raised several new and familiar debates. The first significant question relates to the type of order that hegemonic powers with sovereign claims to truth and knowledge use to reify approaches for ending conflict. In the Westphalian system their application resulted in the preservation of the state-centric, male-dom-inated order, territorial integrity, and very basic human rights.[2] It pre-served a systemic balance of power that resulted in the positivist aspects of order taking precedence over the normative, and state security taking precedence over human security – in other words a negative peace. Have third generation approaches moved beyond this – from the Westphalian into a post-Westphalian order? Debrix has shown how the UN can be compared to a panopticon in which global observation and surveillance, not to mention intervention, occurs to endorse and simulate certain forms of order propagated (though negotiated to a certain extent) by its dominant members and by the universal claims of the Charter within the context of their claims to forms of *global* governance and *global*iza-tion.[3] These practices are aimed at normalizing the practices of sover-eign states within the international system (and a latent international society) and their representations, and the activities of the social groups that find themselves located within these structures. Kaldor argues that terms like 'intervention' peacekeeping and peace-enforcement signify an inability to understand the new forms of warfare that exist.[4] The range of activities examined in this study, including third generation approaches, operate in this manner, though second generation approaches which, through their bottom-up and individual human needs based frameworks, began to deviate, moved some way towards engaging with the concept of a positive peace. Generally speaking, the different approaches to making peace are victims of a performative contradiction, in that the assumptions that lie behind them may prove to exacerbate the issues at the heart of the conflict. States no longer monopolize legitimacy or the means of violence, and therefore cannot monopolize the tools used to end conflict.

Third generation approaches are indicative of a late-Westphalian order in which state security, exclusive sovereign claims and human security are becoming more and more obviously in tension with each other. It is also important to note that the attempt to bring the various approaches to ending conflict together in a hybrid means that it must be assumed that they have similar objectives, methodologies and epistemologies: a similar view of 'order' and what must be done to promote it. The notion of the post-Westphalian order, as developed in particular by Linklater, is useful here as it provides us with a framework with which to critique the three generations of activity I have outlined, and with a normative framework in which post-Westphalian approaches, as opposed to Westphalian and late-Westphalian approaches, can be redefined. The concept allows universal positions to be taken, as approaches to ending conflict must often do, but it endeavours to sensitize them to the inherent pitfalls of doing so. In other words, an intellectual and practical basis for approaches to ending conflict could survive the critiques of modernity, finding a generally accepted basis without becoming totalizing practices.

Three generations, peace and order

An examination of the broader issues and conceptual problems behind making peace indicate that the approaches examined in this study have their roots in the Westphalian international system and are informed by its dominant discourses. They are susceptible to the problems associated with sovereignty and realist claims about it, representation, identity, self-determination and human rights, and how an understanding of these issues inform the negotiating positions of disputants in the context of hegemonic discourses about protecting the status quo. Thus, much of what the UN has done, particularly during the cold war for example, can be characterized as status quo diplomacy, preserving a hierarchical state order by concentrating on national interests to the exclusion of non-state actors, or a human security discourse. This has still been important as part of the UN's role of mediator of the last resort. All three generations endeavour to correct and normalize practices that are seen to lead to conflict, while at the same time not fully comprehending the importance of intersubjective issues such as identity, culture and status.

Approaches to ending conflict can be divided into two main phases, the Westphalian cold war version and the late-Westphalian, post-cold war version. Within these two phases I have identified three main generations of activity: the classical peacekeeping operation in the context of mediation or negotiation; the conflict resolution/facilitation/transformation approach; and the hybrid multidimensional approaches, particularly associated with UN peace operations since the end of the cold war.

First generation Westphalian approaches to ending conflict tend to define non-state-centric conflict as 'intractable' and has produced a zone of conflict/peace position in which certain areas of the world are relegated to long-term conflict. Westphalian approaches characterize issues such as identity, territory, representation and human rights in terms of the responsibility of governments and restoring the integrity of states. Self-determination occurs in rare cases. The role of approaches to ending conflict is therefore one of management and produces order without justice. The neo-liberal addition to this includes the functionalist argument that IOs and ROs are needed to aid in this process in order to reproduce the hegemonic view of order imposed by the great powers. It has been generally argued that a neutral process of mediation and peacekeeping would work best in a stalemate situation – which raises the proposition often associated with Henry Kissinger's diplomacy in the Middle East that to arrive at peace one should aim to produce exhaustion amongst the disputants. The assumption that a compromise on this basis would be the objective of all often obscured the disputants' devious objectives. Thus, peace has often lacked justice, order has often been self-perpetuatingly unjust, and approaches to ending conflict aimed at fine-tuning that order and have often failed because of their tendency to overlook issues beyond state interest and the territorial sovereignty of the Westphalian international system. Such approaches are often normatively hypocritical because normative issues become subservient to strategic interests. Within these approaches there is little or no discussion of the roles and needs of marginalized actors, or broad understanding of the conflict environment (particularly in terms of environmental resources).

Reducing the issues and causes of conflict in this manner to state-centric political communities tends to lead to the replication of conflict in the Westphalian system and hence first generation approaches were generally a failure, even in terms of achieving the limited goals inherent in the realist and neo-liberal discourse. Perhaps they preserved the regional status quo but they never addressed the roots of conflict, legitimacy, identity or justice on anything but their own terms. The term 'intractable conflict' therefore denotes the failure of the Westphalian system and its associated approaches to conflict, which mirrors its own psychosis and in which responsibility is generally limited by states, for states, and within states' borders. The Westphalian system blocks humanitarian objectives and responsibilities and provides little conceptual space to identify the roots of conflict; most work on conflict still replicates this discourse in which theory and practice, subject and object are viewed as separate and binaries are created in which others are subjected to stereotyping and marginalization by dominant and hegemonic actors.

The second generation conflict resolution/peace research framework emerged as a reaction to the failings of peacemaking in a Westphalian realist environment. The work of Burton, Azar, Galtung and many others is essentially positivist but the human needs framework and the notion of structural sources of violence have been very important in shifting peacemaking frameworks towards what has become almost a new ideology – 'human security'. The recognition of structural sources of conflict and of human needs as navigation points for policy-making broadened the spheres in which conflict analysis and resolution operate and retrieved the individual and the intersubjective in conflict, in an attempt to provide a bottom-up influence on state behaviour (though this often tended to occur in reverse), and indicated the need for structural reforms. Such attempts began to recognize the importance of culture and intersubjective understandings of conflict, and through bottom-up methodologies, brought these issues to the fore. The frameworks they suggested have been criticized as being radical, idealistic or indicative of attempts at social engineering, often obscuring local approaches in favour of Western, neo-liberal frameworks based upon indeterminate human needs requirements, and completely separate from the impacts of high-level debates, though facilitating them. However, second generation approaches have constituted an important part of the shift to a late-Westphalian approach to conflict, and potentially, via their reformulation, towards a post-Westphalian framework for the examination of the roots of conflict and alternative forms of political community. This is despite the fact that second generation approaches attempted to provide a scientific basis for understanding the impulses and needs that drive human beings, to reconstruct an international system from the bottom upwards, and pointed to the need for radical structural changes to prevent the reproduction of injustice. It redefined order towards a more human security oriented definition, to which its methodologies for ending conflict were directed.

Third generation approaches arose in the post-cold war, late-Westphalian environment. They consist of multilevel, multidimensional approaches which normally have the objective of rebuilding states via both top-down high-level and bottom-up grassroots methods, and are characterized by a discussion of establishing state administrations that incorporate human security in a broader context than the statecentric approaches of earlier first generation methods. Yet, they are still heavily reliant on neo-liberal versions of functional roles for institutions in the context of a universal discourse about what peace is, and how it should be made. Third generation approaches attempted to unite the very different methodologies, epistemologies and ontologies of first and second generation approaches, ultimately reconstructing and merging a framework which professed to achieve no more than a negative peace in a state security framework within a far more ambitious human security framework.

This third generation approach has given rise to some far-reaching questions. Will it lead to an attempt to generate a universal blueprint and mechanisms for peace to be applied through the UN, subcontracted out to ROs and NGOs? Does this imply a universalist view of international society and would this lead to global governance with or without government? How far can such approaches resolve the tensions between the local and the global, the dominant and the marginalized? So far this third generation approach has tended to ignore such questions, focusing on the operational needs aspects of human security driven interventions in conflicts as we saw in many of the post-cold war UN peace operations. Though such operations were concerned with human security, they were also concerned with the integrity of state and territory and a contribution to international society – which revolves around the interests of its dominant actors. They were multidimensional and multilevel involving different civilian, military, official and non-official actors and focused on human security issues such as human rights, aid, development and democratization. However, the emergence of peace enforcement operations, a logical progression of this mode of thought, illustrated the essentialist, universalist and western-centric nature of such missions in a neo-liberal framework of intervention for the 'greater good'.

Third generation approaches to conflict have become more concerned with the fabric of political communities as both Boutros-Ghali's and Annan's work has illustrated. They have both concerned themselves with reforming the UN peacekeeping framework beyond the limitations of the Westphalian framework and towards long-term settlement processes. There have been several attempts to operationalize this new approach into a coordinated and multidimensional peace regime (the latest being found in the Brahimi Report and with the Secretary-General's support[5]). These frameworks illustrate a reliance on strategic/realist/positivist understandings of political community and their conflicts and run into the trap of potentially imposing western, universalist hegemonic discourses which may only dampen conflict down rather than solve it in the long run. Yet, ending conflict depends on a 'regime of truth'[6] about order, propagated through the tools and approaches used for ending conflict by the actors and institutions involved, and mediated to a greater or lesser degree in the light of their dependence upon access to resources, by the voices and interests of all of the actors involved.

What runs through all approaches is a normative position that there must be order and peace and so methods of propagating that order and peace; the question is upon what basis should these terms be defined – purely political, territorial, economic, philosophical, cultural or humanitarian? Thus, approaches to ending conflict, based on a mutually acceptable definition of peace and order, are totalizing in their very nature, and potentially hegemonic. The paradox in making peace is that it means that consent is delegitimized unless general claims are avoided, and consent is used to attempt to create at least an illusion of consistency while treating each case as unique. As Zolo has argued, what has run through all efforts to make peace and create order has been an attempt by hegemonic actors to preserve their own value systems, through international organization via cosmopolitan structures that freeze the world's cartographies in their dominant members' favour. Zolo wonders if there may have been radical misconceptions in these attempts to achieve universal peace and whether 'any cosmopolitan project [can] ever be anything other than an inherently hegemonic and violent undertaking?'[7] This is the root of the 'weak pacifism' that has recently emerged as an uncertain compromise between cosmopolitan centralism and its counterclaims,[8] seen most recently in selectively low key or 'comprehensive' peacebuilding operations, from Cambodia to Kosovo and East Timor. It must be recognized that peace operations, the institutions that run them, thinking and theorizing about ending conflict, are crucial tasks in a changing world which ultimately reconstitute it. Yet as my examination of numerous instances throughout this study has illustrated, third parties – albeit states, academics, peacekeepers or organizations, despite having shifted their objectives to human security issues and with the best of will, are reluctant to admit that their roles and the impact of their actions are not just about making peace, but are also about exporting order, possibly unwittingly, via the value systems, economic, political, social, cultural and normative models that have shaped their own development. Since this can easily open up the debate to accusations of neo-colonialism on the part of hegemonic powers in a similar manner to the way globalization has often been critiqued from the periphery of the international system, it requires a radical rethink of approaches to making peace, who applies them and where, their objectives, and the types of order they are used to sustain.

The emergence of third generation approaches has been in response to the identification of the multiple roots of contemporary conflict and complex emergencies. It has been predicated on the need for responses at different levels including international and regional arrangements, structural change at the state level, resolution of identity and representational issues, and the need for bottom-up approaches to address cultural issues, as well as the emergence of new normative, non-exclusionary diplomatic cultures. Though the actual practice of such approaches has failed to move far beyond the outer limits which first generation approaches permitted, making peace is now generally conducted by a diverse range of actors, including internal actors or 'indigenous peacemakers' and external actors often support the capacity within societies to manage conflicts in a sustained manner. This means that attention is now being focused on the possibility of the development of domestic peace constituencies and domestic institutions in a socially and culturally non-exclusionary framework of a post-Westphalian order, though at present the practice of third generation approaches is normatively, culturally, and practically, highly unsatisfactory. It is also important to note, however, that peace cannot be produced by formulae which once applied then operate smoothly in perpetuity, but requires long-term commitment, internal and external support and monitoring, and involves political, social, cultural and economic issues, education, and training – as operationalising a broad definition of security would demand.

Though multidimensional peace operations have helped manage political change at the local and sometimes regional levels, they share common characteristics with traditional operations, including a time limitation on mandates, and a dependence upon varying levels of local consent and commitment and external support – whether they are consent-based missions or not. Thus, impartiality and the non-offensive nature of intervention is still often integral to multidimensional operations: they increasingly require the integration of civilian and military tasks and objectives, subcontracting and coordination with humanitarian agencies and NGOs, all of which must ultimately keep all of the disputants committed to a long-term process of peacebuilding, preventive norm-building and the creation of institutions that foster cross-cutting cleavages and interdependence within the context of a local, regional and global normative system in which interaction across the different levels does not create friction. Yet, making peace also depends on the construction and reconstruction of sovereignty, thus reproducing to a greater or lesser degree the binaries that have illustrated the normative, cultural, and operational defunctness of activities derived from within the Westphalian system. Of course, this downplays the realization of the partly structural causes of the issues of group identity and participation, derived from the failings of the Westphalian international system itself. Perhaps, more significantly, it rejects any possibility that the international and regional systems are themselves partly determined by identity and participation factors (ethical issue areas); the fact that there has been so little recognition of this until recently is one of the conflict management/conflict resolution literature's great failings.

The assumptions made by such analyses have created a 'regime of truth' – a discourse about making peace that illustrates how the international system itself may have framed, created, and replicated conflicts and attempts to resolve them. This discourse has presented itself as a single interpretation of what peace is and how it can be understood, and therefore how it can be created. This ignores Foucault's telling assertion that a genealogical method of understanding sees a profusion of complex and interrelated events constituting discourses about power and truth – and therefore peace.[9] Critical approaches to ending conflict argue that its practice is infused by power in the defence of an international order constructed through exclusionary discourses; yet, peace-keeping, peacemaking, and peacebuilding should contest this via normative and emancipatory projects to overcome the binaries that power discourses produce in order to create reciprocal and ethical responsibility and recognition. From a post-modern perspective, however, even this may be suspect, as all approaches to ending conflict may imply a problematic imposition which may result in the further marginalization of the already marginalized in the utilitarian expectations of 'peace' and 'order'.

Hampson has underlined the tension between peace and justice:

> Without peace there can be no justice. Without justice, democratic institutions, and the development of the rule of law, the peace itself will not last. But the political requirements for reaching a peace settlement may well conflict with the desire to lay the foundations for long-term democratic stability. Which model works best when and where: the conflict managers' power-sharing model or the 'democratizers' political justice model? The evidence suggests that a concern for justice must be tempered by the realities of negotiation and the parties' interests in reaching a political settlement.[10]

The descent back into 'pragmatism' that hinges upon a 'sacrifice' of normative peace and human security is justified on the grounds that it is the disputants themselves who, for example, may not want to

> push the frontiers of human rights too far. The challenge for third parties is to advance the cause of human rights without undermining the settlement itself and to foster institutional mechanisms that will advance human rights and democratic development once the political situation has stabilized. Third parties can play a critical role in investigating human rights abuses and other war crimes and in evaluating evidence collected by local authorities before arrests are made. In the fragile political climate that prevails following agreement on a settlement, the temptation to exact retribution and revenge is considerable. International tribunals and commissions bring the element of impartiality necessary to restore faith in the judicial process and the rule of law.[11]

It is easy to see that such pragmatism could lead to oversight of core issues, and that the human security discourse may mean that certain actors feel that they have little to lose by renewing conflict. Yet in the interests of 'effectiveness' and being able to close a chapter, oversights of human rights and justice have frequently been accepted – ironically, as they are often responsible for the breakdown of peace settlements.

Yet Hampson is right to point out on the basis of his work on the cases of Cyprus, Namibia, Angola, El Salvador, and Cambodia that,

> third parties need other third parties if they are to work efficiently and effectively in nurturing the conditions for peace. No single third party alone had the resources or leverage to make the peace process work. In those settlements that . . . succeed, many different laborers tilled the soil so that the peace process could bear fruit. The United Nations required the backing of great powers. Great powers needed the local support of a country's neighbors. Regional actors and groups needed the assistance of sub-regional groups. Governments and international organizations also required the active assistance and involvement of non-governmental organizations and agencies, particularly during implementation of the agreement.[12]

However, pragmatism and the desire to see external involvement in conflicts finally 'ended' often mean that third parties withdraw at certain points. While third generation approaches have begun to respond to the need for sustainable solutions, and have intimated that parties should not withdraw until their role or task had been taken over by a local actor capable of long-term commitment, and peacebuilding processes have become institutionalized as part of the environment, it is apparent that if the peacebuilding process seeks to rebuild exclusionary structures and institutions the long-term sustainability of solutions arising from such processes in the context of the Westphalian state system must be suspect. One of the reasons for this is the link between territory and sovereignty in the imagination of disputants vis-à-vis conflict settlement – a link which is promoted by the Westphalian international system and is in need of rethinking. It is also a serious weakness in traditional thought that ends and beginnings of conflict provide a mythical embarkation and disembarkation point for peace processes.

If a universally acceptable normative and operational framework is not mutually agreed through which mediation between political communities can occur in order to maintain a mutual order, it is clear that the implications of third generation approaches could be construed, because of their increasingly interventionary nature, as leading into a new form of trusteeship system in which IOs, ROs and states stake claims over 'failed states' or regions which are victims of intractable conflict.[13] We need in contrast to move towards an approach to ending conflict which gives authority to groups and communities, as well as the more traditional actors, within a mutually acceptable and sustainable framework that incorporates the intersubjective issues contained with the human security discourse, as well as political and economic interests. This implies a radical overhaul of the international system, that international law must resolve the tension between self-determination and positivist versions of sovereignty (which could be achieved by recognizing multiple claims to sovereignty and legitimacy),[14] and that the link between ending conflict and creating order be more fully explored. Initially, it can be concluded that the only way to avoid UN peace operations being seen as a totalizing practice is, in the short term at least, to recognize the continuing significance of the concept of consent from a majority of directly and indirectly related disputants, covering the local, regional and global environment.[15] Mutual consent-building, at the military, diplomatic and civilian levels across the broader environment should therefore play a significant role in the conduct of peacekeeping and peacemaking, conflict resolution and transformation activities, and in multidimensional peace operations even if they do involve interventionary practices. This may seem to be a step back to the inadequacies of third generation approaches. However, rather than constructing consent within a state security framework, I argue that it should be built up within a human security framework, which includes non-official actors, humanitarian relief, democratization, military, political and social functions.

The criticism levelled here at third generation approaches may open an avenue for the exploration of a fourth generation of approaches to ending conflict which are based on a general normative consensus about what the basis of activities should be, therefore finding local, regional and global commitment, both normatively and in terms of the requisite resources for success. Clearly, such approaches should aim at a just distribution of political, social, and economic resources, operate in a non-exclusionary manner, and export institutions, structures and norms that are welcomed and required by recipients.

Approaches to ending conflict tend to be presented as ways of doing good, but what they are doing more specifically is trying to provide continuity for an international system and an order which has proved not be self-sustaining without the exploitation of coercive practices and therefore lacks sustainability and continuity by itself. Approaches to ending conflict have developed into methods of supporting an order of negative peace rather than positive peace, and this is clear when one takes a more nuanced view which does not assume that the study of ways of ending conflict are merely about method, but are also about its underlying epistemology and ontology. The general assumption that these three generations of approaches to conflict result in a positive peace hides the discontinuity of the international system, particularly in its treatment of peace for non-state actors, ethnic and identity claims, and human security issues.

As with previous approaches, third generation approaches still depend upon containing violent conflict with a regime of truth in which the balance between management and resolution, it is claimed, has shifted towards the resolution of conflict through human security discourses. However, such approaches still tend to be acultural, give rise to the possibility of intervention without consent, based on western models of neo-liberal democratization and human rights as universally prescriptive. This means that a basis for the development beyond such tendencies needs to be examined.

Sensitizing approaches to ending conflict: some proposals for a fourth generation approach

Si vis pacem, para pacem.[16]

The redefinition of approaches to ending conflict is highly contentious, given that any form of involvement must impact upon 'others' and therefore runs the risk of political, economic, social and cultural imposition. Any framework that offers a universal basis for intervention to end conflict therefore runs the risk of having its assumptions used against it by recipients who may be extremely sensitive to the risk of hegemonic practices being imposed upon them to create an external version of 'order' installed upon their 'disorder'.

One strong contender for sensitizing forms of intervention can be found at a theoretical level in the context of the development of an anti-hegemonic, post-Westphalian international society that is able to allow for regional and local pluralism, reaches into all the ethnic corners and states of the world, yet can make a valid claim to a normative basis which is universal without impinging upon social, ethnic, cultural or religious differences.[17] This objective might usefully be made a focal point to critique existing approaches to conflict, along with the deconstruction of local stereotypes that contribute to ethno-politics and insecurity, and the elevation of human security issues and objectives within peace processes. The protection of local distinctiveness must be also part of this system, as long as it is not exclusionary and hegemonic itself. This also requires that approaches to ending conflict are harmonized with projects to rebuild civil societies, related to infrastructure, education and history, and democratization as well as with its local, regional and global, structural, political, economic, social and cultural dynamics. Thus, making peace becomes in this context a trans-state, substate, regional and global activity. In this way the next generation of activity may become part of the fabric of communities engaged in resolving conflict at all levels upon an acceptable and negotiated local and global normative basis, rather than a process of debatable impact or coercive and imposed practices that may reproduce the very conflicts that are being addressed.

The above depiction of the possible post-Westphalian development of approaches to ending conflict processes is dependent upon the elevation of normative issues within our understanding of peace and conflict, and therefore on the role of individuals as perceived as a non-passive part of the development of a fabric of peacebuilding, but without creating a top-down, centralist model that lacks legitimacy at many of the levels of the international system at which international social conflict occurs. In the contemporary environment, the consequences of globalization may both fragment national cultures, and create an impetus for and against a more cosmopolitan culture overall:

> The social bond which unites citizens and divides them from other societies is further weakened by the challenge to a dominant theme in the ideology of state-building namely national-assimilationism. Sub-national groups and indigenous peoples spearhead the politics of identity in which dominant conceptions of national community are challenged and the recognition of group rights is demanded. For these reactions the immanent possibility of new forms of political community has become apparent – a possibility which neo-realism blinkered by the immutability thesis cannot explore. New conceptions of citizenship, community and sovereignty are invited by these changes, and new constructions of community are beginning to appear.[18]

This critical position indicates a radical change in approaches to conflict. Neufeld argues,

> Inevitably, a critical theory of international politics which is committed to working for human emancipation will, virtually by

definition, come into conflict with 'certain vested interests – intellectual, political, economic, social in general'. Even so, there is no alternative. If International Relations theory is to remain 'true to its moral commitment', the restructuring process now underway must be brought to its 'subversive and revolutionary' conclusion. It is only in this way that the discipline of International Relations can hope to make a meaningful contribution to the 'Aristotelian project' of the leading of a good and just life' in our global polis.[19]

Linklater takes the position that all dialogue must incorporate an engagement with the 'other'. In the context of first generation approaches, difference is regarded as a negative factor to be reduced as much as possible by strategy of the hegemonic 'winner', which is ultimately to create a smooth-running system that operates in its favour and reifies and legitimizes the existing order.[20] But, in the context of discourse ethics, the restrictions of sovereignty vis-à-vis the capacity of outsiders to participate in decision-making about issues which concern them is underlined; in the case of first generation approaches, such capacities were regulated by the notion of power, position and citizenship, while second generation approaches attempted to incorporate the 'other' into the process (though 'subjective' issues were dealt with by the sociobiological, and supposedly scientific, human needs framework which carries undertones of social engineering). A clear division existed between first and second track diplomacy in which Track I supposedly had little direct consequence for Track II, thus protecting the interests of first generation actors from the broader issues raised by the presence of non-state actors in conflicts. However, a third generation of activity in which all activities take place in parallel, forming an integrated global, regional, and local fabric of peacebuilding has important implications here: it implies that sovereignty has undergone a metamorphosis, and that intervention in the form of peacemaking and peacekeeping may not require consent. Allegations that this may constitute neo-colonialism in which great powers take the responsibility for the administration of war-torn states and regions are, however, plausible as this implies that there is a universal basis for such activities, which is some cases might necessarily be imposed, as was seen in the case of Somalia. It is this universal basis that needs to be rethought if approaches to ending conflict are not to reify its roots, and sensitized to the needs of identity claims, and to the scarcity of resources such as territory and the environment – and of course, in terms of justice. So far, cosmopolitan approaches to international society seem to offer the most promising way forward, if a universal normative basis can be agreed. Here it is pertinent to examine further Linklater's contribution to the discussion of political community.

Linklater argues that the critical enterprise carries two main implications. The first is the reconstruction of the state and the international states-system to allow the development of universality. The second is the transformation of exclusionary political communities so that respect for cultural differences can replace totalizing projects.[21] This has important implications for approaches to making peace in that it shows that the 'order' envisaged (i.e. the reconstituting of states and the international system) needs to be rethought. Following on from the rethinking of the objectives of making peace on a structural level, its normative basis needs to be developed in order for it to aid in the development of non-exclusionary political communities. In other words, approaches to making peace must not make the mistake of contributing to a totalizing project. First generation approaches can do little more than support the existing system of territorial-sovereign states through diplomatic and military channels; third generation approaches continue this project though they are also concerned with human security issues, curtailed, however, by the territorial limits of the existing state system and precedent therein. The failure of attempts for third generation approaches to move beyond this in the early 1990s underlined their redundancy in reconstituting a failing version of the international system, and the need for a new understanding of 'order' to become the basic goal of approaches to ending conflict. This does not mean that there does not exist a universal basis for approaches to ending conflict to rest upon. As Linklater points out, an elementary, transcendent universalism underpins international society, preventing crude forms of domination in the international system – he provides the examples of the cultural revolt against westernism, the development and independence of former colonies, the delegitimation of racial theories of supremacy, to illustrate the development of a cosmopolitan morality.[22] This new form of universality, however, needs to move beyond the western tendency to use its own version of universality to justify its actions – something which has notably marred its official and unofficial diplomacy, mediation and negotiation, and often UN peace operations. The ethical foundations of political community are under scrutiny as we move towards a post-Westphalian order[23]: making and maintaining peace is a process of re-establishing and maintaining order and this is why its development is so vital – and so problematic if the 'order' that it is bent on establishing and supporting is redundant. Approaches to ending conflict therefore should be seen as contributing to a dialogic order of post-national communities, sensitised to the needs of the systematically excluded.[24] It should enable communities in conflict to progress from an exclusionary position to a universal position on which to build the political, social and economic frameworks for mutual coexistence. This universal position needs to be democratically arrived at, and thus requires a level of democracy in the international system. While this is lacking, approaches ending conflict will be more contested than is necessary.

These cosmopolitan approaches as described in the work of Linklater, though Habermasian discourse ethics and the formation of dialogic communities, provides an important critique here. Habermasian 'communicative reason' is derived from a number of norms that govern political and moral action. For authentic public discourse communicative action should be free from deception, self-deception, power and domination, and any actor who can make a universally defensible proposition should be free to do so. Linklater develops this into his cosmopolitan theory which combines justification and application in a universalism mediated through social processes. Thus, a post-Westphalian order has to honour obligations to 'other' communities even though they may not share its principles of association, in order to strike a balance between the universal and the different. Approaches to making peace could therefore concentrate on introducing, maintaining and enhancing a cosmopolitan communicative ethic.

Fetherston has also made an important contribution to this debate. She argues that objective ways of knowing, uncontaminated by subjectivities, produce totalizing practices within modernity.[25] She argues that peacekeeping and conflict resolution, as consent-based activities, have a symbiosis which can be realized in peacebuilding if such totalizing practices and understanding can be overcome.[26] However, as she points out, most approaches fail to move beyond the debates of modernity in their endeavour to reflect the complexity and diversity of 'the cultures of violence of the social spaces within which these operations take place...' – in war zones.[27] Thus it is crucial to differentiate between emancipation and transformation within modernity – how it constrained debates about peacekeeping, peacemaking and conflict resolution, and to a large extent, peacebuilding – and beyond modernity, which offers a more reflexive social and cultural understanding of conflict and attempts to end it.[28] These critiques are crucial as they underline the fact that the impact of three generations of approaches to conflict have revolved around correction and normalization, and illustrate the need to reformulate approaches to ending conflict, if they are to aid the creation of a positive and sustainable peace.

This raises the question of how multidimensional approaches can avoid the imposition of universalist norms on marginalized actors struggling for human security in the post-Westphalian environment.[29] Though these approaches have opened up a pathway into an understanding of the human security and bottom-up potential of third generation approaches, they have tended to return the emphasis, via their overall contribution to overall high-level peace processes, to mainstream diplomatic discourse which may result in obscuring the impact of multidimensional processes by reproducing zero-sum high-level politics within social groupings. This paradox requires serious attention if the reproducing binaries of mainstream politics are not to reproduce themselves at the civil level, despite peacebuilding processes. Little has been done so far to incorporate intersubjective critiques of the realist and (neo)liberal framework of sovereignty, territory, law, order, justice and history into a discourse which is not hegemonic, and does not marginalize or impose itself.[30] However, this is not to say that the non-state institutions of civil society do not produce the same totalizing and hegemonic discourses, because individual groups also pursue resources and power in the sociopolitical and economic sectors in which they are constituted. This requires that internal civil society practices, associated with the economy, religion and culture, are also addressed in peacebuilding processes. In the Habermasian post-conventional morality of dialogic community, human security rather that state security in international society would be the focus of approaches to ending conflict.[31] The success of such processes would not just be measured in terms of comprehensive agreements but on the establishment of emancipatory discursive practices at the local, regional and global level that allow all actors meaningful exchanges which prevent the recourse to violence. I offer these ideas as criticisms, though it is important to note that I recognize the inherent difficulty of achieving this type of exchange in an environment in which the vast scale of conflict, the scarce resources applied, and the units delineated, provide a stark choice between the relativist trap of doing nothing or else universalizing intervention, and every intervention is experimental and riven by political interests and economic constraints.

Critical approaches to making peace locate first generation approaches in a language/practice engaged in defending an international order – rather than as a normative and emancipatory project to overcome the binaries that power discourses produce. The emergence of

NGOs (and a global civil society) is important here as their activities focus on monitoring and humanitarian activities in the dual context of the local and the global, though not without sometimes chaotic overlap and self-interest. The power politics discourse sees making peace as a way of imposing order by powerful actors to protect the status quo and their own interests. Realists argue that order must be imposed by powerful actors, to protect themselves and their allies, and approaches to making peace reify the order they intend to project. The liberal and neo-liberal addition acknowledges that legitimacy is crucial and that international organizations and economic interests can play an important role by propagating powerful actors' interests (often dressed up as universal norms or economic structures and needs). Critical approaches may help sensitize the practice of ending conflict and peacebuilding to the pitfalls of hegemonic or neo-imperialist discourses, offer the possibility that there can be a viable universalist normative discourse for collective security arrangements and for international and regional organizations to retain their claims to legitimacy, which after all rest on their claim to be representative of an increasing diversity of actors. More radical postmodern critiques, however, would argue that even this presents the danger of marginalizing certain actors, and by implication they offer little room for international organizations to develop their peace apparatus according to their claims to represent universal norms.

As has been argued, there is an element of a totalizing project within Linklater's claims:

> The language of rights as foundational enables the argument to be made for eradicating social practices and inegalitarian norms, not in terms of their intrinsic unpleasantness, but in terms which manifest themselves as somehow *neutral* . . . It is to make this a reality that the activities of the myriad of NGOs and other transnational coalitions of moral activists are directed.[32]

The argument that Linklater's attempt to establish a universal communication community clashes with existing social and cultural norms[33] underlines the main dilemma of such approaches which in calling for universal inclusion also need to set normative standards for candidates to qualify for inclusion. This also clearly applies to approaches to ending conflict and to peacebuilding, which in its function of maintaining and developing 'order' in an international society must tread warily between imposing and judging, and respecting the equal rights of other communities and social, political and culture norms and processes. Indeed the historical practice of making peace would seem to suggest that this cannot be achieved and therefore that it is an inherently flawed approach to the ills of a problematic system.

How can all this help in developing the practice of ending conflict and peacebuilding? There is a clear need to re-examine the objectives of peace processes in the long term – what kind of order should be produced, negotiated by whom and on what basis, and can the political, social, and economic issues of the conflict be resolved? In what way does the long-term order envisaged by all those involved in the conflict help or hinder its short-term progress from violence to negotiation to settlement? Clearly the Westphalian order, as I have sought to illustrate, produces continuities and discontinuities that are problematic in the sustainable resolution of conflict. This might not be the case if a post-Westphalian, dialogic order were to be the long-term framework in which ending conflict and peacebuilding were achieved.

Seen in this light, the three generations of approaches I have outlined show clear linear development, as well as the potential of coexistence as competing research programmes. However, all three approaches also show clear signs of degeneration. First generation approaches remain significant because of the continuing dominance of the state in so many areas, though their operation has become increasingly problematic with the reduction of state influence in many other areas. Second generation approaches have contributed the recognition of individuals, structural violence, humanitarianism and democratization, and their human security concerns, though the scientific claims, and the claim that such approaches are unaffected by state interests are suspect. Third generation approaches have not yet managed to jettison the restrictive and reifying practices of first generation approaches, and have uncritically incorporated the human needs and human security frameworks of second generation approaches. They have raised the political, economic and normative spectres that lie behind grand universal claims to know truth and justice. It is clear that third generation approaches, while offering some hope of facilitating the development of non-exclusionary political communities, also do much to reinforce the exclusionary positions and structures that communities in conflict have adopted. However, much of what already occurs during the third-generation-type processes outlined in Chapter 5 could in fact be sensitized to these needs. What seems to be occurring is that separate activities are being coordinated by an emerging normative human security discourse, in which a variety of actors at different levels and with different mandates turn their attention to different aspects of the same conflict – the global, regional, and local political aspects, as well as its political, social, humanitarian, economic and legal aspects – and are addressing it according to a common normative system revolving around human security. This is implicit, but not direct, and is weakened by the strength of traditional debates about security dilemmas, territorial sovereignty and identity, which as the practice of making peace in the 1990s showed, has made the process highly problematic. But there is an increasing recognition that such debates are inconclusive and unhelpful.

Thus, the charge of neo-colonialism could be answered by the fact that global civil society, a mass of unstructured relationships with a common normative basis, and international society are playing a role in producing a plethora of separate activities aimed at a similar cooperative objective. It is the strengthening of the normative foundations for such activities that is required, and these are arising out of the cobwebs of local, regional and global transactions, interdependencies and organizations. Thus, multidimensional activities may effectively coordinate themselves. While this may be seen to be 'inefficient' it cannot be described as neo-colonial – although the more 'efficient' it becomes, the more the danger of this. The main concern is for outside actors to ensure that all the different levels of the conflict are addressed and that internal actors express their needs and interests, and to prevent spoiling activities where certain direct and indirect actors attempt to prevent different levels of a conflict from actually being addressed by a diversity of actors and organizations. Indications of the latter are a clear sign of obstruction, and have occurred in many of the examples cited in this book. The problem is that the type of order that arises from the application of third generation approaches may not deliver the kind of sensitivity and reflexivity that a post-Westphalian international society would require.

Conclusion

Peacemaking and peacekeeping within the Westphalian system tend to replicate the flaws of that system, particularly if the conflict under scrutiny in some way undermines the conceptual unity of the states-system. Conflict resolution and transformation approaches tend to be constrained by the prevalence of official discourses and by a tendency toward social construction. Third generation approaches as seen after the end of the cold war have failed to move away from such problems and have ultimately continued to be 'normalizing' activities within the exclusive context of territorial sovereignty and state-centricity, though increasingly attention has turned to the sustainability of peace endeavours. This means that third generation approaches are victims of similar problems to the previous generation approaches, something that sits uncomfortably with the 'new ideology' of human security.

Making peace in the international system cannot be examined without some kind of parallel examination of that system. In other words, the international system needs to be conceptualized in order to understand how a peace regime in the context of a normative rather than strategic framework of making peace could be established. This requires that the reproduction of order around which peace processes effectively revolve could be based upon a core system of values, identities, resources and objectives that are themselves sustainable. First generation approaches clearly failed to achieve this; second generation approaches have contributed to this attempt and the development of third generation approaches have endeavoured to do so, but generally have failed to move far from the exclusionary normative, political, social, economic or cultural systems which mar international societies' various cartographies. If approaches to making peace could be sensitized to these requirements, the norm of 'peace' in a Kantian sense of peace with justice, which has been subverted by the Westphalian status quo framework of peace without justice, might remerge as a practical framework.

Traditional diplomacy and the norms of intervention were established with an eye to the realist nature of the international system from the Treaty of Westphalia, lasting until the end of the cold war. Because the post-cold war international system and conflict therein is fundamentally different from that of the previous era, approaches to ending conflict need to be re-examined and reformulated and this is what I have tried to accomplish in this study. The opportunity for new approaches to deal with 'intractable' and non-state conflicts, issues and actors, is now more necessary than ever, given the challenge that non-state conflicts are mounting against the traditional notions of the international system; thus conflict theory itself needs to be reconceptualized as our understanding of the makeup and interrelationships of political community is being rethought. Clearly the normative and strategic tensions that underlie the contemporary practices of ending conflict are pushing it into an either/or situation where intervention either occurs as in Kosovo in 1999, or nothing occurs, as in Rwanda in 1994. This is indicative of the problems the international system itself faces in an era in which injustices are increasingly uncovered, even if they have been shielded by decades or more of state-interest based practice and sovereign assumptions. Both the problems of the increasingly interventionary nature of many types of approaches to making peace, and their absence, need to be discussed within the framework of an acceptable universal and sustainable framework for all actors and issue-areas, without reconstituting claims to sovereignty and statehood as third generation approaches have tended to do. Making peace should be not about the normalization of recalcitrants within the Westphalian state-system. Third generation approaches have moved into the realms of broad human security concerns, but the strain that this has put upon the states-system and the UN in particular has underlined the unsustainability of the current framework, which is interest-oriented more than value-oriented.

Through the critical and cosmopolitan impetus to rethink political communities and to move away from the binaries created by sovereignty and assimilatative states, as well as the increasing awareness of the structural discrimination endemic in the areas of the global economy and local identity, it may well be plausible to create universal frameworks for the conduct of multidimensional approaches to ending conflict, as traditional approaches to diplomacy attempted via Chapter VI of the UN Charter. The modifications provided by *Agenda for Peace* underline this possibility. But this does not mean that local norms and culture have to be subverted or supplanted. By recognizing the intersubjective nature of conflict and its vast and multilevel, social, political, economic, ethnic and cultural implications at local, regional and global levels, and by agreeing on some basic universal normative positions, it may well be possible to see the future of conflict resolution as a vast web of multifarious actors operating upon this framework rather than thoughtlessly imposing their own local norms and objectives in the guise of conflict management, resolution, preventive diplomacy or peacebuilding. In this way, approaches to conflict become sensitized to local conditions and to the need for broad sustainability. Successful conflict resolution in the post-cold war era entails the reform of the international system and the establishment of a permanent, preventive fabric of peacemaking and peacebuilding at local, regional and global levels, through the opening of sufficient space for a diversity of actors to gain access to address the multiple roots of conflict in a culturally sensitive manner, but in a broader normative framework beyond that which the Westphalian system formerly enabled. The final dilemma still remains, however. Approaches to ending conflict which create or restore an order that is even broadly agreed implies an universal normative framework and therefore is open to being characterized by some politicized actors and entrepreneurs open to the use of political violence, as a totalizing project. The 'coming anarchy'[34] could be caused by the employing of ever more extreme forms of violence by the few. This is why the way in which approaches to ending conflict are applied should result in inclusive and broadly sustainable societies rather than enclosed and artificial structures with little local, or contested global, legitimacy.

Notes

Introduction

1 Linklater has noted that a post-Westphalian order, which he frames as dialogic, overcomes the obstruction that sovereignty, territoriality and citizenship has created for this 'universal communication community' – which has important implications, I argue, for the practice of ending conflict. See Andrew Linklater, *The Transformation of Political Community*, University of South Carolina Press, 1998, p.168.

2 A clear tyranny of definitions appears to exist vis-à-vis the extant terminology in the field of conflict resolution and peacemaking. In this book I tend to use the phrases 'making peace' and 'ending conflict' synonymously as generic terms. During the cold war, peacekeeping and peacemaking were clearly differentiated. It must be borne in mind that in dealing with post-cold war approaches, Boutros-Ghali has set out a loose definitional framework including preventive diplomacy, peacemaking, peacekeeping/enforcement, and peacebuilding, though this approach has its limitations. See *Agenda for Peace, A/47/277–S/24111*, 17 June 1992, paras 21 and 57. For the purposes of this project the term 'conflict resolution' is used henceforth to describe 'citizen diplomacy', 'problem-solving workshops' and transformation approaches that have as their objective self-sustaining solutions, as opposed to traditional forms of third-party mediation at the diplomatic level of international relations, which have as their objective settlements based on a balance of power.

3 For an excellent discussion of this see Mary Kaldor, *New and Old Wars: Organised Violence in a Global Era*, Cambridge: Polity Press, 1999.

4 Azar coined the phrase 'protracted social conflict'. See, Edward E. Azar, *The Management of Protracted Social Conflict*, Aldershot: Dartmouth Publishing, 1990.

5 See, Louis Kriesberg, Terrell A. Northrup, Stuart J. Thorson (eds), *Intractable Conflicts and Their Transformation*, Syracuse, NY, Syracuse University Press, 1989.

6 See John Burton, *Resolving Deep Rooted Conflict: A Handbook*, Lanham, MD: University Press of America, 1987.

7 *SIPRI-UNESCO Handbook, Peace, Security, and Conflict Prevention*, OUP, 1998, p. 18.

8 See, for example the well-known argument of Benedict Anderson, *Imagined Communities: Reflections of the Origins and Spread of Nationalism*. Ithaca, NY: Cornell University Press, 1991. Susan Strange has described this as the 'Westfailure System'. See Susan Strange, 'The Westfailure System', *Review of International Studies*, vol. 25, 1999, pp. 345–54.

9 By 'monodimensional' I mean efforts that concentrate mainly on one aspect/level of analysis in the international system. I develop the idea in Chapter 2 that such activities are essentially monodimensional, as mediation, for example, is conceptually chained to the legal, state-centric notions of the

international system, which consequently means that it has great difficulty in operating at other levels.

10 Several models have been used to break down conflict environments, notably Suganami's 'levels of-causation' model in his analysis of causes of war, and Ramsbotham and Woodhouse's 'dimensions-of-conflict' approach, which distinguishes structural, relational and cultural features. Here, I follow Miall, Woodhouse and Ramsbotham's usage of an 'adapted levels-of-analysis' approach in my critical approach 'as it lays bare the complex and controversial relationships between international, state and societal sources of conflict, all of which are prominent in the recent literature and none of which is reducible to the others' in the context of the 'international social conflict' framework. See Hugh Miall, Oliver Ramsbotham and Tom Woodhouse, *Contemporary Conflict Resolution*, Polity Press, 1999, pp. 77–8; See also H. Suganami, *On The Causes of War*, Oxford: Clarendon Press, 1996; Oliver Ramsbotham, and Tom Woodhouse, *Humanitarian Intervention in Contemporary Conflict*, Cambridge, Polity Press, 1996, p. 87.

11 See Oliver P. Richmond, 'Devious Objectives and the Disputants' View of International Mediation: A Theoretical Framework', *Journal of Peace Research*, vol. 35, no. 6, 1998. For a detailed discussion of the Cyprus case as a specific example of this see also, Oliver P. Richmond, *Mediating in Cyprus: The Cypriot Communities and the UN*, London: Frank Cass, 1998.

12 The exploration of how the international system provides for ethnic security and what pressures are constituted by the relationship between identity/ethnic security and the international system forms an important aspect of contemporary international relations. The securitization of identity has been explored by the Copenhagen School. Barry Buzan and Ole Waever's notion that identity is a crucial part of the way that perceptions of security at the societal level influence the operation of the international system is key. See Barry Buzan and Ole Waever, 'Slippery, Contradictory? Sociologically Untenable: The Copenhagen School Replies', *Review of International Studies*, vol. 23, 1997.

13 Kenneth Waltz, 'The Emerging Structure of International Politics', *International Security*, vol. 18., no. 2, 1993, pp. 44–5. Waltz argued that 'peace' prevailed at the centre of the international system and that the cold war bipolar system had demonstrated its structural durability through its ability to survive major wars.

14 It must be pointed out that the term 'citizen' tends to be used in its state context by conflict resolutionists.

15 I differentiate between conflict management (using techniques of mediation and negotiation with some reference to international law and norms in order to arrive at a solution based on a rearrangement of resources and mutual concessions, rather than justice), and conflict resolution (in which a win-win situation is arrived at which also contributes a modicum of justice according to humanitarian norms). This is a fairly standard differentiation, though there often does seem to be some confusion in the literature between management and resolution with the two key terms often being used interchangeable (particularly by diplomats and officials.)

16 See the case on the UN force in Cyprus, for example, where UNFICYP has succeeded in reducing violent incidents but has become almost an institution of division rather than promoting a settlement.

17   These issues are examined in Oliver P. Richmond, 'Devious Objectives and the Disputants' View of International Mediation: A Theoretical Framework', op. cit., pp. 720–1.

18   For a discussion of how this pertains to making peace, see Fen Osler Hampson, 'Third Party Roles in the Termination of Intercommunal Conflict', *Millennium*, vol. 26, no. 3, 1997, pp. 727–40.

19   See Nayef H. Samhat, 'International Regimes as Political Community', *Millennium*, vol. 26, no. 2, 1997, pp. 362–3. 'In describing the characteristics of an international regime that redefine the boundary of political community in a manner consistent with the themes of interpretation and emancipation, three qualities are apparent: (1) the commitment to ethical norms and principles (2) the activation and legitimation of actors other than states at a variety of levels of social activity, and (3) universal membership. In each case, the mode in which local and global actors conduct politics and the ends they seek are oriented towards a convergence through dialogue and discourse – as opposed to an imposition by dominant participants in this process – of shared moral principles that promote the well-being and security of humanity.'

20   Here I concur with Clark's recent argument that the state occupies a middle ground between the internal and the external, and is moulded by, as well as shaping, the process of globalization. See Ian Clark, 'Beyond the Great Divide: globalization and the theory of international relations', *Review of International Studies*, vol. 24, 1998, p. 479.

21   This point draws on Hedley Bull's argument about discussion of the existence of an international society, despite the tendencies of states to follow their own national interests. Hedley Bull, *The Anarchical Society: A Study of Order in World Politics*, London; Macmillan Press – now Palgrave, 1977.

22   It is important to note that discourse at the official level about substate forms of conflict tends to be framed in the language of traditional diplomacy in its realist, neo-realist, or liberal terms.

23   See, for example, David Held, *Democracy and the Global Order*, Cambridge; Polity Press, 1995.

24   Chopra counters the accusation of neo-colonialism by arguing that in instances of 'peace-maintenance' style models, resources are channelled into the local environment rather than removed. This is an important observation though it does not take into account the normal quid pro quo of conditions attached to the inflow of resources and the normative and practical expectations which are attached. However, his objective is the establishment of sustainable governing capabilities that seek not to impose an alien system. Op. cit., pp. 353–4.

25   Tarya Vayrynen, 'Ethnopolitical Meaning in Global Conjunctions: Performative Politics', paper presented at the *Third Pan-European International Relations Conference*, Vienna, 16–19 Sept. 1998, pp. 2–3.

26   This study exploits the debate which has taken place in IR over the nature of its theoretical dimensions. The so-called interparadigm debate exploited the work of Popper, Kuhn and Lakatos, in order to more fully understand the nature of the theoretical debates and frameworks extant in IR. It appears to this author that it would be profitable to apply a similar methodological framework of evaluation and re-evaluation to the development of theory in

the subfield relating to peace in the Westphalian state-centric context. I do not want to indicate that the typology which I put forward in this study, that of grouping approaches to ending conflict into three 'generations', indicates that each generation is incommensurable, or that one runs out of theoretical steam, to be replaced by another soon after. I want to show, that like Lakatos' work on research programmes which are progressive or degenerative, the same is currently true of approaches to making peace. They exist simultaneously, are interconnected and dependent on the nature of the contemporary international environment: they are indeed progressive or degenerative. It seems that classic forms of peacekeeping, international mediation, and conflict resolution, are degenerative when taken separately, in that they cannot alone provide remedies for conflict. The question becomes one of whether there is a synthesis which might replace them. This possibility is examined in the context of third generation approaches and an emerging post-Westphalian perspective which engenders a critical perspective of peace and order. T. S. Kuhn, *The Structure of Scientific Revolutions*, University of Chicago Press, 1970; I. Lakatos, 'Falsification and the Methodology of Scientific Research Programmes' in I. Lakatos and A. Musgrave, *Criticism and the Growth of Knowledge*, Cambridge University Press, 1970, pp. 91–195.; K. P. Popper, *Conjectures and Refutations*, London; Routledge, 1989.

Chapter 1   Order, Security and Conflict in a Changing Global Environment

1 It is important to note that this is a somewhat arbitrary distinction; it is used for the purposes of this book, however, to show how a general shift has occurred in the context of the global shift that the end of the cold war created in providing impetus for a new landscape in world politics. For a critique of the cold war/ post-cold war distinction, see Michael Cox, Ken Booth and Tim Dunne, 'Introduction: the Interregnum: Controversies in World Politics, 1989–1999', *Review of International Studies*, special issue, vol. 25, December 1999, p. 3.; See also Richard Ned Lebow, 'The Rise and Fall of the Cold War in Comparative Perspective', Ibid., p. 21. He argues that the 'end' spanned a process of accommodation lasting for several decades. Chris Brown argues that the cold war was constituted by deep divisions over 'the organisation and content of political, economic and social life at all levels'. Chris Brown, 'History Ends, Worlds Collide', ibid., p. 41. This is partly why I have settled on the Westphalian/post-Westphalian distinction.

2 At the end of every systemic war there has been an attempt to create an institutional framework to prolong order and stability since the Treaty of Westphalia in 1648; yet nothing like this has yet emerged since the end of the cold war, in part because of the politicization of the expansion of the UN Security Council.

3 For a discussion of this 'new' concept, see UNDP, *Human Development Report*, Oxford University Press, 1994.

4 Danilo Zolo, *Cosmopolis: Prospects for World Government*, Cambridge: Polity Press, 1997, p. 1. Zolo describes this order as the 'cosmopolitan model of the Holy Alliance', which depends upon a highly centralized locus of power which

controls the use of force, freezing the status quo in the interests of great powers and their predominant ideology and philosophy. Ibid., pp. 12–13.

5 Ibid., p. 15.

6 Max Singer and Aaron Wildavsky, *The Real World Order*, Chatham House Publishers: New Jersey, 1993, p. 3. Singer and Wildavsky divide the world up into zones of peace and turmoil; in the latter zone stability is a 'meaningless goal', this being a classic example of the problematic analyses that Realist assumptions often produce. Ibid., p. 9.

7 For an excellent account of nationalism, and in particular the contemporary form of ethnonationalism see Walker Conner, *Ethnonationalism: The Quest for Understanding*, Princeton University Press, 1994.

8 Ian Brownlie, *Principles of Public International Law*, Oxford: Clarendon Press, 1990, pp. 64–5.

9 See *Articles 31–117, The Peace Treaty of Versailles*, 28 June, 1919.

10 See *Covenant of the League of Nations*.

11 For an important first-hand account of this see Harold Nicolson, *Peacemaking 1919*, Boston: Houghton Mifflin, 1933.

12 Cecelia Lynch, 'The Promise and Problems of Internationalism', in *Global Governance*, vol. 5, no. 1, 1999, pp. 88–9.

13 See Nicolas White, *Keeping the Peace*, Manchester University Press, 1997, p. 4. White argues that although 'the Covenant of the League of Nations did contain innovative provisions for collective security and provided for the imposition of embargoes and possibly collective military sanctions against offending States, the League was doomed to failure because sovereign States continued to see national interests as paramount over collective interests despite the horror of the First World War, a situation exacerbated by the requirement in Article 5 of the Covenant of unanimity for most substantive decisions of the Council or Assembly of the League.'

14 Christopher Clapham, 'Degrees of Statehood', in *Review of International Studies*, vol. 24, 1998. See also Robert H. Jackson, *Quasi-states: Sovereignty, International Relations and the Third World*, Cambridge University Press, 1990, p. 150.

15 See, for example, *The Declaration on the Granting of Independence to Colonial Countries and Peoples*, UN General Assembly resolution 1514 (XV), 14 December 1960. 'All States shall observe faithfully and strictly the provisions of the Charter of the United Nations, the Universal Declaration of Human Rights and the present Declaration on the basis of equality, non-interference in the internal affairs of all States, and respect for the sovereign rights of all peoples and their territorial integrity'. Parts of UN resolution 1514 reveal the inherent dilemma faced by the General Assembly: '(2) All peoples have the right to self- determination . . . (4) All armed action or repressive measures of all kinds directed against dependent peoples shall cease in order to enable them to exercise peacefully and fully their right to complete independence . . . (6) Any attempt at the partial or total disruption of the national unity and territorial integrity of a country is incompatible with the purposes and principles of the Charter of the UN.'

16 This was to occur only once for each territory. This was somewhat contradictory in that separate self-determination for sub-territorial identity groups could not be exercised.

17   Christopher M. Ryan, 'Sovereignty, Intervention and the Law: A Tenuous Relationship of Competing Principles', *Millennium: Journal of International Studies*, vol. 26, no. 1, 1997, p. 77.

18   David Held, op. cit., pp. 83–5.

19   Ibid., pp. 77–86.

20   Between 1989 and 1996, 96 out of 105 conflicts have been internal. Most of those internal conflicts, 63 in fact, have been 'settled' through negotiations often with third-party assistance. See lecture by T. Sisk, 'Mediation and Negotiation Theory and Practice: Findings from USIP-Sponsored Research', Intercollege Nicosia, Cyprus, 27 January 1998. Sisk argued that this success rate is impressive compared to the rate of less than 20 per cent conflicts ending in negotiated settlements during the Cold War.

21   'Secretary-General's Annual Report to the General Assembly', UN Press Release 20 September 1999; For US President's speech to the General Assembly, see also Press Release GA/9599, 21 September 1999.

22   This section draws on, among others, the following key theoretical texts in the field of IR theory: H. Morganthau, *Politics Amongst Nations*, McGraw-Hill, 1948; E. H. Carr, *The Twenty Years Crisis*, Macmillan, 1966; K. Waltz, *Theory of International Politics*, Reading: MA, 1979; R. Keohane and J. Nye, *Transnational Relations and World Politics*, Cambridge, MA: Harvard University Press, 1972; J. Burton, *World Society*, Cambridge University Press, 1972; R. Gilpin, *War and Change in World Politics*, Cambridge University Press, 1981; C. Brown, *International Relations Theory*, Harvester Wheatsheaf, 1992; G. Modelski, *Long Cycles in World Politics*, Macmillan, 1987; I. Wallerstein, *Geopolitics and Geoculture*, Cambridge University Press, 1991. J. Galtung, 'A Structural Theory of Imperialism', *Journal of Peace Research*, vol. 13, no. 2, 1971.

23   David A. Baldwin, 'The Concept of Security', *Review of International Studies*, vol. 23, 1997, p. 12.

24   Arnold Wolfers, '"National Security" as an ambiguous symbol', *Political Science Quarterly*, vol. 67, 1952, p. 483.

25   Kenneth Waltz, op. cit., p. 126.

26   David A. Baldwin, op. cit., p. 10.

27   Kenneth Waltz, 'The Emerging Structure of International Politics', *International Security*, vol. 18, no. 2, 1993, p. 44.

28   Ibid., p. 45.

29   Ibid., p. 52.

30   Adam Roberts and Benedict Kingsbury, 'The United Nations and Changing World Politics', 'Introduction', in Adam Roberts and Benedict Kingsbury (eds), *United Nations, Divided World*, 2nd. edn, Oxford University Press, 1996, pp. 9–11.

31   For an interesting analysis, see John Baylis, 'European Security in the Post-Cold War Era: The Continuing Struggle between Realism and Utopianism', in *European Security*, vol. 7, no. 3, 1998, p. 16.

32   See David Mitrany, *A Working Peace System*, London: Royal Institute of International Affairs 1946.

33   See Karl Deutsch et al., *Political Community and the North Atlantic Area*, Princeton University Press, 1957. Deutsch based his notion on two categories of security community, the pluralistic in which states integrated at a level where war had become unthinkable, and amalgamated, in which states merged completely.

34   See, for example, A. J. R. Groom and Paul Taylor, *Frameworks for International Co-operation*, London: Pinter, 1990.

35   See Hedley Bull, *The Anarchical Society*, London; Macmillan – now Palgrave, 1977.

36   See, for example, the special issue of *Millennium* on ethics; *Millennium: Ethics and International Relations*, vol. 27, no. 3, 1998.

37   By this I mean that if one defines the limits of responsibility at states' borders, as does the traditional international system, this allows regional and global interests or imperatives to be overlooked. Yet it seems that the lesson that all great powers have had to learn has been that very often much broader interest will transcend the more parochial, state-centric imperatives.

38   J. Rosenau 1990, *Turbulence in World Politics: A Theory of Change and Continuity*, Princeton University Press, 1990, p. 10.

39   Hugh Miall, Oliver Ramsbotham and Tom Woodhouse, *Contemporary Conflict Resolution*, Cambridge: Polity Press, 1999, pp. 15–16.

40   Mary Kaldor, *New and Old Wars: Organised Violence in a Global Era*, Cambridge: Polity Press, 1999, p. 3.

41   See Nicolas Wheeler and Tim Dunne, 'Good international citizenship: a third way for British foreign policy' *International Affairs*, vol. 74, no. 4, 1998, p. 254. 'The problem traditionally has been that the dominant rules of membership-sovereignty and non-intervention have silenced the promotion of human rights abroad. The post-1945 world, however, has witnessed a sea-change in the principles of international legitimacy. Within liberal states, it has become increasingly difficult for state leaders to claim that human rights abroad are of no concern to them. On the other side of the same coin, it is no longer acceptable for states to claim that the way they treat their own citizens is excluded from international scrutiny or censure.'

42   See Nayef H. Samhat, 'International Regimes as Political Community, *Millennium*, vol. 26, no. 2, 1997, p. 377.

43   Nicolas Wheeler and Tim Dunne, op. cit., p. 254.

44   For a discussion of this characterization of the twentieth century political environment, see the recent special issue of the *Review of International Studies* entitled 'The Eighty Years Crisis', vol. 24, December 1998.

45   This point is supported by Christian Reus-Smit, 'The Constitutional Structure of International Society and the Nature of Fundamental Institutions, *International Organisation*, vol. 51, no. 4, 1997, p. 578.

46   Cecelia Lynch, op. cit., pp. 94–5.

47   For an illuminating discussion of what some view as the current transition to an 'international democratic polity', see David Held, *Democracy and the Global Order*, Cambridge: Polity Press, 1995, pp. 266–86. For a discussion of a future state-centric scenario of burgeoning conflict, see Samuel Huntington, *The Clash of Civilisations and the Remaking of World Order*, New York: Simon & Schuster, 1996, final chapter. For a discussion of the changing theoretical debates within International Relations Theory, see Andrew Linklater and John Macmillan (eds), *Boundaries in Question*, London: Pinter, 1995.

48   Mary Kaldor, op. cit., p. 5.

49   See Barry Buzan, 'Rethinking Security after the Cold War', *Cooperation and Conflict*, vol. 32, no. 1, 1997, pp. 5–28.

50   David Baldwin, op. cit., p. 20.

51 Andrew Linklater, *The Transformation of Political Community*, Cambridge: Polity Press, 1998, p. 74.
52 Ibid., p. 34.
53 According to SIPRI data, civil strife and ethic conflict far outweigh international conflict in the post Cold War era. *SIPRI-UNESCO Handbook, Peace, Security and Conflict Prevention*, Oxford University Press, 1998, pp. 13–25.
54 Pierre Hassner, 'Beyond Nationalism and Internationalism', in Michael E. Brown, (ed), *Ethnic Conflict and International Security*, Princeton, NJ: Princeton University Press, 1993, p. 129.
55 Paul Taylor, *International Organisation in the Modern World*, London: Pinter, 1993, p. 80.
56 See David Held, op. cit., pp. 269–79, for a discussion of the way reform of the UN can contribute to the future development of the international system.
57 David Held, ibid., p. 252.
58 Steven L. Burg, 'The International Community', in Esman, Milton and Telhami, Shirley (eds.): *International Organisations and Ethnic Conflict*, Ithaca: Cornell University Press, 1995, p. 267.
59 Adam Roberts and Benedict Kingsbury, op. cit., p. 8.
60 Emanuel Adler, 'Imagined Security Communities: Cognitive Regions in International Relations', *Millennium*, vol. 26, no. 2, 1997, p. 250.
61 Ibid., p. 250. Adler qualifies this by stating that the OSCE may not succeed in these aims across the whole region.
62 Ibid., pp. 269–72.
63 See Charles Krupnik, 'Europe's Intergovernmental NGO: The OSCE in Europe's Emerging Security Structure', *European Security*, vol. 7, no. 2, p. 40. 'The OSCE is at once involved in facilitating arms control agreements, prolonging peace in Bosnia and Chechnya, and monitoring language tests in Latvia. The other major IGOs have broadened their operations as well: NATO is promoting democracy and Western-modelled civil–military relations through its Euro-Atlantic Partnership Council; the EU has become a security player through its many economic initiatives to promote regional stability and with its common foreign and security policy; even the Council of Europe, venerable home to the European unity ideal, promotes "democratic security" as a way to keep Europe at peace.' This latter point is important in that it indicates that traditionally defined and narrow perceptions of security are being replaced, leading to more dynamic and multilevel forms of intervention by more diverse types of actors.
64 Ibid., p. 47.
65 Thomas Weiss and Leon Gordenker (eds), *NGOs, the UN, and Global Governance*, (Boulder, CO: Lynne Rienner 1996) pp. 121–37.
66 David Armstrong, 'Globalisation and the social state', *Review of International Studies*, vol. 24, 1998, p. 96.
67 Ibid., p. 96.
68 Mary Kaldor, op. cit., p. 9.
69 A useful framework in which to examine this is derived from the work of Linklater and based on Habermasian reason and discourse ethics in which a post-conventional awareness leads to a dialogic community. In this context, Linklater discusses a universalism mediated through social processes so that post-Westphalian communities must honour 'other' communities and a

balance can be struck between difference and universalism. Andrew Linklater, op. cit., esp. pp. 179–204.
70 Adam Roberts and Benedict Kingsbury, op. cit., pp. 274–5.

Chapter 2   First Generation Conflict Management: Approaches to Ending Conflict

1 (If you want peace, prepare for war). Latin proverb.
2 This point draws on the debates about an international society despite the tendencies of states to follow their own national interests. See Hedley Bull, *The Anarchic Society: A Study of Order in World Politics*, London; Macmillan – now Palgrave, 1977. See also R. J. Vincent, *Human Rights and International Relations*, Cambridge University Press, 1986.
3 Oliver P. Richmond, *Mediating in Cyprus: The Cypriot Communities and the UN*, London: Frank Cass, 1998.
4 See Thomas Princen, *Intermediaries in International Conflict*, Princeton: Princeton University Press, 1992.
5 Richard Holbrooke, *To End a War*, Random House: New York, 1998.
6 *Montevideo Convention on the Rights and Duties of States*, Article 1, 1933.
7 By this I mean diplomatic activity aimed at preserving fragile military status quos, with little regard to factors of human security or justice.
8 Peter Calvcoressi, 'The Cold War as an Episode', Occasional Paper No. 5, David Davies Memorial Institute of International Studies, London, December 1993, p. 8.
9 *Article 2 (7)*, United Nations Charter.
10 See Alan James, *The Politics of Peacekeeping*, London: Chatto & Windus for the International Institute for Strategic Studies, 1969.
11 Paul F. Diehl, *International Peacekeeping*, Baltimore and London: Johns Hopkins University Press, 1993, pp. 34–7.
12 This became practice with the adoption of the Uniting for Peace Resolution. *United Nations General Assembly Resolution 377*, 3 November 1950.
13 Dag Hammarskjöld defined the principles which laid down the basis for peacekeeping henceforth, including the requirements for consent, non-intervention, impartiality and a temporary mandate. 'Report of the Secretary General', UN GAOR, 13th Sess., UN doc. A/3943, 9 October 1958, pp. 8–27.
14 The term 'generation' with reference to first and second generation peacekeeping refers to the shift towards more complex operations that do not merely patrol ceasefires but are integral parts of a long-term peacemaking process. In contrast, third generation approaches to peacekeeping involved enforcement.
15 Michele Griffin, 'Retrenchment, Reform and Regionalisation: Trends in UN Peace Support Operations', *International Peacekeeping*, vol. 6, no. 1, 1999. pp. 2–3.
16 F. T. Lui, 'Peacekeeping and Humanitarian Assistance', in Leon Gordenker and Thomas G. Weiss (eds), *Soldiers, Peacekeepers and Disasters*, Basingstoke: Macmillan – now Palgrave, 1991, pp. 33–51.
17 United Nations Charter, Chapter 2, Article 3.
18 United Nations Charter, Article 33 (para. 1 & 2).

19 Sydney D. Bailey, *How Wars End: The United Nations and the termination of armed conflict 1946–1964*, Oxford: Clarendon Press, vol. 1, 1982, p. 2.

20 General Assembly resolution 3379 (XXX), 10 November, 1975. This was revoked by General Assembly resolution 46/86, 16 December, 1991.

21 J. O. C. Jonah, op. cit., p. 177.

22 Alan James, *The Politics of Peacekeeping*, London: Chatto & Windus for the International Institute for Strategic Studies, 1969, p. 79.

23 Boutros-Ghali, op. cit., p. 22.

24 J. Bercovitch and A. Houston, op. cit., p. 302.

25 See for example, K. Waldheim, *The Challenge of Peace*, Weidenfeld & Nicolson, 1977, p. 5.

26 William J. Durch (ed.), *The Evolution of UN Peacekeeping*, Basingstoke: Macmillan – now Palgrave, 1994, pp. 1 and 30.

27 UN Press Release SG/1357/8, 26 October 1962, pp. 1 and 2.

28 General Assembly Resolution 3458 A (XXX), 10 December, 1975.

29 Thomas M. Franck and Georg Nolte, 'The Good Offices Function of the Secretary General', in Adam Roberts and Benedict Kingsbury (eds), *United Nations, Divided World*, 2nd edn, London: Oxford University Press, 1996, pp. 179–80.

30 J. Burton, 'The Procedures of Conflict Resolution', in J. Burton and E. A. Azar, *International Conflict Resolution: Theory and Practice*, Brighton: Wheatsheaf, 1986, p. 100.

31 J. Bercovitch and A. Houston, 'The Study of International Mediation: Theoretical Issues and Empirical Evidence', in J. Bercovitch (ed.), *The Theory and Practice of Mediation*, op. cit., p. 28.

32 Jack Donnelly, *The Past, the Present, and the Future Prospects*, in Milton Esman and Shirley Telhami (eds), *International Organisations and Ethnic Conflict*, Ithaca: Cornell University Press, 1995, p. 59.

33 The UN was used in this case to prevent secession. See Alexis Heraclides, *The Self-Determination of Minorities in International Politics*, London: Frank Cass, 1991, p. 69.

34 Ibid., p. 139.

35 Michael C. Hudson, 'The Domestic Context and Perspectives in Lebanon', in Milton Esman and Shirley Telhami (eds), op. cit., pp. 132–3.

36 Steven L. Burg, 'The International Community', in Esman and Telhami, op. cit., p. 267.

37 F. C. Iklé, *How Nations Negotiate*, New York: Kraus Reprint, 1985, p. 2.

38 I. W. Zartman and M. R. Berman, *The Practical Negotiator*, New Haven and London: Yale University Press, 1982, p. 13.

39 Vivienne Jabri, *Mediating Conflict Decision-making and Western Intervention in Namibia*, Manchester; Manchester University Press, 1990, p. 27.

40 This later point is indicative, at least in my opinion, of a crucial weakness in the whole 'negotiation paradigm'; this same weakness also effects international mediation.

41 H. Assefa, *Mediation of Civil Wars*, London: Westview Press, 1987, pp. 89–90.

42 Ibid., p. 191.

43 By this I mean that talks continue without making meaningful progress. This may be a sign of the negotiatiors holding devious objectives towards the mediator.

44   I. W. Zartman and M. R. Berman, op. cit., p. 34.
45   T. Princen, op. cit., p. 9.
46   D. Jones, *Cosmopolitan Mediation*, Manchester: Manchester University Press, 1999, p. 30.
47   Thomas Princen, op. cit., p. 10.
48   Christopher Mitchell and Michael Banks, *Handbook of Conflict Resolution*, Pinter: London, 1996, p. x.
49   Ibid., pp. 3–4.
50   Ibid., pp. 208–9.
51   J. Bercovitch and J. Langley: 'The Nature of the Dispute and the Effectiveness of International Mediation', *Journal of Conflict Resolution*, vol. 37, no. 4, 1993, p. 671.
52   See, for example, J. Bercovitch (ed.), *The Theory and Practice of Mediation*, Boulder and London University of Colorado Press, 1996, p. 4.
53   J. Bercovitch and A. Houston, 'Influence of Mediator Characteristics and Behaviour on the Success of Mediation in International Relations', *International Journal of Conflict Management*, vol. 4, no. 4, 1993, p. 298.
54   Marieke Kleiboer, 'Understanding the Success and Failure of International Mediation', *Journal of Conflict Resolution*, vol. 40., no. 2., June 1996, p. 362.
55   Alan James, op. cit., p. 12.
56   J. Bercovitch and J. Langley, 'The Nature of the Dispute and the Effectiveness of International Mediation', *Journal of Conflict Resolution*, vol. 37, no. 4, 1993, p. 670.
57   L. Kreisberg, *International Conflict Resolution*, 1982, p. 2.
58   O. R. Young, *The Intermediaries: Third Parties in International Crises*, Princeton: Princeton University Press, 1967, p. 35.
59   S. Touval and I. W. Zartman (eds), *International Mediation in Theory and Practice*, School of Advanced International Studies, Johns Hopkins University, 1985, p. 7.
60   D. B. Bendahmane and J. W. McDonald (eds), *Perspectives on Negotiation*, Centre for the Study of Foreign Affairs, Foreign Service Institute, US Department of State, 1986, pp. 217–26.
61   According to Bercovitch and Rubin, mediation is the continuation of negotiation by other means. J. Bercovitch and J. Z. Rubin, *Mediation in IR: Multiple Approaches to Conflict Management*, Basingstoke: Macmillan – now Palgrave, 1992, p. 3.
62   J. Bercovitch and J. Z. Rubin, op. cit., p. 7.
63   Marieke Kleiboer has found that mediation is more successful if the disputants have a democratic relationship with their constituencies. op. cit., p. 366.
64   R. J. Fisher and L. Keashley: 'The Potential Complementarity of Mediation and Consultation within a Contingency Model of Third Party Intervention', *Journal of Peace Research*, vol. 28, no. 1, February 1991, p. 36.
65   Jacob Bercovitch and Jeffrey Langley, 'The Nature of Dispute and the Effectiveness of International Mediation', *Journal of Conflict Resolution*, vol. 37, no. 4, 1993, pp. 670–91.
66   J. A. Wall, 'Mediation', *Journal of Conflict Resolution*, vol. 25 no. 1, March 1981, p. 160.
67   Ibid., pp. 161–2.

68 J. A. Wall and A. Lynn, 'Mediation: A Current Review', *Journal of Conflict Resolution*, vol. 37, no.1, 1993, p. 173.

69 J. A. Wall, op. cit., p. 162.

70 G. Evans, *Cooperating for Peace*, London: Allen & Unwin, 1993, p. 168.

71 J. O. C. Jonah, 'The United Nations and International Conflict: the Military Talks at Kilometre Marker-101', in J. Bercovitch and J. Z. Rubin (eds), op. cit., p. 197.

72 See Richard Holbrooke, op. cit.

73 See J. Bercovitch and J. Z. Rubin, op. cit., p. 20.

74 J. A. Wall, op. cit., p. 165.

75 Donald Rothschild and Caroline Hartzell, 'Interstate and Intrastate Negotiations in Angola', in Zartman, *Elusive Peace*, op. cit., p. 199.

76 Imtiaz H. Bokhari, 'Internal Negotiations among many actors: Afghanistan', in ibid., p. 261.

77 J. Bercovitch and J. Langley, op. cit., pp. 676–7.

78 This discussion was developed further by the conflict resolution/facilitation school, and has become an important part of the more recent critical debates about peacemaking.

79 R. Cohen: 'Deadlock: Israel and Egypt Negotiate', F. Korzenny and S. Ting-Toomey (eds), *Communicating for Peace Diplomacy and Negotiation*, London: Sage, 1990, pp. 137–52.

80 J. A. Wall and A. Lynn, op. cit., p. 174.

81 J. Bercovitch and J. Langley, 'The Nature of the Dispute and the Effectiveness of International Mediation', *Journal of Conflict Resolution*, vol. 37, no. 4, 1993, p. 670., op. cit., p. 675. They argue that the easiest way to measure levels of intensity is through a count of casualties. A less reliable method is through a measurement of the length of the dispute's duration.

82 J. A. Wall and A. Lynn, op. cit., p. 176.

83 J. Bercovitch and A. Houston: The Study of International Mediation: Theoretical Issues and Empirical Evidence, in J. Bercovitch (ed.), op. cit., p. 19.

84 J. Bercovitch and J. Z. Rubin, op. cit., p. 22.

85 Jacob Bercovitch, 'International Mediation: A Study of the Incidence, Strategies and Conditions of Successful Outcomes', *Cooperation and Conflict*, vol. 21, no. 3, 1986, p. 161.

86 Chester A. Crocker and Fen Osler Hampson, 'Making Peace Settlements Work', *Foreign Policy*, no. 104, Fall 1996, pp. 70–1.

87 Alexis Heraclides, 'The Ending of Unending Conflicts; Separatist Wars', *Millennium*, vol. 26, no. 3, 1997, pp. 694–5.

88 Stephen John Stedman, *Peacemaking in Civil War: International Mediation in Zimbabwe, 1974–1980*, London: Lynne Rienner, 1991. Licklider has confirmed this by arguing that the overall success rate of negotiated settlements was around 12 per cent of the internal wars that ended between 1945 and 1989. See Roy Licklider, 'The Consequences of Negotiated Settlement in Civil Wars, 1945–1993', *American Political Science Review*, vol. 89, no. 3, 1995, pp. 681–90.

89 Stephen John Stedman, Peacemaking in Civil War, Boulder, CO: Lynne Rienner, 1991, in note 10, p. 374, cited by David Shearer, 'Exploring the Limits of Consent', *Millennium: Journal of International Studies*, vol. 26, no. 3, 1997, pp. 847–8.

90 S. Touval and I. W. Zartman (eds), op. cit., p. 13.

91 T. Princen, op. cit., p. 214.

92 J. A. Wall and A. Lynn, op. cit., p. 177.

93 Princen has argued that much of what mediators actually do is motivated by attempting to demonstrate their own neutrality in the conflict environment. T. Princen, op. cit., p. 30.

94 C. R. Mitchell and K. Webb (eds), 'Mediation in International Relations: An Evolving Tradition', *New Approaches to International Mediation*, New York: Greenwood Press, 1988, p. 12.

95 Karin Aggestam and Christer Jonsson, '(Un) Ending Conflict: Challenges in Post-War Bargaining', *Millennium*, vol. 26, 1997, pp. 774.

96 Karin Aggestam, 'Two-Track Diplomacy: Negotiations between Israel and the PLO through Open and Secret Channels', *Davis Papers On Israel's Foreign Policy*, no. 53, Leonard Davis Institute for International Relations, 1996, pp. 19–27.

97 Karin Aggestam and Christer Jonsson, op. cit., p. 790.

98 See, for example, ibid., pp. 791–2.

99 Mats Berdal and David Keen, 'Violence and Economic Agendas in Civil Wars: Some Policy Imperatives', *Millennium: Journal of International Studies*, vol. 26, no. 3, 1997, pp. 795–6.

100 I. William Zartman, 'Dynamics and Constraints in Negotiations in Internal Conflicts', in I. William Zartman (ed.), *Elusive Peace*, Washington DC; Brookings Institution, 1995, p. 3.

101 Modelski argues that there are two basic conditions for a settlement in an intrastate war; they are stalemate and a rearrangement of resources. Stalemate can be achieved by international action. George Modelski, 'International Settlement of Internal War', in Rosenau, op. cit., p. 143–4.

102 See A. J. R. Groom and K. Webb, 'Injustice, Empowerment, and Facilitation in Conflict', *International Interactions*, New York: Gordon & Breach, vol. 13, no. 3, 1987.

103 L. Susskind and E. Babbitt, op. cit., p. 33.

104 For an elaboration of this argument, see H. Miall, *The Peacemakers*, Basingstoke: Macmillan – now Palgrave, 1992, p. 61.

105 Vivienne Jabri, op. cit., p. 14.

106 See, for example, I. William Zartman, 'Ripening Conflict, Ripe Moment, Formula and Mediation', in Diane B. Bendhame and John W. McDonald (eds), *Perspectives on Negotiation*, Washington, DC: Center for the Study of Foreign Affairs, 1986, p. 218.

107 See, Christopher R. Mitchell, 'The Right Moment: Notes on Four Models of "Ripeness"', *Paradigms: The Kent Journal of International Relations*, vol. 9, no. 2, 1995, pp. 44–5.

108 See critique in Marieke Kleiboer, 'Ripeness of Conflict: A Fruitful Notion?', *Journal of Peace Research*, vol. 31, no. 1, 1994, pp. 109–16.

109 Karin Aggestam and Christer Jonsson, '(Un)Ending Conflict: Challenges in Post-War Bargaining', *Millennium: Journal of International Studies*, vol. 26, no. 3, 1997, p. 773.

110 Henry Kissinger believed that only a war without victory or defeat could contain the seeds of a settlement. During the October War between Israel and Egypt in 1973, he constantly switched his support from side to side in order to exhaust them, leaving them little choice but to negotiate. John G.

`Stoessinger, *Why Nations Go To War*, New York: St. Martins Press – now Palgrave, 6th edn, 1992, pp. 165–6.

111 Saadi Touval, 'Gaining Entry to Mediation in Communal Strife', Manus Midlarsky (ed.), *The Internalization of Communal Strife*, London and New York: Routledge, 1992, p. 256.

112 T. Princen, op. cit., p. 52.

113 J. B. Bercovitch and J. Z. Rubin, op. cit., p. 9.

114 T. Princen, op. cit., p. 66.

115 C. Mitchell, *Peacemaking and the Consultants Role*, Aldershot: Gower, 1981, p. viii.

116 C. Mitchell, op. cit., p. iii.

117 T. Princen, op. cit., p. 9. and pp. 25–41.

118 Howard Wriggins, 'Sri Lanka; Negotiations in a Secessionist Conflict,' in I. William Zartman (ed.), *Elusive Peace*, Washington DC; Brookings Institution, 1995, p. 35.

119 *The Times*, http://www.the-times.co.uk, 9 May 1998.

120 *The Turkish Daily News*, http://www.turkishdailynews.com, 19 May 1998.

121 Both India and Pakistan regard Kashmir as an internal issue going back to the partition of the subcontinent. The two new countries went to war over the Kashmir's future in October 1947. India insists that the matter is a domestic one while Pakistan refers back constantly to the call by the UN in January 1949 for a plebiscite in the state. India was against unilateral NATO intervention in Kosovo, seeing this as a precedent to justify international involvement in Kashmir. Even the slightest sign of partiality by would-be mediators is seen as a political challenge by the other side. In September of 1999, Pakistan proposed that SAARC should be given a conflict management mechanism. India rejected this and also opposed the US and UN stance on the legitimacy of humanitarian intervention. See *Hindustan Times*, 24 September 1999, p. 1; 27 September p. 18.

122 *Montevideo Convention on the Rights and Duties of States*, Article 1, 1933.

Chapter 3   Second Generation: Conflict Resolution Approaches to Ending Conflict

1 Vivienne Jabri, 'Agency, Structure, and the Question of Power in Conflict Resolution', *Paradigms*, vol. 9, no. 2, winter 1995, p. 51.

2 Alan C. Tidwell, *Conflict Resolved*, London: Pinter, 1998, p. 30.

3 See K. Boulding, 'Future Directions in Conflict and Peace Studies', *Journal of Conflict Resolution*, vol. 22, no. 2, 1978.

4 See David Mitrany, *A Working Peace System*, Oxford: Oxford University Press, 1943; Ernst B. Haas, *The Uniting of Europe*, Stanford, Calif.: Stanford University Press, 1958.

5 Louis Kreisburg, 'The Development of the Conflict Resolution Field', in William Zartman and Lewis Rasmussen (eds), *Peacemaking in International Conflict: Methods and Techniques*, Washington, DC: United States Institute of Peace Press, 1997, p. 56.

6 William Zartman, 'Towards the Resolution of International Conflicts', in William Zartman and Lewis Rasmussen, op. cit., p. 15.

7   See *Treaty of Sèvres*, 1920, Articles 62, 63, 64.
8   Johan Galtung, *Peace by Peaceful Means' Peace and Conflict, Development and Civilization*, London: Sage, 1996, p. viii.
9   Peace research has also been an important part of this debate, though traditionally seen as separate to conflict resolution approaches. This distinction seems to me to be overdone, something which recent literature from both agendas and its crossovers seems to illustrate. See for example, Paul Rogers and Oliver Ramsbotham, 'Then and Now: Peace Research – Past and Future', *Political Studies*, vol. XLVII, 1999, pp. 740–54.
10 See Galtung, op. cit., p. 72.
11 See Hugh Miall, Oliver Ramsbotham, and Tom Woodhouse, *Contemporary Conflict Resolution*, Cambridge: Polity Press, 1999, p. 15.
12 Morton Deutsch, *The Resolution of Conflict, Constructive and Destructive Processes*, New Haven, Conn.: Yale University Press, 1973, p. 17.
13 E. A. Azar, 'Protracted International Conflicts: Ten Propositions', in J. Burton and E. A. Azar, *International Conflict Resolution: Theory and Practice*, Brighton: Wheatsheaf Books, 1986, p. 29.
14 H. Miall (ed.), *The Peacemakers*, Basingstoke: Macmillan – now Palgrave, 1992, pp. 234–7.
15 J. Burton and F. Dukes, *Conflict: Practices in Management, Settlement and Resolution*, Centre for Conflict Management and Resolution, Basingstoke: Macmillan – now Palgrave, 1990, p. 85.
16 J. Burton, *Conflict and Communication*, London: Macmillan – now Palgrave, 1969, p. 161.
17 J. Burton and F. Dukes, op. cit., p. 145.
18 J. Burton, *Conflict and Communication*, op. cit., pp. 61–62.
19 Ibid., pp. 63–73.
20 A. J. R. Groom, 'Problem Solving in International Relations', in R. Thakur (ed.), *International Conflict Resolution* Boulder, CO: Westview Press; Dunedin, New Zealand: University of Otago Press, 1988, p. 88.
21 David Mitrany's work on conflict provides an important contribution to the critique of traditional diplomacy, as does Groom and Taylor's development of his work on functional institutions, which seem to point to an opening for the development of a new form of multidimensional peacemaking, as outlined below. See D. A. Mitrany, *The Functional Theory of Politics*, London: Martin Robertson, 1975; Paul Taylor, 'Functionalism', in A. J. R. Groom and Paul Taylor (eds), *Frameworks for International Co-operation*, London: Pinter, 1990, pp. 125–38.
22 See, for example, William Zartman and Lewis Rasmussen (eds), *Peacemaking in International Conflict: Methods and Techniques*, Washington, DC: United States Institute of Peace Press, 1997, especially pp. 23–80.
23 Kumar Rupesinghe, 'Conflict Transformation', in Kumar Rupesinghe (ed.), *Conflict Transformation*, London: Macmillan – now Palgrave, 1995, pp. 75–6.
24 Dov Ronen, 'Human Needs and the State', in Ho-Won Jeong, *The New Agenda for Peace Research*, Aldershot: Ashgate, 1999, pp. 261–3.
25 Alan C. Tidwell, op. cit., p. 105.
26 See Andrew Linklater, *The Transformation of Political Community*, Columbia: University of South Carolina Press. 1998, D. Jones, *Cosmopolitan Mediation*, Manchester: University of Manchester Press, 1999; Vivienne Jabri, *Discourses*

on Violence: Conflict Analysis Reconsidered, Manchester and New York: Manchester University Press, 1996.

27 See, Louis Kreisberg, Terrell A. Northrup, Stuart J. Thorson (eds), *Intractable Conflicts and Their Transformation*, Syracuse, NY, Syracuse University Press, 1989.

28 Edward E. Azar, *The Management of Protracted Social Conflict*, Aldershot: Dartmouth Publishing, 1990, pp. 10–12.

29 Ibid., p. 7.

30 Ibid., p. 9.

31 Ibid., p. 155.

32 Alan C. Tidwell, op. cit., p. 107.

33 See, Kevin Avruch, Peter W. Black, and Joseph A. Scimecca (eds), *Conflict Resolution: Cross-Cultural Perspectives*, London: Greenwood Press, 1991.

34 M. Lebaron, 'Mediation and Multicultural Reality', *Peace and Conflict Studies*, vol. 5, no. 1, p. 43.

35 Vamik Volkan and Mark Harris, 'Negotiating a Peaceful Separation', *Mind and Human Interaction*, vol. 4, no.1, 1992, pp. 20–39.

36 J. Lewis Rasmussen, 'Peacemaking in the Twenty-First century: New Rules, New Roles, New Actors', in William Zartman and Lewis Rasmussen, op. cit., p. 33.

37 Johan Galtung, 'International Development in Human Perspective', in John Burton (ed.), *Conflict: Human Needs Theory*, New York: St. Martin's Press – now Palgrave, 1990, p. 311. Burton has defined these needs as non-negotiable and including physical and psychological security; basic survival needs; identity needs; economic needs; political participation; and freedom (freedom of speech, movement, religious preference, and association). See John Burton, *Resolving Deep Rooted Conflict: A Handbook*, (Lanham, MD: University Press of America, 1987, p. 23.

38 See A. Rapoport, *The Origins of Violence*, New York: Paragon House, 1989.

39 J. Burton and F. Dukes (eds), *Conflict: Readings in Management and Resolution*, London: Macmillan – now Palgrave, 1990, p. 2.

40 R. A. Baruch Bush and J. P. Folger, *The Promise of Mediation*, London: Jossey-Bass, 1994.

41 Ibid., p. 16.

42 Ibid., p. 20.

43 Ibid., pp. 28–9.

44 Hugh Miall et al., op. cit., p. 22.

45 Louis Kreisberg, Terrell A. Northrup, Stuart J. Thorson (eds), op. cit., p. 57. See also Alan C. Tidwell, op. cit., p. 73.

46 R. Vayrynen, *New Directions in Conflict Theory: Conflict Resolution and Conflict Transformation*, London: Sage, 1991, pp. 4–6.

47 See E. Boulding, *Building a Global Civic Culture: Education for an Interdependent World*, Syracuse, NY: Syracuse University Press, 1990; A. Curle, *Another Way; Positive Response to Contemporary Conflict*, Oxford: John Carpenter, 1994; J. Lederach, *Building Peace – Sustainable Reconciliation in Divided Societies*, Tokyo: United Nations University Press, 1997.

48 Hugh Miall *et al.*, op. cit., p. 19. Caroline Nordstrom's contribution on the 'cultures of violence' is also important here, in unravelling the relationship between knowledge and power in conflict. Carolyn Nordstrom, 'The

Backyard Front', in C. Nordstrom and J. Martin (eds), *The Paths to Domination, Resistance and Terror*, Berkeley: University of California Press, 1992, pp. 269–70.

49 J. Lederach, op. cit., p. 39. See also, J. Lederach, *Preparing for Peace: Conflict Transformation Across Cultures*, Syracuse, NY: Syracuse University Press, 1995.

50 J. Lederach, *Building Peace*, op. cit., pp. 60–1.

51 Ibid., pp. 44–54.

52 Ibid., pp. 60–1.

53 Ibid., pp. 82–4.

54 Kumar Rupesinghe, op. cit., pp. 79–80.

55 Ibid., pp. 87–8.

56 J. Lederach, op. cit., p. 16.

57 This has been reflected in the argument that multidimensional approaches are required, particularly in ethnic conflicts, which address the full range of social forces, including the historical, religious, demographic, political, economic and psychocultural forces. Sean Byrne and Loraleigh Keashly, 'Working with Ethno-political Conflict: A Multi-modal Approach', in Tom Woodhouse and Oliver Ramsbotham, *Peacekeeping and Conflict Resolution*, London: Frank Cass, 2000, pp. 98–9.

58 Christopher Mitchell and Michael Banks, *Handbook of Conflict Resolution*, Pinter: London, 1996, p. x.

59 Ibid.

60 Hugh Miall et al., op. cit., p. 218.

61 V. Jabri, op. cit., p. 150.

62 Ibid., p. 181.

63 H. Miall *et al.*, op. cit., p. 59.

64 They may even become participants in negotiations later on, as was the case in the Israeli–Palestinian negotiations following the Kelman's workshops. See Herbert Kelman, 'Contributions of an Unofficial Conflict Resolution Effort to the Israeli–Palestinian Breakthrough', *Negotiation Journal*, vol. 11, no. 1, 1995, pp. 19–27.

65 J. Burton, *Conflict and Communication*, London: Macmillan – now Palgrave, 1969.

66 See Leonard W. Doob (ed.), *Resolving Conflict in Africa*, New Haven, Conn.: Yale University Press, 1970; Leonard W. Doob, *Intervention: Guides and Perils*, New Haven, Conn.: Yale University Press, 1993.

67 Ronald J. Fisher, 'Interactive Conflict Resolution', in William Zartman and Lewis Rasmussen (eds), op. cit., pp. 241–2.

68 Ronald J. Fisher, op. cit., pp. 258–9.

69 Herbert Kelman, 'Contributions of an Unofficial Conflict Resolution Effort to the Israeli–Palestinian Breakthrough', op. cit., pp. 19–27.

70 Herbert Kelman, 'Social-Psychological Dimensions of International Conflict', in William Zartman and Lewis Rasmussen (eds), op. cit., p. 195.

71 Ibid., p. 211.

72 Herbert C. Kelman, 'An Interactional Approach to Conflict Resolution and its Applications to Israeli–Palestinian Relations', in *International Interactions*, vol. 6, no. 2, 1979; Herbert C. Kelman, 'Informal Mediation by the Scholar-Practitioner', in Jacob Bercovitch and Jeffrey Z. Rubin, *Mediation in International Relations*, Basingstoke: Macmillan – now Palgrave, 1992.

73 Stephen P. Cohen and Edward E. Azar, 'From War to Peace: The Transition between Egypt and Israel', *Journal of Conflict Resolution*, vol. 25, no. 1., 1981, pp. 87–114.
74 Edward E. Azar, op.cit.
75 C. R. Mitchell, *Peacemaking and the Consultant's Role*, Aldershot: Gower, 1981, pp. 8–13.
76 See C. R. Mitchell, 'Problem Solving Exercises and Theories of Conflict Resolution', in J. D. Sandole and Hugo van der Merwe (ed.), *Conflict Resolution Theory and Practice: Integration and Application*, Manchester: Manchester University Press, 1993.
77 For example, see, R. J. Fisher and L. Keashley, 'The Potential Complementarity of Mediation and Consultation within a Contingency Model of Third Party Intervention', *Journal of Peace Research*, vol. 28, no. 1, Feb. 1991, p. 360.
78 See Louise Diamond and John McDonald, *Multi-Track Diplomacy*, Grinnell: Iowa Peace Institute, 1991. Track Two involves nongovernmental conflict resolution activities; Tracks Three to Nine involve various unofficial actors' interactions in the areas of business, research, education, peace and environmental activism, religion, and the media.
79 Loraleigh Keashley and Ronald J. Fisher, 'Complementarity and Coordination of Conflict Interventions: Taking a Contingency Perspective', in J. Bercovitch (ed.), *Resolving International Conflicts: The Theory and Practice of Mediation*, Boulder, CO: Lynne Rienner, 1996, p. 236.
80 D. Jones, op. cit., p. 160.
81 See, for example, Louis Kreisburg, 'Varieties of Mediating Activities and Mediators in International Relations', in Bercovitch, J. (ed.), *Resolving International Conflicts*, op. cit., p. 226.
82 Harold H. Saunders, 'Sustained Dialogue on Tajikistan', *Mind and Human Interaction*, vol. 6, no. 3, 1995, pp. 123–35.
83 Louis Kreisburg, 'The Development of the Conflict Resolution Field', in William Zartman and Lewis Rasmussen, op. cit., pp. 67–8.
84 Harold A. Saunders, *A Public Peace Process*, Macmillan – now Palgrave, 1999, p. 9.
85 Ibid., p. 96.
86 Ibid., p. 224.
87 See Myria Vassiliadou, 'The European Accession and Bicommunal Work on Cyprus', Presentation at Ohio State University, Columbus, 28 June 2000.
88 Cited in William Zartman and Lewis Rasmussen, op. cit., p. 69.
89 Andrew Williams, 'Conflict Resolution after the Cold War: The Case of Moldova', *Review of International Studies*, vol.25, no.1, 1999, p. 72.
90 Ibid., p. 83.
91 Cameron R. Hume, 'A Diplomat's View' in William Zartman and Lewis Rasmussen, op.cit., p. 320.
92 See Oliver P. Richmond, 'Human Security, the "Rule of Law" and NGOs: Potentials and Problems', *Human Rights Review*, forthcoming 2002.
93 Andreas S. Natsios, in I. William Zartman and J. Lewis Rasmussen, op. cit., p. 352.
94 J. Burton, 'The History of Conflict Resolution', *International Conflict Resolution*, op. cit., p. 45.

95 J. Burton, ibid., p. 52. Burton argues that related to this issue is the fact that peacekeeping forces tend to institutionalize conflict, making the search for a solution more difficult.

96 Boutros Boutros-Ghali, *An Agenda for Peace*, para. 55.

97 Ibid., para. 84.

98 Of course the mainstream assertion that non-state conflicts tend to be subjective implies that conflicts between states, over historical borders and territory, for example, are not subjective, though a serious examination of many 'state' conflicts reveals the fallaciousness of such an assertion.

Chapter 4   Critiquing First and Second Generation Approaches

1 See, for example, Inis L. Claude, *Swords into Ploughshares*, 4th edn, New York: Random House, 1964.

2 For a discussion of 'protracted social conflicts' see, among others, Ted Robert Gurr, *Minorities at Risk: A Global View of Ethnopolitical Conflicts*, Washington, DC: United States Institute of Peace Press, 1993; Milton J. Esman, *Ethnic Politics*, Ithaca: Cornell University Press, 1994; Walker Connor, *Ethnonationalism: The Quest for Understanding*, Princeton: Princeton University Press, 1994; Ernest Gellner; *Nations and Nationalism*, Ithaca: Cornell University Press, 1993.

3 Fen Osler Hampson, *Nurturing Peace: Why Peace Settlements Succeed or Fail*, Washington, DC: United States Institute of Peace Press, 1996, p.4.

4 Barry Buzan, 'Third World Regional Security in Structural Perspective,' in Brian L. Job (ed.), *The Insecurity Dilemma: National Security of Third World States*, Boulder, CO: Lynne Rienner, 1992, p.187.

5 Stedman argues that most of these types of conflict have resulted in 'elimination or capitulation'. For details see Stephen John Stedman, *Peacemaking in Civil War International Mediation in Zimbabwe*, Boulder, CO: Lynne Rienner, 1988, p. 9. According to Licklider, only 'one-third of the negotiated settlements of identity civil wars that last for five years "stick."' Furthermore, conflicts that end in military victory may lead to genocide. Roy Licklider, 'The Consequences of Negotiated Settlements in Civil War 1945–1993', *American Political Science Review*, vol. 89, no. 3, September 1995, pp.685–7.

6 N. D. White, *Keeping the Peace*, Manchester: Manchester University Press, 1997, p. 241.

7 Debrix argues that this was ambiguously presented in *Agenda for Peace*, and was exploited in the Bosnia conflict in order to give the UN the illusion of control. François Debrix, *Re-envisioning UN Peacekeeping*, Minneapolis: University of Minnesota Press, 1999, p. 158–9, n. 77 esp.

8 He argues that this is not necessarily wrong, but that it is important not to overlook the role that peace operations may play in importing alien norms and models, albeit unwittingly. Roland Paris, 'Echoes of the *Mission Civilisatrice:* Peacekeeping in the Post-Cold War Era', in Edward Newman and Oliver P. Richmond, *The United Nations and Human Security*, Palgrave, 2001, chapter 6.

9 Alexis Heraclides, 'The Ending of Unending Conflicts; Separatist Wars', in *Millennium: Journal of International Studies*, vol. 26, no. 3, 1997, pp. 694.

10 For this argument in East Timor see Sheila Nair, 'Human Rights, Sovereignty, and the East Timor "Question" ', in *Global Society*, vol. 14, no. 1, 2000.
11 Alexis Heraclides, op. cit., p. 698.
12 Mordechai Bar-on, *In Pursuit of Peace*, Washington: US Institute of Peace, 1996, p. xv.
13 Ibid., pp. 701.
14 Brian Mandell, 'The Limits of Mediation: Lessons from Syria-Israel Experience, 1974–1994', in J. Bercovitch (ed.), *Resolving International Conflicts: The Theory and Practice of Mediation*, London and Boulder, Colo.: Lynne Rienner, 1996, p. 136.
15 Ibid., p. 145.
16 Raymond Cohen, 'Cultural Aspects of International Mediation', in Jacob Bercovitch (ed.), op. cit., pp. 107 and 119.
17 Ibid., p. 108.
18 Cohen mentions the idea of an epistemic community made up of a diplomatic corps who may have cross-cultural skills, but argues that international negotiation tends to be conducted by actors who do not possess such skills. ibid., p. 111.
19 Ibid., p. 146.
20 Francis Mading Deng, 'Negotiating a Hidden Agenda: Sudan's Conflict of Identities', in I. William Zartman (ed.), *Elusive Peace*, Washington, DC: Brookings Institution, 1995, p. 77.
21 I. William Zartman, 'Ripening Conflict, Ripe Moment, Formula, and Mediation,' in Diane B. Bendahmane and John W. McDonald, Jr., eds, *Perspectives on Negotiation*, Washington, DC: Foreign Service Institute, US Department of State, 1986, pp. 217–18.
22 Fen Osler Hampson, *Nurturing Peace*, op. cit., p. 14. See also Brian Tomlin and Brian S. Mandell, 'Mediation in the Development of Norms to Manage Conflict: Kissinger in the Middle East', *Journal of Peace Research*, vol. 28, no. 1, 1991, pp. 43–55.
23 International mediation has tended to result in fragile compromises circumscribed by the interests and resources of great powers with a powerful interest in regional and systemic stability. The case of US mediation in Egypt and Israel is a good example of this. See T. Princen, 'Camp David: Problem-Solving or Power Politics as Usual?', *Journal of Peace Research*, Oslo: Universitetsforlaget, vol. 28, no. 1, Feb. 1991; and also T. Princen, *Intermediaries in International Conflict*, Princeton: Princeton University Press, 1992. However, powerful global and regional actors have not always been able to maintain such balances: the failure of the system of guarantees provided by Britain, Greece and Turkey for the fledgling 1960 constitution in Cyprus is indicative of this.
24 See Dorothy V. Jones, 'The Declaratory Tradition in Modern International Law', in Terry Nardin and David R. Mapel, *Traditions of International Ethics*, Cambridge: Cambridge University Press, 1992, pp. 54–5.
25 David Held, op. cit., pp. 266–86. For a discussion of a future statecentric scenario of burgeoning conflict, see Samuel Huntingdon, *The Clash of Civilizations and the Remaking of World Order*, New York: Simon & Schuster, 1996 (final chapter). For a discussion of the changing theoretical debates within International Relations Theory, see Andrew Linklater and John Macmillan (eds), *Boundaries in Question*, London: Pinter, 1995.

26 For example, see Danilo Zolo, *Cosmopolis: Prospects for World Government*, Cambridge: Polity Press, 1997.

27 Boutros Boutros-Ghali, *Agenda for Peace*, esp. pp. 5–22.

28 See, for example, Michael Mann, 'Authoritarian and Liberal Militarism', in Steve Smith, Ken Booth and Marysia Zalewski, *International Theory: Positivism and Beyond*, Cambridge University Press, 1996, esp. pp. 235–8. This controversy seems to be based partly on a rejection of the triumphalism which the theorem implies for Western civilization, this certainly being a fair criticism. However, as Heraclides has argued, in the West the level of communal violence is markedly reduced because there is a higher degree of political integration, there are more effective means of channelling grievances and redressing inequality, and therefore more peaceful change. See Alexis Heraclides, 'From Autonomy to Secession: Building Down', in A. J. R. Groom and P. Taylor (eds), *Frameworks for International Co-operation*, London: Pinter, 1990, pp. 186–7.

29 David Held, op. cit., p. 73.

30 Michael E. Brown, 'The Causes of Internal Conflict', in Michael E. Brown, Owen R. Cote, Sean M. Lynne-Jones and Steven E. Miller (eds), *Nationalism and Ethnic Conflict*, Cambridge: MIT Press, 1997, p. 8.

31 For an elaboration of this see Fen Osler Hampson, 'Third Party Roles in the Termination of Intercommunal Conflict', *Millennium*, vol. 26, no. 3, 1997, pp. 727–30.

32 Ibid., pp. 734–5.

33 Jacob Bercovitch, Theodore Anagnosen and Donnella Wille, 'Some Conceptual Issues and Empirical Trends in the Study of Successful Mediation in International Relations', *Journal of Peace Research*, vol. 28, no. 1, 1991, pp. 7–17.

34 Fen Osler Hampson, op. cit., pp. 736–40.

35 Inevitably such approaches have responded; the neo-realist attempt to develop an 'ethnic realism', utilizing such concepts as the 'ethnic security dilemma', provides a good example. See, for example, the collection of essays in Michael E. Brown, 'The Causes of Internal Conflict', op. cit. See also Barry Posen, 'The Security Dilemma and Ethnic Conflict', *Survival*, vol. 35, no. 1, 1993, p. 27; Stuart Kaufman, 'Spiralling to Ethnic War: Elites, Masses and Moscow in Moldova's Civil War', *International Security*, vol. 21, no. 2, 1996, pp. 151–2. For an excellent critique of these attempts, see Paul Roe, 'The Intrastate Security Dilemma: Ethnic Conflict as a "Tragedy"?', *Journal of Peace Research*, vol. 36, no. 2, 1999.

36 It is assumed that, in line with the Copenhagen school of thought, that identities are socially constructed (and undergo a process of periodic reconstruction) thus producing a particular hegemonic identity construction around which security processes can take place. Paul Roe, 'The Intrastate Security Dilemma', op. cit. p. 193.

37 See for example, Mervyn Frost, 'A Turn Not Taken: Ethics in IR at the Millennium', *Review of International Studies, special issue*, vol. 24, December 1998, esp. pp. 131–2.

38 See for example, the collection of essays in Michael E. Brown, Owen R. Cote, Sean M. Lynne-Jones & Steven E. Miller, *Nationalism and Ethnic Conflict*, op. cit., p. 8.

39 John Chipman proposes a similar term. See John Chipman, *Managing the Politics of Parochialism. Survival*, vol. 35, no. 1, 1993, p. 162: 'In extreme cases, ethnic conflicts can become so great that they render a state a non-state, create a type of *terra nullius*, in which there may still be recognised frontiers, but everything inside is anarchy.'

40 For the traditional security dilemma's application to ethnic conflict see, for example, Caroline A. Hartzell, 'Explaining the Stability of Negotiated Settlements to Intrastate Wars', in *Journal of Conflict Resolution*, vol. 43, no. 1, 1999, pp. 4–6.

41 Mary Kaldor, *New and Old Wars: Organised Violence in a Global Era*, Cambridge: Polity Press, 1999, p. 7.

42 Stephen Ryan, *Ethnic Conflict and International Relations*, Aldershot: Dartmouth, 1990, p. 4.

43 Ibid., pp. 29–32.

44 For an elaboration of this, see Oliver P. Richmond, 'Mediating Ethnic Conflict: A Task for Sisyphus?', *Global Society*, vol. 13, no. 2, 1999.

45 See, Oliver Richmond, *Mediating in Cyprus*, London: Frank Cass, 1998, pp. 211–20.

46 See press statement by 'TRNC Council of Ministers', 14 December 1997.

47 See, for example, 'Cyprus Country Report', *Economist Intelligence Unit*, pp. 7 and 15.

48 Thomas Princen, *Intermediaries in International Conflict*, Princeton: Princeton University Press, 1992, pp. 84–93.

49 This latter was declared in a statement by Yasser Arafat. *Associated Press Release*, 19 December 1998.

50 It is important to note here that a distinction of uncertain pedigree has been made by the West vis-à-vis the KLA leadership, some of whom are certainly insalubrious characters; yet in the recent case of the Ocalan, the PKK leader, the West decided not to accept his credibility as a leader of his community who could negotiate with the West, and with the leaders of his host state. This was in part related to the strategic importance and political fragility of Turkey and the Turkish democracy, as well as the sheer scale of the Kurdish question in the region.

51 The Serbs responded by going to the Security Council. 'Belgrade Seeks UN Security Council Move On Kosovo', *Reuters*, 19 March 1999.

52 Ibid. See also, *Statement by the Co-Chairs of the Contact Group* (Released following peace conference in Rambouillet), France, 19 March 1999.

53 See, for example, edited transcript of interview given by the British Prime Minister, Tony Blair, *CBS TV*, Chequers, Sunday 18 April 1999.

54 This tendency towards the elevation of humanitarian reasons for intervention has been a growing theme of IR theorizing about the international system. See, for example, Michael Walzer, *Just and Unjust Wars*, New York: Basic Books, 1992: Gene M. Lyons and Michael Mastunduno, *Beyond Westphalia*, Baltimore, MD: Johns Hopkins University Press, 1995.

55 See, for example, 'Macedonia Says It Cannot Accept More Refugees', *Washington Post*, 3 April 1999. 'Saying its fragile democracy and economy were at stake, Macedonia's top government officials said the army would prevent the illegal entry of any more refugees because the country could not handle the influx.' See also *'Human Rights Watch – Current Events: Crisis in Kosovo (Focus*

on Human Rights), *http://www.hrw.org/hrw/press98/sept/kosovo916.htm.* 'On September 11, 1998, in a late evening session the Montenegrin government decided to close the internal boundary between Montenegro and Kosovo to all persons seeking refuge from the armed conflict. The government justified its decision based on the economic strain posed by the incoming displaced persons and its fear that new arrivals would increase ethnic tensions and possibly destabilise the country.'

56 See Nicolas Wheeler and Tim Dunne, 'Good international citizenship: a third way for British foreign policy' *International Affairs*, vol. 74, no. 4, 1998, p. 254. 'The problem traditionally has been that the dominant rules of membership-sovereignty and non-intervention have silenced the promotion of human rights abroad. The post-1945 world, however, has witnessed a sea-change in the principles of international legitimacy. Within liberal states, it has become increasingly difficult for state leaders to claim that human rights abroad are of no concern to them. On the other side of the same coin, it is no longer acceptable for states to claim that the way they treat their own citizens is excluded from international scrutiny or censure.'

57 See Alan J. Bullion, *India, Sri Lanka, and the Tamil Crisis 1976–1994*, London: Pinter, 1995.

58 Ibid., pp. 164–6

59 There were early warnings that local militia against the proposed independence of the territory would cause violence. See *The Times*, 19 April 1999.

60 This was instigated by the May 5th Agreement between Indonesia, Portugal and the UN. The result was 21.5 per cent in favour, and 344,580, or 78.5 per cent, against the proposal of special autonomy. *UN Press Release SG/SM/7119 SC/6722*, 3 September 1999.

61 Yet in interstate wars two-thirds have been settled through negotiations. This seems to indicate that first generation approaches are far more efficient when applied to international conflicts. Alexis Heraclides, 'The Ending of Unending Conflicts; Separatist Wars' in *Millennium: Journal of International Studies* (vol. 26, no. 3, 1997), pp. 681. For this consensus see, among others, George Modelski, 'International Settlement of Internal War', in James N. Rosenau (ed.), *International Aspects of Civil Strife*, Princeton, NJ: Princeton University Press, 1964; Charles King, 'Ending Civil Wars', *Adelphi Paper No. 308* (London: International Institute of Strategic Studies, 1997), p. 12;. Stephen John Stedman, *Peacemaking in Civil War* (Boulder, CO: Lynne Rienner, 1991); Barbara F. Walter, 'The Critical Barrier to Civil War Settlement', *International Organization*, vol. 51, no. 3, 1997, pp. 335–64.

62 Ibid., p. 681

63 See Ian Browlie, *Principles of Public International Law*, 4th edition, Oxford: Oxford University Press, 1990, pp. 567–70.

64 Thomas G. Weiss and Jarat Chopra, 'Sovereignty under Siege: From Intervention to Humanitarian Space', in Gene M. Lyons and Michael Mastunduno, *Beyond Westphalia*, op. cit., 1995, pp. 99–114. Also see the UN Secretary-General's speech at the 1999 General Assembly, 20 September 1999.

65 See Kofi A. Annan, 'Two Concepts of Sovereignty', *The Economist*, 18 September 1999, and http://www.un.org/Overview/SG/kaecon.htm

66 Ibid.

67 Ibid.

68 Ibid.

69 See Richard Holbrooke, *To End a War*, New York: Random House, 1998.

70 Mark Duffield, 'Evaluating conflict resolution – contexts, models and methodology', in Gunnar M. Sorbo, Joanna Macrae and Lennart Wohlegemuth, *NGOs in Conflict – An Evaluation of International Alert*, Chr. Michelsen Institutem CMI Report Series, Bergen, Norway, cited in Tom Woodhouse, 'Conflict Resolution and Peacekeeping: Critiques and Responses', in Tom Woodhouse and Oliver Ramsbotham, *Peacekeeping and Conflict Resolution*, London: Frank Cass, 2000, pp. 12–13.

71 See Tamara Duffey, 'Cultural Issues in Contemporary Peacekeeping', in Tom Woodhouse and Oliver Ramsbotham, op. cit., p. 143–4.

72 Ibid., pp. 160–2.

73 K. Avruch, P. Black and J. A. Scimecca, *Conflict Resolution: Cross-Cultural Perspectives*, London: Greenwood Press, 1991, p. 4.

74 Ho-Won Jeong, 'Research on Conflict Resolution', in Ho-Won Jeong (ed.), *Conflict Resolution: Dynamics, Processes and Structure*, Aldershot: Ashgate, 1999, p. 31. As Dukes has argued, the role of structural forces in conflict resolution has been downplayed: yet they are often responsible for replicating the conflict through inflexible legal frameworks, and claims neutral facilitation to restore social harmony often ignore the wider structural sources of conflict. See E. Franklin Dukes, 'Structural Forces in Conflict and Conflict Resolution in Democratic Society' in ibid., pp. 155–171.

75 See for example, Herbert C. Kelman, 'Informal Mediation by the Scholar/ Practitioner', in Jacob Bercovitch and Jeffrey Z. Rubin (eds), *Mediation in International Relations: Multiple Approaches to Conflict Management*, New York: St. Martin's Press, 1992, pp. 64–96.

76 Often the lure of attendance is the opportunity to attend workshops located abroad, attendance of which tends to be dominated by 'old hands' who jealously guard their privileges.

77 For example, in the Cyprus case, the US funds a large amount of Track II work through the Fulbright Commission. It appears that there is less suspicion of the role of smaller countries and organizations that fund conflict resolution in Cyprus – for example, Norway.

78 This proposal was put forward by a senior official in the Turkish Cypriot administration at a conference held at the London School of Economics by the Association for Greek, Cypriot, and Turkish Affairs, in 1997.

79 See Oliver P. Richmond, Rethinking Conflict Resolution: 'The Linkage Problematic between Track I and Track II', *Journal of Conflict Studies*, forthcoming 2002.

80 Stephen Ryan, *Ethnic Conflict and International Relations*, Aldershot: Dartmouth, 1990, p. 89.

81 Vivienne Jabri, op. cit., p. 54.

82 See for example, the collection of essays in Michael E. Brown, Owen R. Cote, Sean M. Lynne-Jones and Steven E. Miller, *Nationalism and Ethnic Conflict*, op. cit.

83 By this I mean that an extension occurs through the creation of new states: sovereignty therefore is seen to provide security for ethnic actors and minorities (as long as they are homogeneous). It is important to note that sovereignty could provide security by incorporating norms of human rights which

then become part of the package of legitimacy that sovereignty offers, as Barkin has argued, rather than a constraint upon it. J. Samuel Barkin, 'The Evolution of the Constitution of Sovereignty and the Emergence of Human Rights Norms', *Millennium*, vol. 27, no. 2, 1998, pp. 229–31. Barkin extends this point to argue that sovereignty is not in crisis, but is essentially an adaptable concept (as it is also contested).

84 This could involve imprisonment, harassment, phone-taps, the denial of jobs and opportunities, and the general apparatus of oppression applied against political dissenters by authoritarian political organizations and processes (that groups under threat are likely to develop in order to sustain unity and cohesion in the face of the enemy).

85 This has been a common complaint from facilitators in some workshops that have taken place on the Cyprus conflict. See Meron Benvenisti for an anecdote about a similar experience quoted by Tarya Vayrynen, 'Going Beyond Similarity: The Role of the Facilitator in Problem Solving Workshop Conflict Resolution', *Paradigms*, vol. 9, no. 2, winter 1995, p. 71.

86 This is generally regarded as not being a plausible option, as all resources are geared to the communal, ethnic, or interstate conflict, and subgroup disunity is regarded as being suicidal.

87 For example, see Marieke Kleiboer: 'Understanding the Success and Failure of International Mediation', *Journal of Conflict Resolution*, vol. 40, no. 2, June 1996, p. 362.

88 See Oliver Richmond, 'Devious Objectives and the Disputants' Views of International Mediation: A Theoretical Framework', *Journal of Peace Research*, Oslo. vol. 35, no. 6, 1998.

89 See Vivienne Jabri, 'Agency, Structure, and the Question of Power in Conflict Resolution', *Paradigms*, vol. 9, no. 2, winter 1995, p. 57.

90 See Paul Rogers and Oliver Ramsbotham, 'Then and Now: Peace Research – Past and Future', *Political Studies*, vol. XLVII, 1999, pp. 752.

91 Alan C. Tidwell, op. cit., p. 6.

92 See Christopher Clapham, 'Rwanda: the Perils of Peacemaking', *Journal of Peace Research*, vol. 25, no. 2, 1998.

93 See David Shearer, 'Exploring the Limits of Consent: Conflict Resolution in Sierra Leone', *Millennium: Journal of International Studies*, vol. 26, no. 3, 1997.

94 Vivienne Jabri, *Discourses on Violence: Conflict Analysis Reconsidered*, Manchester and New York: Manchester University Press, 1996, p. 150.

95 Ibid., pp. 180–1.

96 M. Hoffman, 'Defining and Evaluating Success', *Paradigms*, vol. 9, no. 2, 1995, p. 9.

97 D. Jones, *Cosmopolitan Mediation*, Manchester: Manchester University Press, 1999, p. 64.

98 See E. Franklin Dukes, 'Structural Forces in Conflict and Conflict Resolution in Democratic Society', in Ho-Won Jeong, op. cit., p. 166. As Dukes has argued, conflict resolution approaches need to recognize the role of structural forces and support social movements facing such problems.

99 For a discussion of the role of culture and class relations and the choices of resolution, reform or revolution, see Richard E. Rubenstein, 'Conflict Resolution and the Structural Sources of Conflict', in Ho-Won Jeong, op. cit., p. 190.

100 Ibid., p. 194.
101 D. Jones, op. cit., p. 3.
102 Jones has argued from a post-positivist and cosmopolitan perspective that mediators should be charged with normative goals relating to enlarging the boundaries of political community and moral responsibility, overcoming divisions, leading to international order based on democratically constructed international law. Ibid., p. 2.
103 Ho-Won Jeong and Tarya Vayrynen, 'Identity Formation and Transformation', in Ho-Won Jeong (ed.), *Conflict Resolution: Dynamics, Processes and Structure*, Aldershot: Ashgate, 1999, p. 63.

Chapter 5   A Third Generation of Multidimensional Approaches to Ending Conflict

1 Kofi Annan, 'Annual Report of the Secretary General on the Work of the Organization', UN doc., A/53/1, 27 August, 1998, para. 28.
2 For further discussion of critical approaches to global order see, Andrew Linklater, *The Transformation of Political Community*, University of South Carolina Press, 1998; Andrew Linklater and John Macmillan (eds), *Boundaries in Question*, London; Pinter, 1995; David Held, *Democracy and the Global Order*, (Cambridge: Polity Press 1995); Steve Smith, Ken Booth and Marysia Zalewski, *International Theory: Positivism and Beyond*, Cambridge University Press, 1996; Mervyn Frost, *Ethics in International Relations: A Constitutive Theory*, Cambridge University Press, 1996; Mervyn Frost, 'A Turn Not Taken: Ethics in IR at the Millennium', *Review of International Studies, special issue*, vol. 24, December 1998; in Gene M. Lyons and Michael Mastunduno, *Beyond Westphalia*, Johns Hopkins University Press, 1995.
3 Vivienne Jabri, *Discourses on Violence: Conflict Analysis Reconsidered*, Manchester University Press, 1996, p. 4.
4 Ibid., p. 7.
5 UN Secretary-General Boutros Boutros-Ghali reacquainted us with this concept, originally from the work of Johan Galtung, which was to identify and reinforce structures which would prevent conflict from re-emerging – to promote positive instead of negative peace. Boutros-Ghali, *Agenda for Peace*, New York: United Nations, 1992, p. 11.
6 See Ingrid A. Lehman, *Peacekeeping and Public Information*, London: Frank Cass, 1999, pp. 1–3. Lehman argues that the UN failed to understand the impact of the media component of globalization on its post-cold war operations.
7 Dorothy V. Jones 'The Declaratory Tradition In Modern International Law' in Terry Nardin and David R. Mapel (eds), *Traditions of International Ethics*, Cambridge University Press, 1992, p. 47.
8 *Locarno Arbitration Treaties, League of Nations Treaty Series* (LTS) 54: 29–301, 30–3, 317–25, 32–39, 34–51.
9 *General Treaty for Renunciation of War (Kellogg-Briand Treaty, 1928)*, LTS 94: 5764.
10 UN Special Committee Reports (1964–1970): UN General Assembly, Official Records, A/7619; 25th sess. (1970), A18018.

11 *International Legal Materials* (ILM) 27 (1988): 1674, 1676. Cited in Dorothy Jones, op. cit., pp. 47–8.
12 Mervyn Frost, op. cit., pp. 106–11.
13 Hedley Bull, cited in Mervyn Frost, ibid., p. 115.
14 Mervyn Frost, ibid., p. 203.
15 Alexis Heraclides, 'The Ending of Unending Conflicts: Separatist Wars', *Millennium: Journal of International Studies*, vol. 26, no. 3, 1997, pp. 680.
16 Global civil society issues include the promotion of universal norms, cosmopolitan versions of justice, human security and rights, development and redistribution of wealth, environment, education, political stability and distribution of resources, political legitimacy, interdependence, regional integration, and freedom of expression and pluralism. Local civil society issues include the sanctity of pluralist constitution and domestic law, observance of regional and international law structures which promote pluralism, communitarian versions of justice, human security and rights, interdependence, development and redistribution of wealth, environment, education, political stability and distribution of resources, political legitimacy, interdependence, local regional integration, freedom of expression and pluralism.
17 See Chris Brown, 'The Idea of World Community', in Ken Booth and Steve Smith (eds), *International Relations Theory Today*, Cambridge; Polity Press, 1995, p. 106.
18 See Terry Nardin, *Law, Morality and the Relations of States*, Princeton, NJ: Princeton University Press, 1983.
19 Chris Brown, op. cit., p. 106.
20 Ibid., p. 106.
21 Ibid., p. 106.
22 Hugh Miall, Oliver Ramsbotham and Tom Woodhouse, *Contemporary Conflict Resolution*, Cambridge: Polity Press, 1999, p. 77.
23 In Sri Lanka, for example, where there is a clear need for a new approach, traditional mediation has been attempted on many occasions since 1957, including the extended mediation of India, which has failed because it was unable to reconcile the conflicting conceptualizations of the conflict by the disputants as well as the third party. See Kumar Rupesinghe, 'Mediation in Internal Conflicts: Lessons from Sri Lanka', in Jacob Bercovitch, op. cit., pp. 161–4.
24 The role of the mediator or the person who 'facilitates' the conflict is often susceptible to the methodological argument within the social sciences that one cannot identify and thus analyse a situation, let alone resolve it, unless one has experience of it: the implication of cultural differences in the understanding of conflicts is thus very obvious.
25 Nayef H. Samhat, 'International Regimes as Political Community', *Millennium*, vol. 26, no. 2, 1997, p. 350. For a discussion of universalism in a post-Westphalian international society, see Andrew Linklater, op. cit., p. 107.
26 Ibid., p. 69.
27 Andrew S. Natsios, in I. William Zartman and J. Lewis Rasmussen, op. cit., p. 338.
28 Pamela Aall, 'Nongovernmental Organisations and Peacemaking', in Chester Crocker, Fen Osler Hampson, and Pamela Aall (eds), *Managing Global Chaos*, Washington, DC: USIP, 1996, p. 434. It is important to note that NGOs differ

in their nature, and whether they work at the grassroots level or with inter-national and regional institutions.

29 Although vague and contested, global civil society can be defined as a trans-national association between economy and state, citizens, voluntary associ-ations and social movements, and forms of public communication. This constitutes the whole framework of global politics as it also incorporates conventional IR and IPE. See Fred Gale, 'Constructing Global Civil Society Actors' in *Global Society*, vol. 12, no. 3, 1998, p. 345. Citing Sandra Maclean, 'Conflicting Boundaries? NGO Partnerships and the Development of Global and National Civil Societies in South Africa', Draft paper presented to the 37th Annual Convention of the International Studies Association. See also Mary Kaldor, '"Civilising" Globalisation', *Millennium*, vol. 29, no. 1, 2000, p. 107. Kaldor argues that this concept can be located within the development of demands for democratization and for interdependence. It has also been described as a 'global humanitarian space'. See Thomas G. Weiss and Jarat Chopra, 'Sovereignty under siege', in Gene M. Lyons and Michael Mastun-duno, *Beyond Westphalia*, Cambridge, MA: Johns Hopkins University Press, 1995 p. 88.

30 François Debrix, *Re-Envisioning UN Peacekeeping*, Minneapolis: University of Minnesota Press, 1999, p. 191.

31 Peter Willets, 'From "Consultative Arrangements" to "Partnership": The Changing Status of NGOs in Diplomacy at the UN,' in *Global Governance*, vol. 6, 2000, p. 196.

32 Ibid., p. 205.

33 Ibid., 206.

34 Oliver Ramsbotham and Tom Woodhouse, *Humanitarian Intervention in Con-temporary Conflict*, Cambridge: Polity Press, 1996, p. 81.

35 General Assembly Resolution 43/131, 8 December 1988; General Assembly Resolution 45/100, 14 December 1990; General Assembly Resolution 46/182, 19 December 1991.

36 Oliver Ramsbotham and Tom Woodhouse, op. cit., p. 84.

37 Margaret Keck and Kathryn Sikkink, *Actors Beyond Borders: Advocacy Networks in International Politics*, Ithaca: Cornell University Press, 1998, p. 215.

38 Louise Diamond and John McDonald, op. cit.

39 However, NGOs may complicate the conflict environment as with the decen-tralization of conflict a wide array of actors become involved in micro and macro-level interventions. For instance, four voluntary agencies (the UN High Commissioner for Refugees (UNHCR), the UN Children's Fund (UNICEF), the World Food Program, and the UN Development Program), and international organizations such as the International Committee of the Red Cross (ICRC), as well as donor-country foreign aid offices, donor-country diplomats, and military forces, often constitute a complex response mechan-ism which suffers from low levels of coordination. Andrew S. Natsios, op. cit., p. 339.

40 See Carnegie Commission on Preventing Deadly Conflict, *Preventing Deadly Conflict*, (Final Report). Washington, 1997, p. 114.

41 See Eftihia Voutira and Shaun A. Wishaw Brown, *Conflict Resolution. A Review of Some Non-Governmental Practices; A Cautionary Tale*, Uppsala: Nordiska Afrikainstituet, 1995.

42   See John Paul Lederach, 'Conflict Transformation in Protracted Internal Conflicts: The Case for a Comprehensive Framework', in Kumar Rupesinghe (ed.), *Conflict Transformation*, Basingstoke: Macmillan – now Palgrave, 1995, pp. 201–22.

43   Op. cit., p. 93.

44   Michele Griffin, op. cit., pp. 19–20.

45   Luis Roninger and Ayse Gynes-Ayata (eds), *Democracy, Clientelism and Civil Society*, Boulder, CO: Lynne Rienner, 1994.

46   The activities of NGOs in Somalia seem to have been somewhat constrained by the lack of security. Somalia Country Report on Human Rights Practices for 1998 (released by the Bureau of Democracy, Human Rights, and Labor, February 26, 1999), U.S. Department of State, http://www.state.gov/www/ global/ humanrights/1998hrpreport/somalia.html. In Bosnia and Herzogovina, NGOs have been relatively unhindered, though there have been instances where they have become politicized.

47   UN Security Council Resolution 794, 3 December 1992; UN Security Council Resolution 814, 26 March 1993.

48   Ozong Agborsangaya, 'Human Rights NGOs and Human Rights Components of Peacekeeping Operations', in *Human Rights, The UN, And Nongovernmental Organisations*, Atlanta, GA: The Carter Center, p. 153.

49   Ibid., p. 155.

50   Ibid., pp. 158–60.

51   S. Nair, 'Human Rights, Sovereignty and the East Timor Question', *Global Society*, vol. 14, no. 1, 2000, pp. 121–2.

52   There were early warnings that local militia against the proposed independence of the territory would cause violence. See The Times, 19 April 1999.

53   This was instigated by the May 5th Agreement between Indonesia, Portugal and the UN. The result was 21.5 per cent in favour, and 344,580, or 78.5 per cent, against the proposal of special autonomy. UN Press Release SG/SM/7119 SC/6722, 3 September 1999.

54   For a fascinating discussion of this see Antonio Donini, 'Asserting Humanitarianism in Peace Maintenance' in Jarat Chopra, *The Politics of Peace-Maintenance*, Boulder, CO: Lynne Rienner, 1998, pp. 81, 96.

55   Oliver Ramsbotham and Tom Woodhouse, op. cit., p. 119.

56   Mary Kaldor, op. cit., p. 124.

57   Thomas G. Weiss, David P. Forsythe, Roger A. Coate, op. cit., p. 39.

58   However, situating crises in their regional historical and political contexts also underlines core issues in regional conflict. For example, the ineffectiveness of the OAU in managing the civil war in Angola reflected internal disagreement about what was engendered by the process of liberation. The capacity of the South Asian Association for Regional Cooperation (SAARC) to act as a neutral mediator of conflict between India and Pakistan over Kashmir weakened by India and Pakistan's contrary stands on the issue and on humanitarian intervention and sovereignty. The capacity of the European Community to respond effectively to the civil war in Croatia was constrained by disagrements amongst its members. Ibid., pp. 40–1.

59   This shift has occurred since the Helsinki Conference in 1992. Emanuel Adler, op. cit., p. 271. In such regions 'people have mastered the practise of peaceful change'. Ibid., p. 276. Articles VII and VIII of the Helsinki Final Act

call for members to respect human rights and fundamental freedoms, and states that all peoples have the right to determine their political status and their political, economic, social and cultural prorities and objectives. Similarly, the EU and the Council of Europe have seen a similar shift within their own structures. At the Lisbon Council, the EU also proposed improving its capacity to address the roots of conflicts and to contribute to the prevention and settlement of conflicts. For further details see John Fry, *The Helsinki Process: Negotiating Security and Co-operation in Europe*, Washington, DC: NDU Press, 1993. See also Charles Krupnick, 'Europe's Intergovernmental NGO: The OSCE in Europe's Emerging Security Structure', *European Security*, vol. 7, no. 2, 1998, pp. 31–2.

60 Emanuel Adler, op. cit., p. 271.

61 See www.oscc.org for further details on the 'OSCE and the Web of Interlocking Institutions'.

62 Charles Krupnik, op. cit., p. 47.

63 See Thomas G. Weiss and Leon Gordenker (eds), *NGOs, the UN, and Global Governance*, Boulder, CO: Lynne Rienner, 1996. See in particular Leon Gordenker and Thomas G. Weiss, 'Pluralizing Global Governance: Analytical Approaches and Dimensions', in ibid., p. 35,

64 Declaration Of The Assembly Of Heads Of State And Government On The Establishment, Within The OAU Of A Mechanism For Conflict Prevention, Management And Resolution, 30 June, 1993. This was funded partly by US contributions. See 'African Conflict Resolution Act', *US Congressional Record*, vol. 140, nos 129–31, 19 September 1994.

65 Michael S. Lund, *Preventing Violent Conflicts*, Washington DC: USIP, 1996, pp. 74–8. Hugh Miall, op. cit., p. 118.

66 See Chairman's Statement: The First Asean Regional Forum, Bangkok, 25 July 1994 and the subsequent document, *The ASEAN Regional Forum : A Concept Paper*, http://www.asean.or.id/amm/progarf1.htm

67 Hugh Miall et al., op. cit., pp. 36–8.

68 Recent Pakistani proposals to incorporate a conflict resolution framework into SAARC met with rejection by India. See *Hindustan Times*, 24 September 1999, p. 1; 27 September p. 18. India has also been reluctant to countenance the concept of humanitarian intervention.

69 Roland Paris, 'Echoes of the Mission Civilisatrice:Peacekeeping in the Post-Cold War Era', in Edward Newman and Oliver P. Richmond, *The United Nations and Human Security*, Basingstoke: Palgrave, 2001, chapter 6.

70 Michele Griffin, 'Retrenchment, Reform, and Regionalisation: Trends in UN Peace Support Operations', in *International Peacekeeping*, vol. 6, no. 1, 1999, p. 4. The author asks whether we might be witnessing the beginning of a fourth generation of peacekeeping operations in which subsidiary becomes a new principle of peacekeeping.

71 Danilo Zolo, *Cosmopolis: Prospects for World Government*, Cambridge: Polity Press, 1997, pp. 27, 39. This reflects the minimalist and maximalist peace research debates. See Paul Rogers and Oliver Ramsbotham, 'Then and Now: Peace Research – Past and Future', *Political Studies*, XLVII, 1999, pp. 744–5.

72 The term 'generation' with reference to first and second generation peacekeeping refers to the shift towards more complex operations along the lines suggested in *Wider Peacekeeping* (London: HMSO, 1995) derived from British

military doctrine, which do not merely patrol ceasefire, but are integral parts of a long-term peacemaking process. In contrast, third generation approaches to peacekeeping involve enforcement and thus diverges from third generation peacemaking which is based on a philosophical approach to building permanent conflict resolution procedures (peacebuilding) within a post-Westphalian international society. *Wider Peacekeeping* outlined a process in which consent could be maintained even in highly volatile environments in which force might have to be used. The French military doctrine of peace restoration required well-armed troops not dependent upon traditional forms of consent in order to fulfil their mission of peace restoration. British military doctrine has now moved closer to this idea. See Peter Viggo Jakobsen, 'The Emerging Consensus on Grey Area Peace Operations Doctrine', *International Peacekeeping*, vol. 7, no. 3, 2000, pp. 37–9.

73   Michele Griffin, op. cit., pp. 2–3. UNGOMAP, which supervised the execution of a peace agreement for Soviet troops from Afganistan and an end to outside assistance of internal factions, was an early indication of the shifts occurring in peacekeeping.

74   Ibid., p. 5.

75   UN doc A/53/1, para.70. Michele Griffin points out the problems of seeing this continuum as chronological and reducing peacemaking to 'calendars' rather than 'objectives', op. cit., p. 5.

76   See, for example, Report of the Secretary General to the UN Security Council Council, A/52/871, 16 April, 1998, para. 63.

77   Tarya Vayrynen, 'Ethnopolitical Meaning in Global Conjunctions: Performative Politics, op. cit., p. 5.

78   Emanuel Adler, op. cit., p. 250.

79   See UN Security Council Resolution 693, 1991.

80   See UN General Assembly, The Situation in Central America: Threats to International Peace and Security and Peace Initiatives, A/45/1055, 16 September, 1991

81   Yvonne C. Lodico, 'A Peace that Fell Apart: The UN and the War in Angola', citing Amnesty International, 'Appeal to Protect Human Rights', *Newsletter*, September 1995, in William J. Durch (ed.), *UN Peacekeeping, American Policy and the Uncivil Wars of the 1990s*, New York: St. Martin's Press – now Palgrave, 1996, p. 126.

82   *The Blue Helmets – A Review of UN Peacekeeping*, 3rd edn, New York: United Nations, 1996, pp. 203–4.

83   See, for example, 'Report of the Secretary General', S/ 15776, 19 May 1983.

84   Oliver Ramsbotham, 'Reflections on UN Post-Settlement Peacebuilding', in Tom Woodhouse and Oliver Ramsbotham, *Peacekeeping and Conflict Resolution*, op. cit., p. 176.

85   James Mayall (ed.), *The New Interventionism 1991–1994*, Cambridge University Press, 1996, p. 8.

86   See, 'Agreement on a Comprehensive Political Settlement of the Cambodia Conflict', *Security Council Letter from the Permanent Representatives of France and Indonesia to the United Nations to the Secretary-General*, 30 October 1991.

87   UN Security Council Resolution 718, 31 October 1991.

88   James A. Shear, 'Riding the Tiger: The UN and Cambodia's Struggle for Peace' in William Durch, op. cit., p. 142.

89 Secretary-General and Prince Sihanouk Press Conference, Phnom Penh, 7 April 1992.
90 Matts Berdal and Michael Leifer, 'Cambodia', in James Mayall, op. cit., pp. 43–4.
91 George Bush, 'Toward a New World Order', Address to Congress, 11 September 1990.
92 François Debrix, op. cit., p. 109.
93 Ioan Lewis and James Mayall, 'Somalia' in James Mayall, op. cit., p. 94.
94 See UN Security Council Resolution 751, 24 April 1992. This resolution provided the framework for Sahnoun's task.
95 For a fascinating discussion of the failures of the UN in Somalia from a cultural point of view, see Tamara Duffey, 'Cultural Issues in Contemporary Peacekeeping', in Tom Woodhouse and Oliver Ramsbotham, *Peacekeeping and Conflict Resolution*, London: Frank Cass, 2000, pp. 153–62.
96 UN Security Council Resolution 866, 22 September 1993.
97 Clement E. Adibe, 'The Liberian Conflict and the Ecowas–UN Partnership', in Thomas G. Weiss, *Beyond UN Subcontracting*, London: Macmillan – now Palgrave, 1998, p. 76.
98 UN Security Council Resolution 872, 5 October 1993.
99 French Operation Turquoise was endorsed under Chapter VII of the UN Charter for humanitarian purposes, but undermined UN impartiality. Ingrid A. Lehman, op. cit., p. 93.
100 UN Security Council Resolution 912, 21 April 1994. See also *Comprehensive Report on Lessons Learned from UNAMIR*, Lessons Learned Unit, Department of Peacekeeping Operations, New York: United Nations, 1996. See also, *Report of the Independent Enquiry into the Actions of the UN during the 1994 Genocide in Rwanda*, New York: United Nations, December 1999.
101 James Mayall, op. cit., p. 8.
102 For a review of these events until late 1994, see Spyros Economides and Paul Taylor, 'Former Yugoslavia', in James Mayall (ed.), *The New Interventionism 1991–1994*, Cambridge University Press, 1996, pp. 59–63.
103 UN Security Council adopted Resolution 713, 25 September 1991: UN Security Council Resolution 743, February 1992.
104 UN Security Council Resolution 749, 7 April 1992.
105 UN Security Council Resolution 769, 7 August 1992.
106 UN Security Council Resolution 816, 31 March 1993: UN Security Council Resolution 824, 6 May 1993.
107 François Debrix, op. cit., pp. 158–9. Debrix argues that this was a 'simulation of enforcement'-move to provide the UN with a façade of authority as it was increasingly stretched beyond its means and its former basis of legitimacy.
108 Boutros-Ghali, op. cit., para. 20.
109 François Debrix, op. cit., p. 159, note 77.
110 Ibid., pp. 159–60.
111 Spyros Economides and Paul Taylor, 'Former Yugoslavia', in James Mayall, op. cit., p. 92.
112 Security Council Resolution 983, 31 March 1995.
113 Hugh Miall et al., op. cit., pp. 121–3.
114 Security Council Resolution 1101, 28 March 1997.
115 Hugh Miall et al., op. cit., pp. 121–3.

116 See *Security Council Resolution 1199*, 23 September 1998.
117 There were early warnings that local militia against the proposed independence of the territory would cause violence. See *The Times*, 19 April 1999. See also the May 5th Agreement between Indonesia, Portugal and the UN. The result was 21.5 per cent in favour, and 344 580, or 78.5 per cent, against the proposal of special autonomy. UN Press Release SG/SM/7119 SC/6722, 3 September 1999.
118 Alan Bullion, 'India in Sierra Leone: A Case of Muscular Peacekeeping', conference paper presented at the Political Studies Association (PSA) annual conference at the London School of Economics in April 2000.
119 Security Council Resolution 1270, 22 October 1999; Security Council Resolution 1289, 7 February 2000.
120 Hugh Miall, op. cit., p. 129. Miall et al. argue that 'peacekeepers and the various humanitarian and development agencies working in war zones need to be aware of the conflict resolution dimension of their work'.
121 Dimitris Bourantonis and Jarrod Weiner, *The UN in the New World Order*, Basingstoke: Macmillan – now Palgrave, 1995, p. x.
122 See, for example, UN Secretary General Report, 'Renewing the United Nations: A Programme for Reform', SG/2037 ORG/1239, 16 July 1997.
123 W. Andy Knight, 'Establishing Political Authority in Peace Maintenance', in Jarat Chopra, op. cit., p. 22.
124 See Pamela Aall, op. cit., p. 441.
125 Miall, op. cit., pp. 150–1.
126 For a discussion of this see Alan Bullion, op. cit. These principles have found support, both from Richard Holbrooke, the UN Ambassador to the UN and from the British Military Doctrine. Indeed, as Bullion points out, British intervention in Sierra Leone was along these lines and to 'expunge the memory of Somalia'.
127 For a development of this line of thought see François Debrix, *Re-Envisioning UN Peacekeeping*, Minneapolis: University of Minnesota Press, 1999, p. 56.
128 For an outline of this life-cycle, see, Stephen Ryan, 'United Nations Peacekeeping: A Matter of Principles', in Tom Woodhouse and Oliver Ramsbotham, op. cit., p. 34.
129 Boutros Boutros-Ghali, op. cit., para. 15.
130 Ibid., para. 16. Paragraph 17 reiterates that the foundation-stone of the organization remains the state, but the implications are clear, though Boutros-Ghali also points out that fragmentation of the state system must be curtailed.
131 Ibid., para. 45.
132 Ibid., para. 34.
133 Here it is important to note that the coordination of such strategies may be problematic. Initially space must be made for diverse peacemaking actors to become involved independently, even though they may recognize their common basic goals.
134 Ibid., para. 55.
135 Ibid., para. 84.
136 Boutros Boutros-Ghali, 'Supplement to An Agenda for Peace' A/50/60, S.1995/1, 3 January 1995.

137 Stephen Ryan, op. cit., p. 31. Ryan argues that Agenda was too broad and PDD-25 too narrow.

138 Kofi Annan, cited by Philip Wilkinson, 'Shaperning the Weapons of Peace: Peace Support Operations and Complex Emergencies', in Woodhouse and Ramsbotham, op. cit., p. 63. Annan argues that UN must be able to counter force with force regardless of the traditional norms of sovereignty.

139 Letters from the Secretary-General to the President of the General Assembly and the President of the Security Council, *Report of the Panel on UN Peace Operations*, A/55/305– S/2000/809, 21 August 2000.

140 Ibid., para. 28.

141 Ibid., paras. 49–52.

142 Michael S. Lund, op. cit., pp. 169–202.

143 See C. R. Mitchell, 'Problem Solving Exercises and Theories of Conflict Resolution', in J. D. Sandole and Hugo van der Merwe (eds), *Conflict Resolution Theory and Practice: Integration and Application*, Manchester University Press, 1993; Loraleigh Keashley and Ronald J. Fisher, 'Complementarity and Coordination of Conflict Interventions: Taking a Contingency Perspective', in J. Bercovitch (ed.), op. cit.

144 Oliver Ramsbotham, 'Reflections on UN Post-Settlement Peacebuilding', in Tom Woodhouse and Oliver Ramsbotham, *Peacekeeping and Conflict Resolution*, op. cit., p. 170.

145 As Gill has pointed out with respect the violent protests in Seattle in late 1991 a new form of political agency has emerged which he calls the 'post-modern Prince', which he understands as 'something plural and differentiated, although linked to universalism and the construction of a new form of globalism, and of course, something that needs to be understood as a set of social and political forces in movement.' Stephen Gill, 'Towards a Post-Modern Prince?' *Millennium*, vol. 29, no. 1, 2000, p. 137. This is also crucial for the development of peacemaking.

146 Michael S. Lund, op. cit., p. 10 (see also Boutros- Ghali, op. cit., para.1. cited in Lund, ibid.)

147 Ibid., p. 87.

148 Ibid., pp. 178–80.

149 Robert Keohane, 'International Institutions: Two Approaches', *International Studies Quarterly*, vol. 32, no. 4, pp. 379–96.

150 Michael S. Lund, op. cit., p. 183.

151 Ibid., p. 185.

152 Ibid., p. 188.

153 Ibid., p. 192.

154 Ibid., p. 193.

155 S. Stedman, 'Alchemy for a New World Order: overselling "preventative diplomacy"', *Foreign* Affairs, vol. 74 (May/ June), 1995; Raimo Vayrynen, 'Preventing Deadly Conflicts: Failures in Iraq and Yugoslavia', *Global Society*, vol. 14, no.1, 2000, p. 31.

156 Ibid., p. 32.

157 Cited by H. Miall et al., op. cit., p. 114.

158 Jarat Chopra, 'The Space of Peace Maintenance', *Political Geography*, vol. 15, no. 3/4, 1996, p. 338.

159 Ibid., pp. 353–4.

160 J. Lederach, *Building Peace – Sustainable Reconciliation in Divided Societies*, Tokyo: United Nations University Press, 1997, pp. 44–7.
161 Ibid., p. 60–1.
162 Ibid., p. 75.
163 Ibid., pp. 82–4.
164 Ibid., p. 99.
165 Ibid., p. 152.
166 Oliver Ramsbotham, 'Reflections on UN Post-Settlement Peacebuilding', in Tom Woodhouse and Oliver Ramsbotham, *Peacekeeping and Conflict Resolution*, op. cit., p. 179.
167 See Nayef H. Samhat, 'International Regimes as Political Community', *Millennium*, vol. 26, no 2, 1997, pp. 362–3.
168 See J. Samuel Barkin, 'The Evolution of the Constitution of Sovereignty and the Emergence of Human Rights Norms', *Millennium*, vol. 27, no. 2, pp. 229–31. Barkin argues that sovereignty is not in crisis as it is an adaptable concept which can incorporate human right norms. However, I would argue that this may well occur, but only because of the need to prevent inflexible forms of sovereignty leading to a breakdown of the international system. In other words, incorporation of human rights norms may occur by default.

Chapter 6   Conclusion: Rethinking Approaches to Ending Conflict

1 Who shall guard the guardians? Juvenal, Satire 6. 347–8, *The Sixteen Satires*, London: Penguin, 1999. Cited in Thomas G. Weiss, David P. Forsythe, Roger A. Coate, *The United Nations and Changing World Politics*, Westview Press: Boulder, Colorado, 1997, p. 143.
2 I am very aware of the fact that one major omission from this study, which would add weight to my critique of the failure of 'Westphalian' approaches to ending conflict relates to the role of women in conflict, gender, and the continuing marginalization that is reified through such approaches. I fear this omission in my own work illustrates how difficult it is to move beyond the limiting assumptions often made in trying to understand and end conflict. See Tom Woodhouse, 'Conflict Resolution and Peacekeeping: Critiques and Responses', in Tom Woodhouse and Oliver Ramsbotham, *Peacekeeping and Conflict Resolution*, London: Frank Cass, 2000, p. 21, notes 37 and 38.
3 See, for example, François Debrix, *Re-envisioning Peacekeeping: the UN and the mobilization of ideology*, Minneapolis: University of Minnesota Press, 1999. p. 91.
4 Mary Kaldor, *New and Old Wars: Organised Violence in a Global Era*, Cambridge: Polity Press, 1999, p. 113.
5 Report of the Panel on UN Peace Operations, A/55/305–S/2000/809, 21 August 2000.
6 See Richard Ashley, 'The Geopolitics of Geopolitical Space: Towards a Critical Social Theory of International Politics', *Alternatives*, vol. 12, no. 4, 1987.
7 Danilo Zolo, *Cosmopolis: Prospects for World Government*, Cambridge: Polity Press, 1997, pp. 14–15.

8   Ibid., p. 128.
9   Michel Foucault, 'What is Enlightenment', in P. Rabinow (ed.), *The Foucault Reader*, London: Penguin, 1989, p. 46.
10 Fen Osler Hampson, *Nurturing Peace*, Washington DC: USIP, 1996, p. 230.
11 Ibid., p. 231.
12 Ibid., p. 233.
13 It is important to note, as Kaldor has done, that outside involvement in conflict in different guises is so common that there 'is no such thing as non-intervention', Mary Kaldor, *New and Old Wars: Organized Violence in a Global Era*, Cambridge: Polity Press, 1999. p. 118.
14 See Tonya Langford, 'States Fall Apart: State Failure and the Politics of Intervention', *International Studies Review*, vol. 1, no. 1, spring 1999, p. 74.
15 John Mackinlay's assessment of the changing nature of peacekeeping also reached a similar conclusion about consent. See John Mackinlay and Jarat Chopra, 'Second Generation Multinational Operations', *Washington Quarterly*, Summer 1992.
16 Paul Rogers and Oliver Ramsbotham, 'Then and Now: Peace Research – Past and Future', *Political Studies*, vol. XLVII, 1999, p. 742.
17 This of course, could also be interpreted as anti-hegemonic hegemony.
18 Andrew Linklater, 'The Achievements of Critical Theory', in Steve Smith, Ken Booth and Marysia Zalewski, *International Theory: Positivism and Beyond*, Cambridge: Cambridge University Press, 1996, p. 288.
19 Mark A. Neufeld, *The Restructuring of International Relations Theory*, Cambridge: Cambridge University Press, 1995, p. 125.
20 Robert Cox with T. Sinclair, *Approaches to World Order*, Cambridge: Cambridge University Press, 1996, p. 88.
21 Andrew Linklater, *The Transformation of Political Community*, Columbia: University of South Carolina Press, 1998, p. 16. See also Christopher Farrands, 'Language and the Possibility of Inter-community Understanding', *Global Society*, vol. 14, no. 1, 2000.
22 Ibid., p. 24.
23 Ibid., p. 34.
24 Ibid., p. 51.
25 A. B. Fetherston, 'Peacekeeping, Conflict Resolution and Peacebuilding: A Reconsideration of Atheoretical Frameworks', in Tom Woodhouse and Oliver Ramsbotham, *Peacekeeping and Conflict Resolution*, London: Frank Cass, 2000, p. 192.
26 Ibid., p. 192.
27 Ibid., p. 194.
28 Ibid., p. 195.
29 Dunane Bratt has argued that the UN placed peace over justice in the Charter (peace, Article 1:1; justice, Article 1:3) and needs to continue to do so to avoid the spectre of imperialism. Dunane Bratt, 'Peace over Justice: Developing a Framework for UN Peacekeeping Operations in Internal Conflicts', in *Global Governance*, vol. 5, no. 1, 1995, pp. 63–6.
30 For a discussion of the establishment of new discursive relations in ethnic conflict along these lines, see Ho-Won Jeong and Tarya Vayrynen, 'Identity Formation and Transformation', in Ho-Won Jeong (ed.), *Conflict Resolution: Dynamics, Processes and Structure*, Aldershot: Ashgate, 1999.

31   For a ground-breaking contribution to this debate, see A. B. Fetherston, op. cit., pp. 208–14.

32   Stephen Hopgood, 'Reading the Small Print in Global Civil Society', *Millennium*, vol. 29, no. 1, 2000, p. 23.

33   Ibid., p. 11. See also Beate Jahn, 'One Step Forward, Two Steps Back: Critical Theory as the Latest Edition of Liberal Idealism', *Millennium*, vol. 27, no. 3, 1998, p. 641.

34   Robert D. Kaplan, *The Ends of the Earth: A Journey at the Dawn of the Twenty First Century*, London: Papermac, 1997.

Bibliography

Abiew, Francis Kofi, and Tom Keating, 'Strange Bedfellows: NGOs and UN peace-keeping operations', *International Peacekeeping*, vol. 6, no. 2, 1999.

Adler, Emanuel, 'Imagined Security Communities: Cognitive Regions in International Relations', *Millennium*, vol. 26, no. 2, 1997.

Aggestam, K., 'Reframing International Conflicts: "Ripeness in International Mediation"', *Paradigms*, vol. 9, no. 2, 1995.

——, 'Two-Track Diplomacy: Negotiations between Israel and the PLO through Open and Secret Channels', *Davis Papers on Israel's Foreign Policy*, no. 53, Leonard Davis Institute for International Relations, Hebrew University of Jerusalem, 1996.

Aggestam, Karin and Christer Jonsson, '(Un)Ending Conflict: Challenges in Post-War Bargaining', *Millennium*, vol. 26, no. 3, 1997.

Akashi, Yasushi, 'The Challenge of Peacekeeping in Cambodia', *International Peacekeeping*, vol. 1, no. 2, 1994.

Alagappa, Muthiah, 'Regionalism and Conflict Management: a framework for analysis', *Review of International Studies*, vol. 21, no. 4, Oct. 1995.

Alger, Chadwig F. and J. Balacz(eds), *Conflict and Crisis of International Order*, Budapest: Centre for Peace Co-ordination of the Hungarian Academy of Sciences, 1985.

Alker, Hayward R., *International Conflict Episodes*, Ann Arbor, MI: Inter-University Consortium for Political and Social Research, 1980.

Allesbrook, M., *Prototypes of Peacemaking*, Chicago and London: St James Press, 1986.

Anderson, Benedict. *Imagined Communities: Reflections of the Origins and Spread of Nationalism*, Ithaca, NY: Cornell University Press, 1991.

Anderson, Malcom, *Frontiers*, Cambridge: Polity Press, 1996, p. 2.

Annan, Kofi A., 'Two Concepts of Sovereignty', *The Economist*, 18 September 1999, and http://www.un.org/Overview/SG/kaecon.htm

Arend, Anthony Clark and Robert J. Beck, *International Law and the Use of Force*, London: Routledge, 1993.

Armstrong, David, 'Globalisation and the social state', in *Review of International Studies*, vol. 24, no. 4, 1998.

Army field manual, *Wider Peacekeeping*, London: HMSO, 1995.

Arrow, Kenneth J., et. al., *Barriers to Conflict Resolution*, New York: W.W. Norton, 1995.

Ashley, Richard 'The Geopolitics of Geopolitical Space: Towards a Critical Social Theory of International Politics', *Alternatives*, vol. 12, no. 4, 1987.

Ashrawi, Hanan, *The Side of Peace: A Personal Account*, New York: Simon & Schuster, 1995.

Assefa, H., *Mediation of Civil Wars*, London: Westview Press, 1987.

Austin, Dennis, *Democracy and Violence in India and Sri Lanka*, London: Pinter, 1994.

Avruch, Kevin, Peter W. Black and Joseph A. Scimecca (eds), *Conflict Resolution: Cross-Cultural Perspectives*, London: Greenwood Press, 1991.

Axford, Barrie, *The Global System*, Cambridge: Polity Press, 1995.

Azar, Edward E., *The Management of Protracted Social Conflict*, Aldershot: Dartmouth, 1990.

Bailey, Sydney Dawson, *How Wars End: The United Nations and the termination of armed conflict 1946–1964*, Vols 1 and 2, Oxford: Clarendon Press, 1982.

—— *The United Nations: A Short Political Guide*, 2nd edn, Basingstoke: Macmillan now Palgrave, 1989.

Baker, James, *The Politics of Diplomacy: Revolution, War and Peace, 1989–1992*, New York: Simon & Schuster, 1995.

Baldwin, David A., 'The Concept of Security', *Review of International Studies*, vol. 23, no. 1, 1997.

Barkin, J. Samuel, 'The Evolution of the Constitution of Sovereignty and the Emergence of Human Rights Norms', *Millennium*, vol. 27, no. 2. 1998.

Barnett, Michael, 'Partners in Peace? The United Nations, regional organisations, and peacekeeping', *Review of International Studies*, vol. 21, no. 4, Oct. 1995.

Bar-on, Mordechai, *In Pursuit of Peace*, Washington, DC: US Institute of Peace, 1996.

Bar-Siman-Tov, Yaacov, *Israel and the Peace Process 1977–1982: In Search of Legitimacy for Peace*, Albany, NY: State University of New York Press, 1994.

Baruch Bush, R. A., and J. P. Folger, *The Promise of Mediation*, London: Jossey-Bass, 1994.

Baylis, John, 'European Security in the Post-Cold War Era: The Continuing Struggle between Realism and Utopianism', in *European Security*, vol. 7, no. 3, 1998.

Beitz, Charles R., *Political Theory and International Relations*, Princeton, NJ: Princeton University Press, 1979.

Bell-Fialkoff, Andrew. *Ethnic Cleansing*, New York: St. Martin's Press – now Palgrave, 1996.

Bendahmane, D. B., and J. W. McDonald (eds), *Perspectives on Negotiation*, Center for the Study of Foreign Affairs, Foreign Service Institute, US Dep of State, 1986.

Bennet, Christopher. *Yugoslavia's Bloody Collapse*, London: Hurst, 1995.

Bercovitch, Jacob, 'International Mediation: A Study of the Incidence, Strategies and Conditions of Successful Outcomes', *Cooperation and Conflict*, vol. 21, no. 3, 1986.

Bercovitch, J., 'International Mediation', *Journal of Peace Research*, Oslo: Universitetsforlaget, vol. 28, no. 1, Feb. 1991.

Bercovitch, J. (ed.), *Resolving International Conflicts: The Theory and Practice of Mediation*, Boulder: Lynne Rienner, 1996.

Bercovitch, J., Theodore Anagnosen and Donnella Wille, 'Some Conceptual Issues and Empirical Trends in the Study of Successful Mediation in International Relations', *Journal of Peace Research*, vol. 28, no. 1, 1991.

Bercovitch, J. and P. Diehl, 'Conflict Management of Enduring Rivalries: The Frequency, Timing and Short-Term Impact of Mediation', *International Interactions*, vol. 22, no. 4, 1997.

Bercovitch, J. and A. Houston, 'Influence of Mediator Characteristics and Behaviour on the Success of Mediation in International Relations', *International Journal of Conflict Management*, vol. 4, no. 4, 1993.

Bercovitch, J. and J. Langley, 'The Nature of the Dispute and the Effectiveness of International Mediation', *Journal of Conflict Resolution*, University of Michigan: Ann Arbor, vol. 37, no. 4, 1993.

Bercovitch, J. and J. Z. Rubin *Mediation in IR: Multiple Approaches to Conflict Management*, Basingstoke: Macmillan – now Palgrave 1992.

Berdal, Matts and David Keen, 'Violence and Economic Agendas in Civil Wars: Some Policy Imperatives', *Millennium*, vol. 26, no. 3, 1997.

Berridge, G. R., *Return to the United Nations: UN diplomacy in regional conflicts*, Basingstoke: Macmillan – now Palgrave, 1991.

——*Diplomacy: Theory and Practice*, Hemel Hempstead: Harvester Wheatsheaf, 1995.

Black, C. E. and Richard A. Falk, eds, *The Future of the International Legal Order, Volume 3*, Princeton, NJ: Princeton University Press, 1972.

Bloomfield, Lincoln P., 'Why Wars End: A Research Note', in *Millennium*, vol. 26, no. 3, 1997.

Bloomfield, Lincoln P. and Amelia C. Leiss, *Controlling Small Wars*, New York: Alfred Knopf, 1969.

Boerma, M., 'The United Nations Interim Force in the Lebanon: Peacekeeping in a Domestic Conflict', *Millennium*, vol. 8, no. 1, 1988.

Booth, Ken and Steve Smith (eds), *International Relations Theory Today*, Cambridge: Polity Press, 1995.

Boulding, E, *Building a Global Civic Culture: Education for an Interdependent World*, Syracuse, NY: Syracuse University Press, 1990.

Boulding, K., *The Image: Knowledge in Life and Society*, Ann Arbor, MI: Michigan University Press, 1956.

Bourantonis, D. and M. Evriviades (eds), *A UN for the Twenty-First Century: Peace Security and Development*, The Hague: Kluwer Law International, 1996.

Bourantonis, Dimitris, and Jarrod Weiner: *The UN in the New World Order*, Basingstoke: Macmillan – now Palgrave, 1995.

Boutros-Ghali, Boutros, *An Agenda for Peace: Preventive Diplomacy, Peacemaking and Peacekeeping*, New York: United Nations, 1992.

——, 'Supplement to An Agenda for Peace', A/50/60, S.1995/1, 3 January 1995.

Boyd, Andrew, *Fifteen Men on a Powder Keg: A History of the United Nations Security Council*, London: Methuen, 1971.

Bratt, D., 'Peace over Justice: Developing a Framework for UN Peacekeeping Operations in Internal Conflicts', *Global Governance*, vol. 5, no. 1, 1995.

Brecher, Michael, *Crisis, Conflict and Instability*, New York: Oxford University Press, 1989.

Brinkley, Douglas, *Dean Acheson, the Cold War Years*, New Haven, CT: Yale University Press, 1992.

Broome, Benjamin, 'Overview of Conflict Resolution Activities in Cyprus', *Cyprus Review*, vol. 10, no. 1, spring 1998.

Boulding, K., 'Future Directions in Conflict and Peace Studies', *Journal of Conflict Resolution*, vol. 22, no. 2, 1978.

Brown, C., *International Relations Theory*, Brighton: Harvester Wheatsheaf, 1992.

Brown, Michael E. (ed.), *Ethnic Conflict and International Security*, Princeton, NJ: Princeton University Press, 1993.

Brown, Michael E., Owen R. Cote, Sean M. Lynne-Jones and Steven E. Miller, *Nationalism and Ethnic Conflict*, Cambridge, Mass.: MIT Press, 1997.

Brownlie, Ian, *Principles of Public International Law*, Oxford: Clarendon Press, 1990.

Buchanan, Allen, *Secession: The Morality of Political Divorce from Sumter to Lithuania and Quebec*, Boulder, CO: Westview, 1990.

Bulchheit, Lee C, *Secession: The Legitimacy of Self- Determination*, New Haven, CT: Yale University Press, 1978.

Bull, Hedley, The Anarchical Society, London: Macmillan – now Palgrave, 1977.

—— (ed.), *Intervention in World Politics*, Oxford: Clarendon Press, 1984.

Bullion, Alan, 'India in Sierra Leone: A Case of Muscular Peacekeeping', conference paper presented at the Political Studies Association (PSA) annual conference at the London School of Economics, April 2000.

Bullion, Alan J., *India, Sri Lanka, and the Tamil Crisis 1976–1994*, London: Pinter, 1995.

Burton, J., *Conflict and Communication*, London: Macmillan – now Palgrave, 1969.

Burton, J., *World Society*, Cambridge University Press, 1972.

Burton, J., *Resolving Deep Rooted Conflict: a Handbook*, Lanham, MD: University Press of America, 1987.

Burton, J., *Conflict Resolution and Provention*, Basingstoke: Macmillan – now Palgrave, 1992.

Burton, J., and E. A. Azar, *International Conflict Resolution: Theory and Practice*, Brighton: Wheatsheaf Books, 1986.

Burton, J. and F. Dukes (eds), *Conflict: Practices in Management, Settlement and Resolution*, Basingstoke: Macmillan – now Palgrave, 1990.

Burton, J. and F. Dukes (eds), *Conflict: Readings in Management and Resolution*, London: Macmillan – now Palgrave, 1990.

Burton, John, (ed.), *Conflict: Human Needs Theory*, New York: St. Martin's Press – now Palgrave, 1990.

Burton, John W., *Deviance, Terrorism and War*, Oxford: Martin Robertson, 1979.

Buzan, Barry, 'Rethinking Security after the Cold War', *Cooperation and Conflict*, vol. 32, no. 1, 1997.

Buzan, Barry and Ole Waever, 'Slippery, Contradictory? Sociologically Untenable: The Copenhagen School Replies', *Review of International Studies*, vol. 23, 1997.

Callaghan, James, *Time and Chance*, London: Collins, 1987.

Calvcoressi, Peter, 'The Cold War as an Episode', Occasional Paper no. 5, David Davies Memorial Institute of International Studies, London, December 1993.

Carment, David and Patrick James, 'The International Politics of Ethnic Conflict: New Perspectives on Theory and Policy', *Global Society*, vol. 11, no. 2, 1997.

Carnegie Commission on Preventing Deadly Conflict, *Preventing Deadly Conflict (Final Report)*. Washington, DC, 1997.

Carr E. H., *The Twenty Years Crisis*, London: Macmillan – now Palgrave, 1966.

Chazan, Naomi (ed.) *Irredentism and International Politics*, Boulder, CO: Lynne Rienner, 1991.

Chipman, John, *Managing the Politics of Parochialism, Survival*, vol. 35, no. 1, 1993.

Chopra, Jarat, 'The Space of Peace Maintenance', *Political Geography* 15, no. 3/4, 1996.

——, *The Politics of Peace-Maintenance*, Boulder, CO: Lynne Rienner, 1998.

Clapham, Christopher, 'Degrees of Statehood', *Review of International Studies*, vol. 24, 1998.

——, 'Rwanda: the Perils of Peacemaking', *Journal of Peace Research*, vol. 25, no. 2, 1998.

Clark, Ann Marie, Elisabeth J. Friedman, and Kathryn Hochesteller, 'The Sovereign Limits of Global Civil Society: A Comparison of NGO Participation in UN World Conferences on the Environment, Human Rights, and Women', in *World Politics*, vol. 51, no. 1, 1998.

Clark, Ian, 'Beyond the Great Divide: globalisation and the theory of international relations', *Review of International Studies*, vol. 24, 1998.

Claude, Inis, *Swords into Ploughshares*, 4th edn, New York: Random House, 1964.

——, 'Collective Legitimisation as a Political Function of the United Nations', *International Organisation*, vol. 21, summer 1966.

Clements, Kevin P., and Robin Ward (eds), *Building International Community: Cooperating for Peace Case Studies*, Canberra: Allen & Unwin, 1994.

Coakley, John (ed.), *The Territorial Management of Ethnic Conflict*, London: Frank Cass, 1993.

Cohen, Stephen P. and Edward E. Azar, 'From War to Peace: The Transition between Egypt and Israel', *Journal of Conflict Resolution*, vol. 25, no. 1, 1981, pp. 87–114.

Connor, Walker, *Ethnonationalism: The Quest for Understanding*, Princeton, NJ: Princeton University Press, 1994.

Corbin, Jane. *The Norway Channel: The Secret Talks that Led to the Middle East Peace Accords*, New York: Atlantic Monthly Press, 1994.

Cox, Michael, Ken Booth and Tim Dunne, 'Introduction: The Interregnum: Controversies in World Politics, 1989–1999', *Review of International Studies*, special issue, vol. 25, December 1999, p. 3.

Cox, Robert, with Sinclair, T, *Approaches to World Order*, Cambridge University Press, 1996.

Craig, Gordon A. and Alexander L. George, *Force and Statecraft*, New York: Oxford University Press, 1983.

Crocker, Chester A. and Fen Osler Hampson with Pamela Aall, (eds), *Managing Global Chaos: Sources of and Responses to International Conflict*, Washington, DC: United States Institute of Peace Press, Fall 1996.

——, and Fen Osler Hampson, 'Making Peace Settlements Work', *Foreign Policy*, no. 104, 1996.

Curle, A., *Another Way; Positive Response to Contemporary Conflict*, Oxford; John Carpenter, 1994.

Davidson, Nicol (ed.), *Paths to Peace: The United Nations Security Council and its Presidency*, New York: Pergamon Press, 1981.

Debrix, François, *Re-Envisioning UN Peacekeeping*, Minneapolis, MN: University of Minnesota Press, 1999.

De Silva and S. W. R. Samarasinghe, *Peace Accords And Ethnic Conflict*, London: Pinter, 1993.

Deutsch, Karl, et al., *Political Community and the North Atlantic Area*, Princeton, NJ: Princeton University Press, 1957.

Deutsch, Morton, *The Resolution of Conflict, Constructive and Destructive Processes*, New Haven, Conn.: Yale University Press, 1973.

Diamond, Louise, and John McDonald, *Multi-Track Diplomacy*, Grinnell: Iowa Peace Institute, 1991.

Diehl, Paul and Harry Goert, *War and Peace In International Rivalries*, Urbana, IL: University of Illinois Press, 1990.

Diehl, Paul F., *International Peacekeeping*, Baltimore and London: Johns Hopkins University Press, 1993.

Dobinson, K, *Mediatory Power and Small States*, MA Dissertation, Canterbury: University of Kent, 1995, http://ukc.ac.uk

Doob, Leonard W., (ed.), *Resolving Conflict in Africa*, New Haven, CT: Yale University Press, 1970.

——, *Intervention: Guides and Perils*, New Haven Conn.: Yale University Press, 1993.

Doyle, Michael W., *Ways of War and Peace: Realism, Liberalism, and Socialism*, New York: W. W. Norton, 1997.

Doyle, Michael, Ian Johnston, and Robert Orr (eds), *Keeping the Peace: Multidimensional UN Operations in Cambodia and El Salvador*, Cambridge: Cambridge University Press, 1997.

Duke, S., 'The United Nations and Intra-state Conflict', *International Peacekeeping*, vol. 1, no. 4, winter 1994.

Durch, William J. (ed.), *The Evolution of UN Peacekeeping*, Basingstoke: Macmillan – now Palgrave, 1994.

Eden, Anthony, *The Eden Memoirs: Full Circle*, London: Cassell, 1960.

Eriksen, Thomas Hylland: *Ethnicity and Nationalism*, London: Pluto Press, 1993.

Esman, Milton, *Ethnic Politics*, Ithaca, NY: Cornell University Press, 1994.

Esman, Milton and Shirley Telhami (eds), *International Organisations and Ethnic Conflict*, Ithaca, NY: Cornell University Press, 1995.

Evans, G., *Cooperating for Peace*, London: Allen & Unwin, 1993.

Evans, Peter, Harold K. Jacobson, and Robert D. Putnam (eds), *Double-Edged Diplomacy: International Bargaining and Domestic Politics*, Berkeley, CA: University of California Press, 1993.

Fabian, L. L., *Soldiers Without Enemies*, Brookings Institution, Washington DC, 1974.

Falk, Richard A., S. Samuel, Kim and Saul H. Mendlovitch (eds), *The United Nations and a Just World Order*, Boulder, CT: Westview Press, 1991.

Farrands, Christopher, 'Language and the Possibility of Inter-Community Understanding', *Global Society*, vol. 14, no. 1, 2000.

Fawcett. J. E. S., *The Law of Nations*, 2nd. edn, Harmondsworth: Penguin, 1971.

Festinger, Leon and Morton Deutsch, *The Resolution of Conflict*, New Haven, CT: Yale University Press, 1973.

Fisk, Robert, *Pity the Nation : Lebanon at War*, Oxford: Oxford University Press, 1991.

Fisher, R., *Interactive Conflict Resolution*, Syracuse, NY: Syracuse University Press, 1997.

Fisher, R. J. and L. Keashley, 'The Potential Complementarity of Mediation and Consultation within a Contingency Model of Third Party Intervention', *Journal of Peace Research*, Oslo: Universitetsforlaget, vol. 28, no. 1, Feb. 1991.

Flamhaft, Ziva. *Israel on the Road to Peace: Accepting the Unacceptable*, Boulder, CO: Westview Press, 1996.

Foucault, Michel, *The Archaeology of Knowledge and the Discourse on Language*, New York: Pantheon Books, 1972.

Franck, Thomas and Inis Claude, *The Power of Legitimacy*, New York: Oxford University Press, 1990.

Freedman, Robert O. (ed.), *Israel under Rabin*, Boulder, CO: Westview Press, 1995.

Frost, Mervyn, 'A Turn Not Taken: Ethics in IR at the Millennium', *Review of International Studies*, special issue, vol. 24, Dec. 1998.
——, *Ethics in International Relations: A Constitutive Theory*, Cambridge: Cambridge University Press, 1999.
Fry, John, *The Helsinki Process: Negotiating Security and Co-operation in Europe*, Washington DC: NDU Press, 1993.
Gale, Fred, 'Constructing Global Civil Society Actors', *Global Society*, vol. 12, no. 3, 1998.
Galtung, J., 'A Structural Theory of Imperialism', *Journal of Peace Research*, vol. 13, no. 2, 1971.
Galtung, Johan, *Peace by Peaceful Means: Peace and Conflict, Development and Civilization*, London: Sage, 1996.
Gellner, Ernest, *Nations and Nationalism*, Ithaca, NY: Cornell University Press, 1993.
——, *Nations and International Security*, Princeton, NJ: Princeton University Press, 1993.
Gill, Stephen, 'Towards a Post-Modern Prince?' *Millennium*, vol. 29, no. 1, 2000.
Gilpin, R., *War and Change in World Politics*, Cambridge: Cambridge University Press, 1981.
Glenny, Misha, *The Fall of Yugoslavia : the Third Balkan war*, 3rd edn, London: Penguin, 1996.
Gobbi, H. J., *Building Peace and Development*, New York: United Nations, 1994.
Gordenker, Leon, and Thomas G. Weiss (eds), *Soldiers, Peacekeepers and Disasters*, Basingstoke: Macmillan – now Palgrave, 1991.
Gottlieb, Gidon, *Nation against State*, New York, NY: Council for Foreign Relations Press, 1993.
Gow, James, *Triumph of Lack of Will: International Diplomacy and the Yugoslav War*, London: Hurst, 1997.
Griffin, Michele, 'Retrenchment, Reform, and Regionalisation: Trends in UN Peace Support Operations', *International Peacekeeping*, vol. 6, no. 1, 1999.
Groom, A. J. R, *Peacekeeping*, Department of International Relations, Bethlehem, PA.: Lehigh University, 1973.
——, 'Approaches to Conflict and Cooperation in International Relations: Lessons from Theory and Practise', *Kent Papers in Politics and IR*, Series 2, no. 2, 1993.
——, *Global Governance in a World of Ethnic Violence*, Unpublished Paper, 1996.
Groom, A. J. R, and Keith Webb, 'Injustice, Empowerment, and Facilitation in Conflict', *International Interactions*, New York: Gordon & Breach, vol. 13. no. 3, 1987.
Groom, A. J. R, and Paul Taylor (eds), *Frameworks for International Co-operation*, London: Pinter, 1990.
Gurr, Ted Robert, *Minorities at Risk: A Global Wew of Ethnopolitical Conflicts*, Washington, DC: United States Institute of Peace Press, 1993.
Gurr, Ted Robert, and Barbara Harff, *Ethnic Conflict in World Politics*, Boulder: Westview Press, 1994.
Haas, Ernst B., *The Uniting of Europe*, Stanford, CA: Stanford University Press, 1958.
Haass, Richard N., *Conflicts Unending: The United States and Regional Disputes*, New Haven, CT: Yale University Press, 1990.
——, *Intervention: The Use of American Military Force in the Post-Cold War World*, Washington, DC: Carnegie Endowment for International Peace, 1994.

Habermas, Jurgen, *Moral Consciousness and Communicative Action*, Cambridge: MIT Press, 1990.

Halperin, Morton H. and David J. Scheffer, *Self-Determination in the New World Order*, Washington, DC: Carnegie Endowment for International Peace, 1992

Hampson, Fen Osler, *Nurturing Peace: Why Peace Settlements Succeed or Fail*, Washington, DC: United States Institute of Peace Press, 1996.

——, 'Third Party Roles in the Termination of Intercommunal Conflict', *Millennium*, vol. 26, no. 3, 1997.

Harbottle, M, 'The Strategy of Third Party Interventions in Conflict Resolution', *International Journal*, vol. XXXV, no. 1, winter 1979–1980.

Harriss, John (ed.), 'The Politics of Humanitarian Intervention', London: Pinter, 1995.

Hartzell, Caroline A., 'Explaining the Stability of Negotiated Settlements to Intrastate Wars' *Journal of Conflict Resolution*, vol. 43, no. 1, 1999.

Hassner, Pierre, 'Beyond Nationalism and Internationalism', in Michael E. Brown (ed), *Ethnic Conflict and International Security*, Princeton, NJ: Princeton University Press, 1993.

Held, David, *Democracy and the Global Order*, Cambridge: Polity Press, 1995.

——, *The Self-Determination of Minorities in International Politics*, London: Frank Cass, 1991.

Heraclides, Alexis, 'The Ending of Unending Conflicts; Separatist Wars', *Millennium*, vol. 26, no. 3, 1997.

Higgins, R., *UN Peacekeeping: Europe 1946–79*, Oxford: Oxford University Press, 1981.

Hoffman, M., 'Defining and Evaluating Success,' *Paradigms*, vol. 9, no. 2, 1995.

Holbrooke, Richard, *To End a War*, New York: Random House, 1998.

Hollis, Rosemary and Nadim Shehadi (eds), *Lebanon On Hold: Implications for Middle East Peace*, London: Royal Institute of International Affairs in association with Oxford Centre for Lebanese Studies, 1996.

Holm, H., and G. Sorensen (eds), *Whose World Order? Uneven Globilization and the End of the Cold War*, Boulder, CO: Westview, 1995.

Holsti, K. J., *Peace and War: Armed Conflicts and International Order 1648–1989*, Cambridge: Cambridge University Press, 1991.

——, *The State, War, and the State of War*, Cambridge: Cambridge University Press, 1996.

Hopgood, Stephen, 'Reading the Small Print in Global Civil Society', *Millennium*, vol. 29, no. 1, 2000.

Horowitz, Donald L., *Ethnic Groups in Conflict*, Berkeley: University of California Press, 1985.

Huntington, Samuel P., *Political Order in Changing Societies*, New Haven, CT: Yale University Press, 1969.

——, *The Clash of Civilizations and the Remaking of World Order*, New York: Simon & Schuster, 1996.

Iklé, F. C., *How Nations Negotiate*, New York: Kraus Reprint, 1985.

Iklé, Fred Charles, *Every War Must End*, New York: Columbia University Press, 1991.

Inbar, E, 'Great Power Mediation: The USA and the May 1983 Israeli–Lebanese Agreement', *Journal of Peace Research*, Oslo: Universitetsforlaget, vol. 28, no. 1, Feb. 1991.

Inbari, Pinhas, *The Palestinians between Statehood and Terrorism*, Brighton: Sussex Academic Press, 1996.

Jabri, V., *Mediating Conflict Decision-making and Western Intervention in Namibia*, Manchester: Manchester University Press, 1990.

——, 'Agency, Structure, and the Question of Power in Conflict Resolution', *Paradigms*, vol. 9, no. 2, winter 1995.

——, *Discourses on Violence: Conflict Analysis Reconsidered*, Manchester and New York: Manchester University Press, 1996.

Jackson, Robert H., *Quasi-states: Sovereignty, International Relations and the Third World*, Cambridge: Cambridge University Press, 1990.

Jacquin Berdal, Dominique, 'Ethnic Wars and International Intervention', *Millennium*, vol. 27, no. 1, 1998.

Jahn, Beate, 'One Step Forward, Two Steps Back: Critical Theory as the Latest Edition of Liberal Idealism', *Millennium*, vol. 27, no. 3, 1998.

Jakobsen, Peter Viggo, 'The Emerging Consensus on Grey Area Peace Operations Doctrine', *International Peacekeeping*, vol. 7, no. 3, 2000.

James, A., *The Politics of Peacekeeping*, London: Chatto & Windus for the International Institute for Strategic Studies, 1969.

——, 'The United Nations Force in Cyprus', *International Affairs*, 65(3), summer 1989.

——, 'International Peacekeeping: The Disputants' View', *Political Studies*, Oxford: Clarendon Press, vol. XXXVIII, 1990.

——, *Peacekeeping in International Politics*, International Institute for Strategic Studies, Macmillan – now Palgrave, 1994.

——, 'United Nations Peacekeeping: Recent Developments and Current Problems', *Paradigms: The Kent Journal of International Relations*, Canterbury: UKC International Relations Society, vol. 8, no. 2, winter 1994.

Jervis, R., *Perception and Misperception in International Politics*, Princeton, NJ: Princeton University Press, 1976.

Jeong, Ho-Won (ed.), *The New Agenda for Peace Research*, Aldershot: Ashgate, 1999.

—— (ed.), *Conflict Resolution: Dynamics, Processes and Structure*, Aldershot: Ashgate, 1999.

Job, Brian L. (ed.), *The Insecurity Dilemma: National Security of Third World States*, Boulder, CO.: Lynne Rienner, 1992.

Jones, D., *Cosmopolitan Mediation*, Manchester: University of Manchester Press, 1999.

Jupp, James, *Sri Lanka: Third World Democracy*, London: Frank Cass, 1978.

Kaldor, Mary, *New and Old Wars: Organised Violence in a Global Era*, Cambridge: Polity Press, 1999.

——, ' "Civilising" Globalisation', *Millennium*, vol. 29, no. 1, 2000.

Kaplan, Robert D., *The Ends of the Earth: A Journey at the Dawn of the Twenty First Century*, London: Papermac, 1997.

——, *Balkan Ghosts: A Journey through History*, New York: Vintage, 1994.

Kass, Ilan and Brad O'Neill, *The Deadly Embrace: The Impact of Israeli and Palestinian Rejectionism on the Peace process*, Fairfax, VA: National Institute for Public Policy, 1997.

Kaufman, J., *The World in Turmoil: Testing the UN's Capacity*, Academic Council on the United Nations System, 1991.

Kaufman, S. and G. T. Duncan, 'A Formal Framework for Mediator Mechanisms and Motivations', *Journal of Conflict Resolution*, University of Michigan, Ann Arbor:, vol. 36, no. 4, 1992.

Kaufman, Stuart J., 'Spiraling to ethnic war: elites, masses, and Moscow in Moldova's civil war', *International Security*, fall 1996, vol. 21, no. 2, 1996.

Keashley, Loraleigh and Ronald J. Fisher, 'Complementarity and Coordination of Conflict Interventions: Taking a Contingency Perspective', in J. Bercovitch (ed.), *Resolving International Conflicts: The Theory and Practice of Mediation*, Boulder, CO: Lynne Rienner, 1996.

Keegan, John, *A History of Warfare*, London: Pimlico, 1993.

Kelidar, A., *Lebanon: the Collapse of a State: Regional Dimensions of the Struggle*, 1976.

Kellas, James G.: *The Politics of Nationalism and Ethnicity*, London: Macmillan – now Palgrave, 1991.

Kellerman, Barbara and Jeffrey Z. Rubin (eds) *Leadership and Negotiation in the Middle East*, New York: Praeger, 1988.

Kelman, Herbert C., 'An Interactional Approach to Conflict Resolution and its Applications to Israeli–Palestinian Relations', *International Interactions*, vol. 6, no. 2, 1979.

Kelman, Herbert, 'Contributions of an Unofficial Conflict Resolution Effort to the Israeli–Palestinian Breakthrough', *Negotiation Journal*, vol. 11, no. 1, 1995.

Kelsen, Hans, *The Law of the United Nations*, London, 1950.

Keohane, R., and J. Nye, *Transnational Relations and World Politics*, Cambridge, MA: Harvard University Press, 1972.

Keohane, Robert O., *After Hegemony: Cooperation and Discord in the World Economy*, Princeton, NJ: Princeton University Press, 1984.

Keohane, Robert, 'International Institutions: Two Approaches', *International Studies Quarterly*, vol. 32, no. 4. 1988 (December): 379–96.

King, Charles, 'Ending Civil Wars', *Adelphi Paper* 308, London: Oxford University Press for International Institute for Strategic Studies, 1997.

Kleiboer, Marieke, 'Ripeness of Conflict: A Fruitful Notion?', *Journal of Peace Research*, vol. 31, no. 1, 1994.

——, 'Understanding the Success and Failure of International Mediation', *Journal of Conflict Resolution*, vol. 40, no. 2, June 1996.

Korzenny, F., and S. Ting-Toomey (eds), *Communicating for Peace Diplomacy and Negotiation*, London: Sage, 1990.

Kozyrev, Adrie, *NATO Review*, vol. 42, no. 4, 1994.

Krasner, Stephen D. (ed.), *International Regimes*, Ithaca, NY: Cornell University Press, 1983.

Kreisburg, L., 'Formal and Quasi Mediators in International Disputes: An Exploratory Analysis', *Journal of Peace Research*, Oslo: Universitetsforlaget, vol. 28, no. 1, Feb. 1991.

Kreisburg, L., T. A. Northrup, and S. J. Thorson, *Intractable Conflicts and their Resolution*, Syracuse, NY: Syracuse University Press, 1984.

——, *Intractable Conflicts and Their Transformation*, Syracuse, NY: Syracuse University Press, 1989.

Kreisburg, L., and S. J. Thorson, (eds), *Timing the De-escalation of Intractable Conflicts*, Syracuse, NY: Syracuse University Press, 1991.

Krepon, Michael and Amit Sevak (eds), *Crisis Prevention, Confidence Building, and Reconciliation in South Asia*, Basingstoke: Macmillan – now Palgrave, 1995.

Kritz, Neil J. (ed.) *Transitional Justice: How Emerging Democracies Reckon with Former Regimes, Volume 1*, Washington, DC: United States Institute of Peace Press, 1995.

Krupnick, Charles, 'Europe's Intergovernmental NGO: The OSCE in Europe's Emerging Security Structure', *European Security*, vol. 7, no. 2, 1998.

Kuhn, T. S., *The Structure of Scientific Revolutions*, Chicago, IL: University of Chicago Press, 1970.

Lakatos, I., and A. Musgrave, *Criticism and the Growth of Knowledge*, Cambridge: Cambridge University Press, 1970.

Lall, A. S., (ed.), *Multilateral Negotiation and Mediation*, Oxford: Pergamon Press, 1985.

Langford, Tonya, 'States Fall Apart : State Failure and the Politics of Intervention', *International Studies Review*, vol. 1, no. 1, spring 1999.

Lapidoth, Ruth, *Autonomy: Flexible Solutions to Ethnic Conflict*, Washington, DC: United States Institute of Peace, 1996.

LaRose-Edwards, Paul, *UN Human Rights Operations: Principles and Practice in United Nations Field Operations*, Ottawa: Human Rights and Justice Division, Department of Foreign Affairs and International Trade, 1996.

Lebaron, M., 'Mediation and Multicultural Reality', *Peace and Conflict Studies*, vol. 5, no. 1, p. 43.

Lebow, Richard Ned, *The Art of Bargaining*, Baltimore, MD: Johns Hopkins University Press, 1996.

Lederach, J. *Preparing for Peace: Conflict Transformation Across Cultures*, Syracuse, NY: Syracuse University Press, 1995.

Lederach, John Paul, *Building Peace: Sustainable Reconciliation in Divided Societies*, Washington, DC: United States Institute of Peace Press, 1997.

Lehman, Ingrid A., *Peacekeeping and Public Information*, London: Frank Cass, 1999.

Lewicki, Roy, J. et al., *Negotiation*, 2nd edn, Burr Ridge, IL: Irwin, 1994.

Licklider, Roy (ed.), *Stopping the Killing: How Civil Wars End*, New York: New York University Press, 1993.

——, 'The Consequences of Negotiated Settlements in Civil Wars 1945–1993,' *American Political Science Review*, vol. 89, no. 3, Sept. 1995.

Lijphart, Arend, *Democracies: Patterns of Majoritarian and Consensus Government in Twenty-One Countries*, New Haven, CT: Yale University Press, 1984.

Linklater, Andrew, *The Transformation of Political Community*, Columbia University of South Carolina Press, 1998.

Linklater, Andrew, and John Macmillan, *Boundaries in Question*, London: Pinter, 1995.

Lister, F, 'The Recent Revival of the United Nations', *International Relations*, London: David Davies Memorial Institute of International Studies, vol. IX, no. 5, May 1989.

——, 'The Role of International Organisations in the 1990s and Beyond', *International Relations*, London: David Davies Memorial Institute of International Studies, vol. X, no. 2, Nov. 1990.

Little, David, *Sri Lanka: The Invention of Enmity*, Washington, DC: United States Institute of Peace Press, 1994.

Luard, Evan, *Conflict and Peace in Modern International System*, Albany, NY: State University of New York Press, 1988.

——, *A History of the United Nations: Volume 2 The Age of Decolonization, 1955–1965*, Basingstoke: Macmillan – now Palgrave, 1989.

——, *The Globalization of Politics*, Basingstoke: Macmillan – now Palgrave, 1990.

Luis Roninger and Ayse Gynes-Ayata (eds), *Democracy, Clientelism and Civil Society*, Boulder CO: Lynne Rienner, 1994.

Lund, Michael S., *Preventing Violent Conflict: A Strategy for Preventive Diplomacy*, Washington, DC: United States Institute of Peace Press, 1996.

Lynch, Cecelia, 'The Promise and Problems of Internationalism', *Global Governance*, vol. 5, no. 1, 1999.

Lyons, Gene M., and Michael Mastunduno, *Beyond Westphalia*, Baltimore, MD: Johns Hopkins University Press, 1995.

Mackinlay, John, and Jarat Chopra, 'Second Generation Multinational Operations', *Washington Quarterly*, summer 1992.

Macmillan, Harold, *Riding the Storm*, London: Macmillan, 1971.

MacQueen, N., 'Ireland and the United Nations Peacekeeping Force in Cyprus', *Review of International Studies*, Harlow: Longman, 1983.

Mandell, B. S. and B. W. Tomlim: 'Mediation in the Development of Norms to Manage Conflict: Kissinger in the Middle East', *Journal of Peace Research*, Oslo: Universitetsforlaget, vol. 28, no. 1, Feb. 1991.

Massoud, Tansa G., 'War Termination', *Journal of Peace Research*, vol. 33, no. 4, 1996.

Mayall, James (ed.), *The New Interventionism, 1991–1994 : United Nations Experience in Cambodia, former Yugoslavia, and Somalia*, Cambridge and New York, Cambridge University Press, 1996.

——, *Nationalism and International Society*, Cambridge: Cambridge University Press, 1990.

McDowall, David, *A Modern History of the Kurds*, London: I. B. Tauris, 1997.

Miall, H., (ed.), *The Peacemakers*, Basingstoke: Macmillan – now Palgrave, 1992.

Miall, Hugh, Oliver Ramsbotham, and Tom Woodhouse, *Contemporary Conflict Resolution*, Cambridge: Polity Press, 1999.

Midlarsky, Manus (ed.), *The Internalization of Communal Strife*, London and New York: Routledge, 1992.

Mitchell, C., and Michael Banks, *Handbook of Conflict Resolution*, London: Pinter, 1996.

Mitchell, C. and K. Webb (eds), 'Mediation in International Relations: An Evolving Tradition', *New Approaches to International Mediation*, New York: Greenwood Press, 1988.

Mitchell, C., *Peacemaking and the Consultant's Role*, Aldershot: Gower, 1981.

Mitchell, C. R., *The Structure of International Conflict*, Basingstoke: Macmillan – now Palgrave, 1981.

Mitchell, Christopher R., 'The Right Moment: Notes on Four Models of "Ripeness" ', *Paradigms: The Kent Journal of International Relations*, vol. 9, no. 2, 1995.

Mitra, S. and A. Lewis (eds) *Subnational movements in South Asia*, Boulder, CO: Westview Press, 1996.

Mitrany, D. A., *The Functional Theory of Politics*, London: Martin Robertson, 1975.

Mitrany, David, *A Working Peace System*, Oxford: Oxford University Press, 1943.

Modelski, G., *Long Cycles in World Politics*, London; Macmillan, 1987.

Montevideo Convention on the Rights and Duties of States, Article 1, 1933.

Montville, Joseph (ed.) *Conflict and Peacemaking in Multi-Ethnic Societies*, Lexington, MA: Lexington Books, 1990.

Morganthau, H., *Politics Amongst Nations*, McGraw-Hill, 1948.

Morphet, Sally, 'The influence of states and groups of states on and in the Security Council and General Assembly, 1980–1994', *Review of International Studies*, Harlow: Longman, vol. 21, no. 4, Oct. 1995.

Nardin, Terry, *Law, Morality and the Relations of States*, Princeton, NJ: Princeton University Press, 1983.

Nardin, Terry, and David R. Mapel, *Traditions of International Ethics*, Cambridge: Cambridge University Press, 1992.

Navartna-Bandara, Abysinghe M., *The Management of Ethnic Secessionist Conflict: The Big Neighbour Syndrome*, Aldershot: Dartmouth, 1995.

Netanyahu, Benjamin, *A Place Among the Nations: Israel and the World*, New York. Bantam Books, 1993.

——, *Fighting Terrorism: How Democracies Can Defeat Domestic and International Terrorists*, New York: Farrar Straus Giroux, 1995.

Neufeld, Mark A., *The Restructuring of International Relations Theory*, Cambridge: Cambridge University Press, 1995.

Newman, Edward, and Oliver P. Richmond, *The United Nations and Human Security*, Basingtoke: Palgrave, 2001.

Nicolson, Harold, *Peacemaking 1919*, Boston: Houghton Mifflin, 1933.

Nordstrom, C. and J. Martin (eds), *The Paths to Domination, Resistance and Terror*, Berkeley, CA: University of California Press, 1992.

Organization of African Unity, *Declaration Of The Assembly Of Heads Of State And Government On The Establishment, Within The OAU Of A Mechanism For Conflict Prevention, Management And Resolution*, 30 June 1993.

Osterud, Oyvind, 'The Narrow Gate: Entry to the Club of Sovereignty States', *Review of International Studies*, vol. 23, 1997.

Ovendale, Ritchie, *The origins of the Arab–Israeli wars*, 2nd edn, London: Longman, 1992.

Parsons, Anthony, *From Cold War to Hot Peace – United Nations Interventions 1947–1994*, London: Penguin, 1995.

Perry, Mark, *A Fire in Zion: The Israeli–Palestinian Search for Peace*, New York, NY: William Morrow, 1994.

Pillar, Paul, *Negotiating Peace: War Termination as a Bargaining Process*, Princeton, NJ: Princeton University Press 1983.

Popper, K. P., *Conjectures and Refutations*, London; Routledge, 1989.

Posen, Barry, 'The Security Dilemma and Ethnic Conflict', *Survival*, vol. 35, no. 1, 1993.

Premdas, Ralph, S. W. R. de A. Samarasinghe, and Alan B. Anderson (eds), *Secessionist Movements in Comparative Perspective*, London: Pinter, 1990.

Princen, T, 'Camp David: Problem-Solving or Power Politics as Usual?', *Journal of Peace Research*, Oslo: Universitetsforlaget, vol. 28, no. 1, Feb. 1991.

——, *Intermediaries in International Conflict*, Princeton, NJ: Princeton University Press, 1992.

P. Rabinow (ed.), *The Foucault Reader*, London: Penguin, 1989.

Ramet, Sabrina Petra, *Nationalism and Federalism in Yugoslavia, 1962–1992*, 2nd edn, Bloomington, IN: Indiana University Press, 1992.

Ramsbotham, Oliver and Tom Woodhouse, *Humanitarian Intervention in Contemporary Conflict*, Cambridge, Polity Press, 1996.

Rapoport, A, *The Origins of Violence*, New York: Paragon House, 1989.

Ratner, Steven, R., 'The New UN Peacekeeping', London: Macmillan – now Palgrave, 1997.

Reus-Smit, Christian, 'The Constitutional Structure of International Society and the Nature of Fundamental Institutions, *International Organisation*, vol. 51, no. 4, 1997.

Richmond, Oliver P. 'Negotiating Out Fear and Fearing to Negotiate: Implications of the Dynamics of Peacemaking in Cyprus for Theoretical Approaches to the Ending of Conflict', *Cyprus Review*, Nicosia: Intercollege, fall 1996.

——, *Mediating in Cyprus: The Cypriot Communities and the UN*, London: Frank Cass, 1998.

——, 'Devious Objectives and the Disputants' View of International Mediation: A Theoretical Framework', *Journal of Peace Research*, vol. 35, 1998.

——, 'The Linkage Problematic Between "Track I" and Track II and The Emergence of a Third Generation of Multi-dimensional Peacemaking in Intractable Conflict', INCORE, www.incore.ulst.ac.uk, 1999.

——, 'Mediating Ethnic Conflict: A Task for Sisyphus?', Global Society, vol. 13, no. 2, 1999.

——, 'States of Sovereignty, Sovereign States, and Ethnic Conflict', *Review of International Studies*, forthcoming, 2002.

Rikhye, I. J., Harbottle, M., Egge, B., *The Thin Blue Line*, New Haven, CT: Yale University Press, 1974.

Rittberger, Volker (ed.) *Regime Theory and International Relations*, Oxford: Oxford University Press, 1995.

Rivlin, B., 'The UN Secretary-Generalship at Fifty', *Paradigms*, Canterbury: University of Kent International Relations Society, vol. 8, no. 2, winter 1994.

Roberts, Adam, 'Communal Conflict as a challenge to international organisation: the case of former Yugoslavia', *Review of International Studies*, Harlow: Longman, vol. 21, no. 4, Oct. 1995.

Roberts, Adam, and Benedict Kingsbury (eds), *United Nations, Divided World*, 2nd edn, London: Oxford University Press, 1996.

Robins, P., *Turkey and the Middle East*, London: Royal Institute of International Affairs and Pinter, 1991.

Roe, Paul, 'The Intrastate Security Dilemma: Ethnic Conflict as a "Tragedy"?' *Journal of Peace Research*, vol. 36, no. 2, 1999.

Rogel, C., *Breakup of Yugoslavia*, Westport, CT: Greenwood Press, 1998.

Rogers, Paul, and Oliver Ramsbotham, 'Then and Now: Peace Research – Past and Future', *Political Studies*, vol. XLVII, 1999.

Rosenau, J., *Turbulence in World Politics: A Theory of Change and Continuity*, Princeton, NJ: Princeton University Press, 1990.

Rosenau, James N. (ed.), *International Aspects of Civil Strife*, Princeton, NJ: Princeton University Press, 1964.

Rothschild, Donald K., *Managing Ethnic Conflict in Africa: Pressures and Incentives for Co-operation*, Washington, DC: Brookings Institution, 1997.

Rothschild, Joseph, *Ethnopolitics*, New York: Columbia University Press, 1980.

Rubin, Barry, Joseph Ginat and Moshe Ma'oz, *From War to Peace: Arab–Israeli Relations 1973–1993*, Brighton: Sussex Academic Press, 1994.

Rupesinghe, Kumar (ed.), *Conflict Transformation*, London: Macmillan – now Palgrave: 1995.

Rupesinghe, Kumar and Khawar Mumtaz (eds), *Internal Conflict in South Asia*, London: Sage, 1996.

Russett, Bruce, *Grasping the Democratic Peace*, Princeton, NJ: Princeton University Press, 1993.

Ryan, Christopher M., 'Sovereignty, Intervention and the Law: A Tenuous Relationship of Competing Principles', *Millennium*, vol. 26, no. 1, 1997.

Ryan, S, 'Explaining Ethnic Conflict: The Neglected International Dimension', *Review of International Studies*, vol. 14, 1988.

Ryan, Stephen, *Ethnic Conflict and International Relations*, Aldershot: Dartmouth, 1990.

Saaty, T. J. and J. M. Alexander, *Conflict Resolution*, New York and London: Praeger, 1989.

Sahadevan, P., 'Lost Opportunities and Changing Demands: Explaining the Ethnic Conflict in Sri Lanka', *Kent Papers in Politics and IR*, www.ukc.ac.uk/gsir/ 1998.

Said, Edward W., *Peace and Its Discontents: Gaza-Jericho 1993–1995*, London: Vintage, 1995.

———, *The Politics of Dispossession. The Struggle for Palestinian Self-Determination, 1969–1994*, London: Vintage, 1995.

Samarasinghe, S. W. R de A. and Alan B. Anderson (eds), *Secessionist Movements in Comparative Perspective*, London: Pinter, 1990.

Samhat, Nayef H., 'International Regimes as Political Community', *Millennium*, vol. 26, no. 2, 1997.

Sandole, D. J. D., and I. Sandole-Staroste (eds), *Conflict Management and Problem Solving*, London: Pinter, 1987.

Saunders, Harold, *A Public Peace Process*, London: Macmillan – now Palgrave, 1999.

Saunders, Harold H. 'Sustained Dialogue on Tajikistan', *Mind and Human Interaction*, vol. 6, no. 3, 1995.

Schultz, Helena Lindholm, *Between Revolution and Statehood: Reconstruction of Palestinian Nationalisms*, Göteborg: Padrigu Papers, 1996.

Seyersted, F., *UN Forces and the Law of Peace and War*, Leyden: A. W. Stazhoff, 1966.

Shearer, David, 'Exploring the Limits of Consent', *Millennium*: vol. 26, no. 3, 1997.

Sherman, Richard, *Eritrea: The Unfinished Revolution*, New York: Praeger, 1980.

Singer, David, *The Correlates of War*, New York: Free Press, 1980.

Singer, Max and Aaron Wildavsky, *The Real World Order*, NJ Chatham House Publishers: New Jersey, 1993.

SIPRI-UNESCO Handbook, *Peace, Security and Conflict Prevention*, Oxford: Oxford University Press, 1998.

Sirriyeh, Hussein, *Lebanon: Dimensions of Conflict*, London: Brassey's, for the International Institute of Strategic Studies, 1989.

Sisk, T., *Power Sharing and International Mediation in Ethnic Conflicts*, Washington DC: United States Institute of Peace, 1996.

Skjelsbaek, Kjell, 'The United Nations Secretary-General and the Mediation of International Disputes', *Journal of Peace Research*, Oslo: Universitetsforlaget, vol. 28, no. 1, Feb. 1991.

Skogmo, Bjorn, *UNIFIL: International Peacekeeping in Lebanon*, 1978–1988, Boulder, CO, and London, Lynne Rienner, 1989.
Small, Melvin and J. David Singer, *Resort to Arms*, Beverly Hills, CA: Sage, 1982.
Smith, Anthony D, *The Ethnic Origin of Nations*, Oxford: Blackwell, 1986.
Smith, James D, 'Mediator Impartiality: Banishing the Chimera', *Journal of Peace Research*, vol. 31, no. 4, Nov. 1994.
Smith, Steve, Ken Booth and Marysia Zalewski, *International Theory: Positivism and Beyond*, Cambridge: Cambridge University Press, 1996.
Smock, David R. (ed.), *Making War and Waging Peace: Foreign Intervention in Africa*, Washington, DC: United States Institute of Peace, 1993.
Sorenson, Georg, 'An Analysis of Contemporary Statehood: Consequences for Conflict and Cooperation', *Review of International Studies*, vol. 23, 1997.
Soto, Alvaro de and Graciana del Castillo, 'Implementation of Comprehensive Peace Agreements: Staying the Course in El Salvador', *Global Governance*, vol. 1, no. 2, 1995.
Stearns, Monteagle, *Entangled Allies: US Policy towards Greece, Turkey, and Cyprus*, New York: Council on Foreign Relations, 1992.
Stedman, Stephen John, *Peacemaking in Civil War: International Mediation in Zimbabwe*, Boulder, CO.: Lynne Rienner, 1991.
Stegenga, James A., *The United Nations Force in Cyprus*, Columbus: Ohio State University, 1968.
Stein, Janice Gross and Louis W. Pauly (eds), *Choosing to Cooperate: How States Avoid Losses*, Baltimore, MD: Johns Hopkins University Press, 1993.
Stoessinger, John G., *Why Nations Go To War*, 6th edition, New York: St. Martins Press, 1992.
Strange, Susan, 'The Westfailure System', *Review of International Studies*, vol. 25, no. 3, 1999.
Suganami, Hugh, *On The Causes of War*, Oxford: Clarendon Press, 1996.
Suhrke, Astri and Lela Garner Noble (eds), *Ethnic Conflict and International Relations*, New York: Praeger, 1977.
Sutterlin, J. S., *The United Nations and the Maintenance of International Security*, New York: Praeger, 1995.
Symynkywicz, Jeffrey B., *Civil War in Yugoslavia*, Parsippany, NJ, Dillon Press, 1997.
Taylor, Paul, *International Organisation in the Modern World*, London: Pinter, 1993.
Thakur, R. (ed.), *International Conflict Resolution*, Boulder, CO, Westview Press; Dunedin, New Zealand: University of Otago Press, 1988.
The Peace Treaty of Versailles, 28 June 1919.
Theophlyactou, D., *Security, Identity and Nation Building*, Aldershot: Avebury, 1995.
Tidwell, Alan C., *Conflict Resolved*, London: Pinter, 1998.
Tomlin, Brian, and Brian S. Mandell, 'Mediation in the Development of Norms to Manage Conflict: Kissinger in the Middle East,' *Journal of Peace Research*, vol. 28, no. 1, 1991.
Tomuschat, Christian (ed.), *Modern Law of Self-Determination*, Dordrecht: Martinus Nijhoff, 1993
Touval, S. and I. W. Zartman, (eds), *International Mediation in Theory and Practice*, School of Advanced International Studies, Baltimore, MD, Johns Hopkins University Press, 1985.

Touval, Saadia, 'Why the UN. fails', *Foreign Affairs*, vol. 73. no. 5. Sept.-Oct. 1994.
UN Secretary General Report, 'Renewing the United Nations: A Programme for Reform', SG/2037 ORG/1239, 16 July 1997.
UN, *The Blue Helmets – A Review of UN Peacekeeping*, 3rd edn, New York: United Nations, 1996.
UN, *Comprehensive Report on Lessons Learned from UNAMIR, Lessons Learned Unit*, Department of Peacekeeping Operations, New York, United Nations, 1996.
UNDP, *Human Development Report*, Oxford: Oxford University Press, 1994.
Urquhart, B., *A Life in Peace and War*, London: Weidenfeld & Nicolson, 1987.
Usher, Graham, *Palestine in Crisis: The Struggle for Peace and Political Independence after Oslo* London, Pluto Press, 1995.
Vasquez, John A., *The War Puzzle*, Cambridge: Cambridge University Press, 1993.
——, (ed.), *Beyond Confrontation: Learning Conflict Resolution in the Post-Cold War Era*, Ann Arbor, MI: University of Michigan Press, 1995.
Vayrynen, R. (ed.), *New Directions in Conflict Theory*, London: Sage, 1991.
Vayrynen, Tarya, 'Going Beyond Similarity: The Role of the Facilitator in Problem Solving Workshop Conflict Resolution', *Paradigms*, vol. 9, no. 2, winter 1995.
——, 'Ethnopolitical Meaning in Global Conjunctions: Performative Politics', paper presented at the Third Pan-European International Relations Conference, Vienna, 16–19 Sept. 1998.
Vincent, J. R., *Nonintervention and International Order*, Princeton, NJ: Princeton University Press, 1974.
Vincent, R. J., *Human Rights and International Relations*, Cambridge: Cambridge University Press, 1986.
Vizhi, Gower, 'Ethnic Conflict and Political Accommodation in Pluralistic Societies: Cyprus and Other Cases', *Journal of Commonwealth and Comparative Politics*, vol. 31, no. 1, Mar. 1993.
Volkan, Vamik, *The Need to Have Enemies and Allies*. Northvale, NJ: Jason Arson, 1988.
Volkan, Vamik and Itykowitz, N, *Turks and Greeks – Neighbours in Conflict*, Huntingdon: Eothen Press, 1994.
Volkan, Vamik and Mark Harris, 'Negotiating a Peaceful Separation', *Mind and Human Interaction*, vol. 4, no. 1, 1992.
Voutira, Eftihia, and Shaun A. Wishaw Brown, *Conflict Resolution. A Review of Some Non-Governmental Practices; 'A Cautionary Tale'*, Uppsala: Nordiska Afrikainstituet 1995.
Wai, Dunstan M., *The Afro-Arab Conflict in the Sudan*, New York: Africana Publishing, 1981.
Wainhouse, D. W., *International Peacekeeping at the Crossroads*, Baltimore, MD: Johns Hopkins University Press, 1973.
Waldheim, K., *The Challenge of Peace*, London: Weidenfeld & Nicolson, 1977.
Waldheim, K., *In the Eye of the Storm*, London: London: Weidenfeld & Nicolson, 1985.
Wall, J. A., 'Mediation', *Journal of Conflict Resolution*, vol. 25 no. 1, March 1981.
Wall, J. A. and A. Lynn, 'Mediation: A Current Review', *Journal of Conflict Resolution*, Ann Arbor MI: University of Michigan Press, vol. 37 no. 1, 1993.
Wallensteen, Peter (ed.), *Peace Research: Achievements and Challenges*, Boulder, CO: Westview Press, 1988.

Wallerstein, I., *Geopolitics and Geoculture*, Cambridge: Cambridge University Press, 1991.

Walt, Stephen M., *The Origins of Alliances*, Ithaca, NY: Cornell University Press, 1987.

Walter, Barbara F., 'The Critical Barrier to Civil War Settlement', *International Organization*, vol. 51, no. 3, 1997.

Waltz, Kenneth N., *The Theory of International Politics*, New York: McGraw-Hill, 1979.

——, 'The Emerging Structure of International Politics', *International Security*, vol. 18, no. 2, 1993.

Walzer, Michael, *Just and Unjust Wars*, New York: Basic Books, 1992.

Webb, K., 'Third Party Intervention and the Ending of Wars', *Paradigms*, Canterbury: University of Kent International Relations Society, vol. 9, no. 2, winter 1995.

Wehr, P. and J. P. Lederach, 'Mediating Conflict in Central America', *Journal of Conflict Resolution*, Ann Arbor, MI: University of Michigan Press, vol. 28, no. 1, Feb. 1991.

Wehr, Paul, *Conflict Regulation*, Boulder, CO: Westview Press, 1979.

Weiss, Thomas G., David P. Forsythe, Roger A. Coate, *The United Nations and Changing World Politics*, Boulder, CO: Westview Press, 1997.

Weiss, Thomas G., and Leon Gordenker (eds), *NGOs, the UN, and Global Governance*, Boulder, CO: Lynne Rienner, 1996.

Weiss, Thomas G., *Beyond UN Subcontracting*, London: Macmillan – now Palgrave, 1998.

Wheeler, Nicolas, and Tim Dunne, 'Good International Citizenship: a Third Way for British Foreign Policy' *International Affairs*, vol. 74, no. 4, 1998.

White, N. D., 'U.N. Peacekeeping Development or Destruction?', *International Relations*, London: David Davies Memorial Institute of International Studies, vol. XII, no. 1, 1994.

White, Nicolas, *Keeping the Peace*, Manchester: Manchester University Press, 1997.

Willets, Peter, and Fay Wright, 'From "Consultative Arrangements" to "Partnership": The Changing Status of NGOs in Diplomacy at the UN,' *Global Governance*, vol. 6, no. 2, 2000.

Williams, Andrew, *Failed Imagination? New World Orders of the Twentieth Century*, Manchester: Manchester University Press, 1998.

——, 'Conflict Resolution after the Cold War: The Case of Moldova', *Review of International Studies*, vol. 25, no. 1, 1999.

Wilmer, Franke, 'Identity, culture and historicity: the social construction of ethnicity in the Balkans', *World Affairs*, vol. 160, no. 1, summer 1997.

Wilson, Jeyaratnam, 'Ethnic Strife in Sri Lanka: The Politics of Space', in John Coakley (ed.), *The Territorial Management of Ethnic Conflict*, London: Frank Cass, 1993.

Wilson, A. Jeyaratnam, *Politics in Sri Lanka 1947–1973*, London: Macmillan – now Palgrave, 1974.

Winham, G. R., 'Practitioners' Views of International Negotiation', *World Politics*, vol. 32, no. 1, Oct. 1979.

Winham, G. R., 'Negotiation as a Management Process', *World Politics*, Princeton, NJ: Princeton University Press, vol. 30, no. 1, 1977.

Wirsing, Robert, *India, Pakistan and the Kashmir Dispute*, New York: St. Martin's Press – now Palgrave, 1994.

Wizeman, H., *Peacekeeping*, New York: Pergamon Press, 1983.

Wolfers, Arnold, ' "National Security" as an ambiguous symbol', *Political Science Quarterly*, vol. 67, 1952.

Woodhouse, Tom and Oliver Ramsbotham, *Peacekeeping and Conflict Resolution*, London: Frank Cass, 2000.

Woodward, Susan L., *Balkan Tragedy: Chaos and Dissolution after the Cold War*, Washington, DC: Brookings Institution, 1996.

Wright, John F. R., Suzanne Goldberg, and Richard Schofield (eds), *Transcaucasian Boundaries*, London: UCL Press, 1996.

Wright, Quincy, *A Study of War*, Chicago, IL: University of Chicago Press, 1965.

Yaacov Bar-Siman-Tov, *Israel and the Peace Process 1977–1982: In Search of Legitimacy for Peace*, Albany, NY: State University of New York Press, 1994.

Young, O. R. *The Intermediaries: Third Parties in International Crises*, Princeton, NJ: Princeton University Press, 1967.

Zartman, I. William, *Ripe For Resolution: Conflict and Interaction in Africa*, 2nd edn, New York: Oxford University Press, 1989.

Zartman, I. W., and M. R. Berman, *The Practical Negotiator*, New Haven and London: Yale University Press, 1982.

Zartman, William (ed.), *Elusive Peace: Negotiating and End to Civil Wars*, Washington, DC: Brookings Institution, 1995.

Zartman, William and Victor Kremenyuk (eds), *Cooperative Security: Reducing Third World Wars*, Syracuse, NY: Syracuse University Press, 1995.

Zartman, William 'Ripening Conflict, Ripe Moment, Formula and Mediation', in Diane B. Bendahmane and John W. McDonald (eds), *Perspectives on Negotiation*, Washington, DC: Center for the Study of Foreign Affairs, 1986.

Zartman, William, and Lewis Rasmussen (eds), *Peacemaking in International Conflict: Methods and Techniques*, Washington, DC: United States Institute of Peace Press, 1997.

Zartman, William, 'Negotiations and Prenegotiations in Ethnic Conflict: The Beginning, the Middle, and the Ends', in Joseph Montville (ed.), *Conflict and Peacemaking in Multiethnic Societies*, Lexington, MA: D.C. Heath, Lexington Books, 1990.

Zartman, William, 'The Unfinished Agenda: Negotiating internal Conflicts', in Roy Licklider (ed.), *Stopping the Killing: How Civil Wars End*, New York: New York University Press, 1993.

Zartmann I. and M. R. Berman, *The Practical Negotiator*, New Haven and London: Yale University Press, 1982.

Zolo, Danilo, *Cosmopolis: Prospects for World Government*, Cambridge: Polity Press, 1997.

Zubek, M. Z., D. G. Pruitt, R. S., Pierce, N. B. Mcgillicuddy and H. Syna, 'Disputant and Mediator', *Journal of Conflict Resolution*, Ann Arbor, MI: University of Michigan Press, vol. 36, no. 3, 1992.

Index